Praise for *The Art of Hold*

T0109837

"Heather Plett brings so much grace, care, and accountability to this book and her teachings. She leaves us with hard-earned lessons and skills intended to support people and help lead us toward repair."

DESIREE ADAWAY, trainer, facilitator, and principal of The Adaway Group

"*The Art of Holding Space* provides the missing link for those of us who do any kind of transformational work. Heather Plett has done a great service by writing this book, which should be required reading for anyone who does work with other human beings."

PAMELA SLIM, author of *Body of Work*

"Reading this book will teach you to engage in the possibilities for transformational listening and speaking as they appear in daily life. Read it. Trust yourself. Show up. Repeat."

CHRISTINA BALDWIN, author of *Life's Companion* and *Storycatcher*

"This beautifully written book will give you a reason to discover your authenticity, and hold space for yourself and those around you. As our world continues to change, *The Art of Holding Space* is a road map to negotiate the future."

TUBEARS, author, poet, and artist

"What I love about Heather Plett is that she brings so much compassion to her own mistakes and traumas, which she shares with deep honesty and courage. This book is a great gift to the world in this time of turmoil and crisis, and is exactly what we need."

DR. ROBIN YOUNGSON, author of *Time to Care: How to Love Your Patients and Your Job*

"I recommend this book to anyone who is seeking to foster connections and conversations in a world that often feels fractured. It will help restore your faith in what is possible."

DR. DAVID DRAKE, author of *Narrative Coaching: The Definitive Guide to Bringing New Stories to Life*

"There is deep and timely wisdom in these pages. With uncommon tenderness and care, Heather Plett has managed to write a book that seems to be the very thing it is pointing us toward."

STEVE BELL, singer-songwriter and author

"Building on the foundation of her own grounded authenticity, Heather Plett has offered us a floodlight to illuminate our path through the dark spaces of human exchange. Plett walks us through academic as well as historical and cultural roots within the practice. We cannot help but be left with the impression that as we were reading *The Art of Holding Space*, we were being artfully held."

FRANCESCA MASON BORING, facilitator and author of *Connecting to Our Ancestral Past*

"*The Art of Holding Space* will transform your relationships with friends, family, colleagues, strangers—and yourself. Here you will find insightful and practical guidance, elegantly illustrated through Heather Plett's personal experiences, research, and professional path, to bring more kindness, curiosity, and meaning to all your interactions. I can't think of an 'art' we need more right now."

CHRISTA COUTURE, author of *How to Lose Everything*

"This wise and compassionate book has the potential to forever change the way we show up for each other as individuals and in community. Read it, absorb it, practice it. Repeat."

ALANA SHEEREN, documentary filmmaker of *Listen Closely*

the art of
holding space

a practice of love,
liberation, and leadership

the art of
holding
space

heather plett

PAGE TWO

Cataloguing in publication information is
available from Library and Archives Canada.
ISBN 978-1-989603-47-5 (paperback)
ISBN 978-1-989603-75-8 (ebook)

Page Two
pagetwo.com

Edited by Brenda Dammann
Copyedited by John Sweet
Proofread by Alison Strobel
Cover and interior design by Taysia Louie
Cover and part opening illustrations by Brian Tong
Additional graphics by Michelle Clement
Printed and bound in Canada by Friesens
Distributed in Canada by Raincoast Books
Distributed in the US and internationally by Macmillan

23 24 25 26 27   8 7 6 5 4

heatherplett.com

For my daughters, Nicole, Julie, and Madeline,
who teach me new things every day.

And for my son, Matthew, whose birth
and death set me on this path.

contents

introduction

THE FIRST TIME I heard the term "holding space" was at Authentic Leadership in Action (ALIA) Summer Institute in Halifax, Nova Scotia, in June 2010. I arrived at this gathering feeling a complex mixture of brokenness, despair, fear, longing, and hopefulness. I was hungry for healing, connection, inspiration, and relief.

At the time, I was the director of resources and public engagement for Canadian Foodgrains Bank, a national nonprofit whose byline was "A Christian Response to Hunger." I ran a national team of seventeen staff and volunteers responsible for the fundraising, communication, education, and public engagement work for the international development organization. It was a challenging and demanding job with a team that was equally complex and (sometimes) challenging. I was burnt-out and on the verge of quitting.

A month before I attended ALIA, my husband and I had decided it was finally my turn to quit my job and launch my business. Years prior, when he quit his job to go to university, we had made an agreement that once he had stable work, it would be his turn to be the major income-earner. It took him longer than expected to find a stable job, but he was finally in a term position that looked as if it would lead to something more permanent.

However, only a week after making that decision, my husband went into an emotional tailspin because of something that happened at work. Depression and anxiety set in and he couldn't work. He'd dealt with mental illness throughout our marriage, and this was a repeat of an episode that had taken place earlier, just before I gave birth to our first child. As then, it ended with a suicide attempt that landed him in the psych ward at the hospital.

As a result, he lost his term position and we went back to where we'd started, with me stuck in a job that had begun to suck the energy and optimism out of me. With a mortgage to pay and three kids to feed, I had few options.

That's how I arrived at ALIA. I convinced my boss to let me attend, partly because I needed to go somewhere that would take my mind off my overwhelming life and partly because, if I had to stay in this job after all, I needed something to inspire me so I could recommit my energy into good leadership.

At the dinner on opening night, Michael Chender, one of the founders of ALIA, got up to speak. His opening words were, "This is the kind of place where you bring your fears, your pain, and your brokenness." I started to cry. With those words, he opened a release valve on the pressure cooker that my life had become. I could finally breathe. He went on to say that ALIA was a place for vulnerability and truth telling, where each of us agreed to do our best not to sit in judgment of each other.

I don't know if Chender used the term "holding space" in his talk, but he was certainly describing what later became my understanding of it. I *do* know I heard the term elsewhere that week, and it cracked my life open in a way I could never have anticipated. Those who spoke of it were talking about something I'd craved my whole life but didn't know how to express. I'd even offered it to others but didn't know how to give it to myself.

I made a lot of friends that week who remain some of my favourite people. These were people who spoke my language, wrestled with the same questions I wrestled with, and chose authentic, open-hearted lives. It was an environment like I'd never experienced before, where people were intentional about how they hosted conversations, how they asked big questions, and how they sat with brokenness and discomfort. I felt as though I had finally come home.

Before I left that gathering, I knew I had found the kind of work—and the kind of people—I wanted to dedicate the rest of my life to.

Four months later, I finally walked away from that job. Our life was not yet stable (my husband still didn't have a permanent job), but I couldn't wait any longer. I cashed in my retirement savings, hoping and praying that the new work I was about to create, which felt closer to a calling than anything I'd ever experienced, would eventually sustain me and my family.

A week after I left my job, I travelled to Ontario to learn The Circle Way with Christina Baldwin. When I'd read her book ten years earlier, I'd felt as if she lit a candle in a dark place for me at a time when I was in an even more soul-destroying job with the federal government, coping with a toxic leadership environment. As I told her when we met, I knew that the circle held a key to the work I needed to do for the rest of my life.

That week with Baldwin solidified the experience from ALIA and took me even deeper into what it meant to hold space. There was no turning back—I was fully invested. Just as I expected, the circle changed my life.

Since that time at ALIA, I've probed deeper and deeper into what it means to hold space. I don't know its exact origins (though I will share an interesting theory on that in the last chapter), but most people I ask point in two directions.

The people I met who used the term at ALIA point in the direction of Harrison Owen. Owen is a teacher and facilitator who developed the concept of Open Space, a facilitation practice where participants have autonomy and control over what is discussed, what direction the agenda takes, and how they will participate. Rather than controlling or directing the conversation, facilitators in this practice "hold space" for what wants to emerge from the group. Facilitation of an Open Space dialogue requires the facilitator to have a lot of trust in themselves and in the group. It's not something that can be done well if you are nervous or too control-oriented.

In his book *Open Space Technology: A User's Guide*, Owen describes holding space as one of the roles of the facilitator:

> *The job of holding space and time does not fit neatly within a precise job description or linear specification of tasks. It is an opportunistic role, depending upon a close reading of the meeting environment, a clear sense of self and purpose, and a capacity for sensitive and innovative response. Done well, the role manifests what I see as the essential qualities of a good facilitator: total presence and absolute invisibility.*
>
> *Holding space and time requires that you be in that space and time as fully present, available, open, truthful, and having no agenda of your own, except that the time and space be held and honored.*[1]

When I reached out to Owen recently to let him know I was naming him in the lineage of the concept, his brief response was, "Actually I think it might go back to 1200 B.C. in China. Tao Te Ching... or whatever." In other words, he has no interest in claiming it.

Others in the education field point to Donald Winnicott. He first spoke the words in his book *The Child, the Family, and the Outside World*,[2] so it's possible that Owen's work was influenced by Winnicott. Winnicott did, however, normally speak of "holding" rather than "holding space," so perhaps it was a precursor. In Winnicott's work, "holding" is what teachers and parents do when they create safe and supportive environments for children to learn while not jeopardizing the autonomy and individuality of those children.

> *Winnicott and his wife used the term "holding" to refer to the supportive environment that a therapist creates for a client. The concept can be likened to the nurturing and caring behavior a mother engages in with her child that results in a sense of trust and safety. Winnicott believed that this "holding environment" was critical to the therapeutic environment and could be created through the therapist's direct engagement with a client. Winnicott also believed that antisocial behaviors developed from a person's having been deprived of a holding environment in childhood and from feelings of insecurity.*[3]

Though I have less knowledge of Winnicott's work than I do of Owen's teachings, I think it's valuable to reflect on the influences of the educational field on this concept. An educational thread in the tapestry implies that the act of holding space is not just about backing away while a person stays stuck in one place; it's about creating a healthy environment where **growth and development** can naturally occur. When we see this as part of the equation, it can change how we show up, and where we'll place limitations and boundaries if no growth is evident.

As we'll see in the coming chapters, the concept of holding space is like a tapestry with many threads that each tell a story. It can be both a very simple concept (i.e., I hold space for you when I listen deeply to your story) and a very complex concept (i.e., holding space for systemic changes or in situations of racial injustice). It's something you can do for yourself, for a friend, for a community, or for a crowd of thousands.

When I approach the concept of holding space, I approach it as an *inquiry* rather than an *expertise*. It's not something to be mastered, but rather something into which I will inquire for the rest of my life. It is multi-layered, and I trust that everyone who also inquires into it will add a layer to the collective understanding. Just as I may bring nuances to it that Owen or Winnicott didn't include in their works, *you* will bring nuances that I haven't yet encountered in my work.

We are weaving this tapestry together, bringing our stories and ideas to the conversation to add contour, depth, colour, and clarity. I may have arrived here before you, but you may take it further. This is evolving work and it is my hope that this book will open new doors for its continued evolution.

Let us begin our weaving...

PART ONE

the
fundamentals of
holding
space

1

what is "holding space"?

MOM WAS DYING. We knew that, but we kept hoping we had time—six months to a year—as the doctor said we should expect. But here we were, less than three months in, and she was deteriorating quickly.

On Monday morning, I stepped out of the university class I was teaching to call my brother Brad, who had flown in from Calgary and was with Mom. "Should I come now?" I asked. "It would probably be a good idea," he said. I picked up my sister, Cynthia, and we drove out to the small town where Mom lived with her husband (the man she'd married after my dad died). My other brother, Dwight, came from his home a couple of hours away.

Close to Mom's home, Cynthia and I spotted a bald eagle perched in a tree, watching us. In Indigenous spirituality, I later learned from a student in my university classroom, an eagle, which flies higher than any bird, is believed to bring our prayers to God.

I don't remember any verbal agreement between us that we would care for Mom at home and keep her out of the hospital. My siblings and I all just seemed to assume that we would. A palliative care nurse named Anne came to visit, and she walked us through what to expect in the coming days. She inserted a stent in Mom's arm and showed me how to inject a small syringe of morphine whenever Mom was in pain. She left a zip-lock bag of syringes on Mom's dresser.

"There are some things that will probably be hard for you to do for your mom, and that she might not want you to do," she said. "I'll come every few days to bathe and change her. And you can call me with any questions or concerns."

Then she left, and we were alone, waiting with Mom as she gradually left us.

There's a strange liminal space between "she's dying" and "she's dead." We wanted to soak up every moment we had with her, and yet, in those long hours when all we could do was sit and bear witness to the way her body and mind were gradually shutting down, we felt restless for the end to come.

The five of us—me, my siblings, and Mom's husband, Paul— were all in that liminal space, waiting, like the characters in the Dr. Seuss book, *Oh, The Places You'll Go!* In the book, people get stuck in "The Waiting Place," where they're waiting for a train, or a bus; the mail, or the rain; a yes or a no; or their hair to grow.[4] We were there—with no choice but to wait.

At the beginning of the week, there were moments when Mom was still with us, when her sense of humour would spark, or her concern for her family would rise to the surface. In some of those moments, true to form, she still felt responsible for making sure we all had enough to eat, or that we weren't giving up too much of our lives for her sake. And there were moments when she'd worry about her funeral (as when she wondered which dress in her closet might show less of her emaciated body) or moments when she'd wonder what heaven would be like. Increasingly, though, there were times when she seemed to already be visiting another plane, where none of us in the room could go with her. In those moments, her eyes would take on an empty sheen, and her voice would nearly disappear.

Once, when she was curled up in the big reclining chair in the living room, I was sitting next to her when she made a motion to me, as though she wanted to say something. I leaned in and she looked deeply into my eyes. She said nothing, but simply placed her hand on the top of my head, like a priest offering a blessing.

Another time she became restless and, thinking she wanted to be moved, I bent my head and prepared to pick her up. Instead, she wrapped her arms around me, kissed the top of my head several times, and smiled. I smiled back.

A third time, in that same chair, I leaned in to hear her whisper, "I don't know how to do this." With my voice cracking and tears obliterating my view, I said, "I don't know how to do this either." And then we were silent, because there was nothing more to say.

She was in her own liminal space while we were helpless bystanders in the middle of our own.

A liminal space is a threshold, the space of ambiguity or disorientation that occurs when we find ourselves transitioning from who we once were to who we are becoming. We were not yet orphans, and yet we were no longer Mom's children (at least not in the way we'd once been). She was not yet dead, and yet not quite living.

We were waiting.

Waiting for her breath to change
or the pain to come
or the song to end
or the light to change

or the birds to visit

or the night to come

or the nurse to say, "It's almost over."

Just waiting.

Nine and a half years earlier, when Dad was killed suddenly in a farm accident, we didn't have this same kind of liminal space. When the tractor rolled over him and tore a gaping hole across his back, we were thrust instantly into our new identities as fatherless adult children. Instead, the liminal space came after his death, when we were selling the farm and grappling with the suddenness of it all. The journey then was to discover what identity we would have once the grief settled into our bones. At the time, I wrote a poem called "I Can't Find Normal Anymore." Normal had vanished instantly and caught us all off guard in its ruthless departure. This time, with Mom, Normal was making a slow exit.

Anne visited again, once with a doctor who gave us more details about what was happening from a medical perspective, and once to give Mom a sponge bath in her bed. We badly wanted Anne to give us a timeline or perhaps a *What to Expect When You're Expecting Death* guidebook that would walk us step by step through the process, but there was nothing she could give us. "There's just no way of knowing," she said repeatedly. "It could be tonight, or it could be three weeks from now. It could be shortly after she stops eating and drinking, or her body could hang on quite a while after that. I can't tell you whether you should sit here and wait with her or try to go back to your lives for a while. You'll simply have to decide what feels best."

Though she gave us few of the answers we thought we needed, Anne gave us more of something else. She gave us comfort and encouragement and—most importantly—the confidence to trust ourselves in supporting our mother in the way Mom needed us to. We couldn't avoid the liminal space, but at least we knew that we were being held in it by someone with the right strength and skills.

Sitting at Mom's bedside, in moments when she was sleeping peacefully, I read *When Women Were Birds* by Terry Tempest Williams. One of the last activities Mom and I were able to do together was to sit and watch the birds that visited the bird feeder just outside her window, so it seemed the right book to read in those long hours of waiting.

The book is about a chest full of journals Williams's mother passed on to her daughter while on her deathbed. Every one of the journals turned out to be completely empty. Williams was left wondering what this meant about her mother's lack of voice and what she was meant to carry forward from it as her own voice grew in resonance. All of this is set against a back-drop of birdwatching and bird listening. Birds, after all, never question whether or not they should sing, and they never try to sing in a voice that's not their own.

I wondered, too, as I read it, how this final silencing of Mom's voice would change my own voice, and how the blank pages of what Mom didn't write might inform my future. Like Williams's mother, Mom was a product of a patriarchal, reli-gious tradition that left little room for women's voices. As her daughter, I'd bristled against these culturally imposed restric-tions, and yet they still had power in my life. I was more silent than I wanted to be. I knew that this threshold at Mom's death-bed would undoubtedly change who I was and how much I trusted my own voice (and indeed it has).

On Thursday evening, after too many nights on couches and reclining chairs, interrupted by Mom's restlessness, I went home to spend time with my daughters and attempt to get a decent night's sleep. Shortly after 3 a.m., the phone rang and Cynthia was on the other end of the line. "You'd better come quickly. She won't be with us much longer." I raced back to

Mom's apartment. In the deep darkness of the sparsely populated prairie highway, a deer darted across my path and I veered onto the shoulder to avoid it. My heart was pounding when I finally arrived at Mom's door.

Cynthia greeted me at the door with a look of astonishment on her face. "Mom died," she said, but the look on her face said that wasn't the end of the story. "She wasn't breathing for a couple of minutes. But I told her, 'You're supposed to wait for Heather to get here!' and she started breathing again."

"But . . ." I shrieked, louder than I meant to, caught in the fear that this liminal space would go on forever, "she needs to go! This needs to be over!"

Mom's body kept breathing, but her spirit was gone. Just before it left her, before I'd arrived on the scene, she'd had a moment of lucidity when her voice became louder. Dwight and Cynthia were there, talking with her, but it was clear she was speaking to someone else. "She started greeting people," they told me, "like she was arriving in heaven and saying hello to Dad and all of the other people who've gone before her. She was reaching toward something and there was a light in her eyes, like the future was right in front of her."

For the next four hours, we listened to Mom's rasping breath. The liquid in her lungs made her breath sound like the coffee pot she had when we were children, where the boiling water gurgled up into the glass bubble at the top, signalling that the coffee was ready. It was horrible to listen to it boiling to the surface, again and again, like a coffee pot perpetually boiling that nobody could take off the stove. Each time it paused, we held our own breath, wondering if this would be the end.

When the soft light of dawn filled the room, the gurgling stopped and then there was only silence and death and emptiness. Outside, large white snowflakes were carpeting the earth, and at Mom's bird feeder, a red-headed woodpecker landed.

"It's a messenger from heaven," one of us said, "telling us all will be well."

Yes, all would eventually be well, but not in that moment. In that moment we had to face the waves of grief that threatened to drown us.

A few months after Mom died, I spoke with my friend Maaianne in Zimbabwe about the vision quest she'd just completed, when she'd journeyed into the woods to spend four days alone. What surprised her about the experience was how intense the fear was. It was like a companion who just wouldn't leave her alone. It wasn't until the third day, when she'd fallen to the ground, weeping in utter surrender, that the fear finally subsided and she found some peace. It was only then that she was able to enter into the deeper spiritual work she had hoped for.

Listening to her describe the experience, I was struck by how much her four-day experience mirrored the four days we'd spent with Mom. In a sense, I too was on a vision quest during those four days, wrestling with fear and denial and having no choice but to surrender before I could emerge to discover the new identity and new voice that Mom's death brought.

There was, in that liminal space, both brokenness and opportunity, both emptiness and openness. There was the surrendering of one identity and the waiting for the next. While one story died, the next had yet to be born.

In the years following Mom's death, I kept coming back to that liminal space, wondering what it meant and how it would inform my life. There was a universality to it that went far beyond the death of a parent. I saw the same patterns as I worked with clients. Everyone I talked to seemed to go on their own version of the vision quest as they let go of one story and waited for the next to emerge. Grief, transition, loss, birth, divorce, trauma, job loss, bankruptcy, marriage, betrayal, relocation, graduation, conflict—nearly every human experience had within it some element of vision quest and liminal space.

Three months before Mom died, I'd co-facilitated a women's retreat and was excited about doing more of that kind of work. While at that retreat, however, I'd received news from Mom that her doctor had said there was nothing more they could do for her, and that we should prepare for her death. Before I'd left the retreat, I'd said to the women at the circle, "I was sure that I was going to leave this retreat and step into bigger and bigger circles of work and influence. But now I have found that my mom is dying, and instead of a bigger circle, I need to settle into a smaller circle, with my family at my mom's bedside. I am certain, though, that that small circle has something to teach me about the work I will do."

I didn't know then just how prophetic those words would be. Journeying through Mom's death would teach me more about my work than any other experience in my life. And one of the most significant lessons it taught me was the value—and challenge—of holding liminal space.

Holding space was what we were doing for Mom as we sat with her and waited for her new story to emerge. Holding space was also what Anne, our palliative care nurse, was doing for us as we waited for our new story to emerge. In a sense, holding space was what Mom was doing for herself in that moment when she whispered, "I don't know how to do this."

Imagine, if you will, that Identity A—where we are before the liminal space—is represented by a house built of Lego bricks. The Lego house serves us very well when we need it, but now we've outgrown the walls and it's time for something new. We can't build the new identity, though, or even imagine what it needs to be, until we dismantle the original Lego house.

Perhaps it's a bridge we need. But before the bridge can be built, there are a lot of loose Lego pieces that can easily get lost, broken, or stepped on. We need something to hold those little pieces, to guard them and keep them safe while they wait to become the bridge. We need a bowl, a container to keep the pieces together.

When we hold space for people who are between Identity A and Identity B, we become that bowl.

We hold their brokenness with gentle compassion. We help them to see that they are not alone in their sense of loss. We give them boundaries so they are protected from further hurts. We give them space for the waiting they must do before the new story emerges.

When Mom was dying, we served as her bowl. We held the space while she transitioned out of this life and into the next. We kept her safe and made sure she had what she needed. We helped however we could, but mostly we trusted that she would take the journey in the way she needed to. In the end, she journeyed away from us.

At the same time, Anne, the palliative care nurse, served as our bowl, holding the space for our transition. She gave us guidance and support when we needed it, and she withdrew when we needed to trust our own judgment. She didn't make the process her own, but rather gave us space to make our own decisions. She let us be broken without casting judgment on our brokenness. Deeply transformed by the grief of it all, we found our way into a new, post-Mom identity.

At some point in our lives, each of us is given the opportunity to be the bowl for someone else. It might be a death, or it might be a birth. It might be a career change, or it might be a divorce. It might be a car accident, or it might be a coming out. It might be a faith-shaking moment when someone no longer knows what they believe in. Or it might be someone's emerging realization that they don't identify with the gender they were assigned at birth. It could be any number of moments in a life when an old identity is taken away or no longer serves a purpose.

Holding space is a gift we give and receive, again and again, throughout our lives. Sometimes we do it well, and sometimes we fail. Sometimes it requires much of us, and sometimes it requires only a simple phone call.

> For the purpose of this book, we will define "holding space" this way: Holding space is what we do when we walk alongside a person or group on a journey through liminal space. We do this without making them feel inadequate, without trying to fix them, and without trying to impact the outcome. We open our hearts, offer unconditional support, and let go of judgment and control.

Here, based on what Anne did for my family as we held space for Mom, are some of the things we can do to hold space for people in our lives:

1 **Give people permission to trust their own intuition and wisdom.** We had no experience to rely upon and yet, intuitively, we knew what was needed. We knew how to carry Mom's shrinking body to the washroom, we knew how to sit and sing hymns to her, and we knew how to love her. We even knew when it was time to inject the morphine to help ease her pain. In a very gentle way, Anne let us know that we didn't need to do things according to some arbitrary health care protocol; we simply needed to trust our intuition and accumulated wisdom from the many years we loved Mom.

2 **Give people only as much information as they can handle.** Anne gave us simple instructions and left us with a few handouts, but did not overwhelm us with far more than we could process in our tender time of grief. Too much information would have left us feeling incompetent and unworthy.

3 **Don't take their power away.** When we take decision-making power out of people's hands, we leave them feeling useless and incompetent. There may be some times when we need to step in and make hard decisions for other people (i.e., when they're dealing with an addiction and an intervention may be the only thing that will save them), but in almost every other case people need the autonomy to make their own choices (even our children). Anne knew we needed to feel empowered to make decisions on our mom's behalf, and so she offered support, but never tried to direct or control us.

4 **Keep your own ego out of it.** We all get caught in that trap now and then, when we believe someone else's success is dependent on our intervention, or when we think their failure reflects poorly on us, or when we're convinced that whatever emotions they choose to unload on us are about us instead of them. It's a trap I've occasionally found myself slipping into when I teach. I can become more concerned about my own success (Do the students like me? Do their marks reflect on my ability to teach?) than about the success of my students. But that doesn't serve anyone, not even me. To truly support their growth, I need to keep my ego out of it and create the space where they have the opportunity to grow and learn.

5 **Help them feel safe enough to fail.** When people are learning, growing, or going through grief or transition, they are bound to make some mistakes along the way. When we, as their space-holders, withhold judgment and blame, we offer them the opportunity to reach inside themselves to find the courage to take risks, and the resilience to keep going even when they fail. When we let them know that failure is simply a part of the journey and not the end of the world, they'll spend less time beating themselves up for it and more time learning from their mistakes.

6   **Give guidance and help with humility and thoughtfulness.**
A wise space-holder knows when to withhold guidance (i.e.,
when it makes a person feel foolish and inadequate) and when
to offer it gently (i.e., when a person asks for it, or is too lost
to know what to ask for). Though Anne did not take our power
or autonomy away, she did offer to come and give Mom baths
and do some of the more challenging parts of caregiving. This
was a relief to us, as we had no practice at it and didn't want to
place Mom in a position that might make her feel shame (i.e.,
having her children see her naked). This is a careful dance we
all must do when we hold space for other people. Recognizing
areas in which they feel most vulnerable and incapable, and
offering the right kind of help without shaming them, takes
practice and humility.

7   **Create a container for complex emotions, including fear,
trauma, etc.** When people feel that they are held in a deeper
way than they are used to, they feel safe enough to allow complex emotions to surface that might normally remain hidden.
Someone who is practised at holding space knows that this can
happen and will be prepared to hold the emotions in a gentle,
supportive, and non-judgmental way.

We cannot hold this space if we are overly emotional ourselves, if we haven't done the hard work of looking into our
own shadows, or if we don't trust the people for whom we are
holding space. In Anne's case, she did this by showing up with
tenderness, compassion, and confidence. If she had shown up
in a way that didn't offer us assurance that she could handle
difficult situations, or that suggested she was afraid of death,
we wouldn't have trusted her as we did.

8   **Allow them to make different decisions and to have different experiences than you would.** Holding space is about
respecting each person's differences and recognizing that
those differences may lead to them making choices we would

not make. Sometimes, for example, they make choices based on cultural norms that we can't understand from within our own experience. When we hold space, we release control and honour differences. This showed up, for example, in the way Anne supported us in making decisions about what to do with Mom's body after her spirit was no longer housed there. If there had been some ritual we felt was necessary to conduct before releasing her body, we were free to do that in the privacy of Mom's home.

HOLDING SPACE is not something we can master overnight, nor can it be adequately addressed in a list of tips like the ones just given. Holding space is a complex practice that evolves as we practise it. It's unique to each person and each situation.

In the chapters that follow, we'll delve into the nuances of what it means to hold space—both as an act of service to others and as a commitment to ourselves.

2

liminal space

IN ORDER TO understand the concept of holding space, we need to peer deeper into the **space we're holding** to catch a glimpse of what it is.

When we hold space in the simplest of ways—such as when we're listening to a friend tell us about a disappointing first date—the space may not seem very complex or deep. It's simply a space for a story, a space for some emotion, a space for truth telling. It requires kindness and empathic listening, but it's the kind of space-holding we've been doing since childhood, so it likely doesn't require a deep understanding or skill level.

I have a collapsible bowl (made from silicon and sold at camping stores as a portable container) that helps me teach the ways we hold space at varying depths. Sometimes we hold only "shallow" space (such as when a friend tells a story about how tired she is from having a new baby), sometimes we hold "medium" space (such as when that friend admits to how her tiredness is making her susceptible to having some old trauma triggered), and sometimes we hold "deep" space (such as when that friend's baby has just died and she is lost in despair).

When we hold deep space in more complex situations, what we're holding is an in-between place that is strange, vast, and sometimes uncomfortable, a space full of complex and often overlapping emotions. I call this **liminal space**.

The word "liminal" originates from the Latin word *limen*, which means "a threshold." In anthropology, liminality is "the quality of ambiguity or disorientation that occurs in the middle stage of rituals, when participants no longer hold their pre-ritual status but have not yet begun the transition to the status they will hold when the ritual is complete. During a ritual's liminal stage, participants 'stand at the threshold' between their previous way of structuring their identity, time, or community, and a new way, which the ritual establishes."[5]

Liminal space, then, is a period in which something—social hierarchy, culture, belief, tradition, identity, etc.—has been dissolved and a new thing has not yet emerged to take its place (i.e., the journey your friend makes through grief from expectant mother to a new identity as a childless mother after suffering a miscarriage). It's that period of uncertainty, ambiguity, restlessness, fear, discomfort, and anguish. It's the space between, when a trapeze artist lets go of one bar and doesn't yet know whether they will be able to catch the other bar.

There is nothing shallow or easy about liminal space. In the article "Grieving as Sacred Space," Richard Rohr describes liminal space as

> *a unique spiritual position where human beings hate to be but where the biblical God is always leading them. It is when you have left the "tried and true" but have not yet been able to replace it with anything else. It is when you are finally out of the way. It is when you are in between your old comfort zone and any possible new answer. It is no fun.*[6]

In the summer of 2016, along with millions of Canadians, I watched an example of liminal space unfold in front of me on the TV screen as singer-songwriter Gord Downie performed his final concert. In a remarkable show of courage and strength, he'd gone out on tour with his band, The Tragically Hip, even though he had inoperable brain cancer that has since killed him. In a moment I don't think I'll ever forget, with pure anguish written on his face and tears rolling down his cheeks, he screamed a primal scream that ripped through the air and left a scar across the whole country. This was not a scream that could be resolved. It was not a cry for help or for pity. It was a scream that emerged from the deepest place in him and touched the deepest places within us. It was a scream from the depths of liminal space.

When we hold liminal space, we must be willing to hold that kind of scream, to witness it without judging or resolving it. We are willing to be in both the darkest and lightest of places with each other, to be alongside that kind of anguish and terror in tandem with the profound joy and celebration of a life well lived. We are willing to crack open and be at our rawest and most vulnerable. We are willing to hold each other in that unresolved place.

That is what I mean when I talk about holding space. This is not the kind of "holding space" that's tossed about on social media, when people want to say something meaningful in response to someone's pain without getting too involved. It's something much deeper and more profound. It can rip you apart and leave you breathless. It can require much more of you than you knew you had to give. It can take strength and courage and resilience and a fierce commitment to love.

Holding that kind of space is one of the most sacred acts we can perform for each other. When we do it, we stand on holy ground. And we can't do it well unless we are well-grounded and well-supported ourselves.

For a better understanding of the journey through liminal space, look at the transformation of a caterpillar to a butterfly. Though this metaphor is not without its limitations (i.e., it's a one-time-only transformation that ends with more beauty than it started with, neither of which is necessarily true for humans), it has a lot of value as an analogy. In order for a caterpillar to fulfill its destiny as a butterfly, it must first surrender to, and pass through, the liminal space of the chrysalis phase. Though I've never cut one open, I'm told that inside the chrysalis is a gel-like substance that resembles neither caterpillar nor butterfly. It's liminal: empty, void, expectant. It's complex— both pleasant and claustrophobic, comforting and frightening. It's dark and enclosed, but also warm and secure.

It's also absolutely necessary, because the transformation to butterfly cannot happen without the void of the chrysalis in between.

Below is a whimsical little story, "Let Go of the Ground," that may help you to understand the butterfly's transformation.

Let Go of the Ground

"How do you get to be so free?" Caterpillar asks wistfully of Butterfly.

"Surrender," Butterfly whispers as she flutters by.

"But... I've read all the books, taken all the classes, and I just can't seem to get off the ground."

"Surrender."

"What do you mean, 'surrender'? Surrender to what?"

"To the Mystery. To your Creator. To your own DNA."

"How do I do that?" Caterpillar frowns.

"Climb up in that tree, let go of the branch, and spin."

"Spin?"

"Yes, spin."

"But I don't know how to spin. Do I need to take a course? Is there a manual?"

"You'll know. Once you're up there on the branch."

"I'll know? How will I know?"

"It's written in your DNA."

"What happens next? Do I have to spin my own wings?"

"No, silly," Butterfly giggles. "You spin a cocoon."

"A cocoon? I've never heard of that before. What do I do with it once I've spun it?"

"You don't do anything. You just wait. Inside the cocoon."

"What good does waiting do? I have too much work to do to sit around waiting in a cocoon. I have housework to do and children to feed and . . . well, that's just ridiculous." Caterpillar turns away, her eyes back on the ground.

"Well, then you'd better give up your dream of flying, because that's the only way to get up here." Butterfly's wings carry her a little higher.

Caterpillar glances back at the sky. Her eyes fill with tears. "But . . . I really want to fly. Can you tell me a little more? Please. What comes next?"

"The hard part. The surrender."

"So we're back to surrender again. That doesn't seem very help-ful. And it's kind of confusing. What am I surrendering?"

"Everything you ever knew. Every cell of your body. Every story you've ever told yourself."

"I have to give up EVERYTHING?! Isn't that asking a bit much?"

"Yes, but it's worth it."

"Does it hurt?"

"Oh yes. It hurts."

"How do you handle the pain?"

"You won't like the answer."

"Tell me anyway."

"Surrender. And trust. You have to surrender to the pain and trust the process. You have to give up control and let your body turn to an ugly, gooey, mushy substance while you wait for transformation to happen. Your friends—those who haven't learned to spin yet—will turn away because they won't rec-ognize you. It will be the hardest thing you'll ever have to do."

"I don't know if I can do it. I can't handle that much pain."

"You can."

"But..."

"Do you want to taste the sky?"

"Oh yes. I really, really do."

"Then you have to let go of the ground."

FIGURE 1 is a diagram I developed to help us better understand the journey through liminal space. In the diagram, you'll see that the passage through liminal space is never linear or direct. Instead, it's a *spiral* pathway through a complexity of emotional states and experiences. (In truth, I am even more fond of the path of the labyrinth, with its way of moving you close to the destination and then, with a simple turn, taking you far away from where you think you're meant to be. But that's harder to demonstrate in a two-dimensional image.)

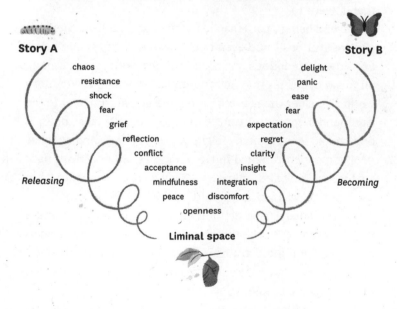

FIGURE 1. THE JOURNEY THROUGH LIMINAL SPACE

Story A

Story B

Story A	Story B
chaos	delight
resistance	panic
shock	ease
fear	fear
grief	expectation
reflection	regret
conflict	clarity
acceptance	insight
mindfulness	integration
peace	discomfort
openness	

Releasing

Becoming

Liminal space

The first spiral is the "releasing" (or, as suggested in the caterpillar story above, the "surrender"). It's a time of letting go, of admitting we do not have control of the outcome. There is much resistance in the releasing. It's a time when we fantasize, with fondness, of the way things used to be. Weren't things simpler back then? Wasn't I happier? Can't I go back and reclaim what once was?

A person can get stuck in resistance and spend much of their life there. They can also be influenced by leaders and friends who want to keep them stuck. (The forty-fifth president of the United States speaks to those resisters when he promises to "make America great again.") A resister doesn't want the world to change, even if there is significant evidence that it needs to.

Beyond being a path that individuals get stuck on, there are also institutions—and even countries—that resist evolution. Consider the religious organizations, for example, that hang on to old doctrines that no longer make sense in the modern world. Consider the resistance to same-sex marriage or to the transgender community, for example; these social structures don't make sense to many in the religious world, and so those people most entrenched in the religion's old doctrines fight against the new and unknown. They want to return to what they thought was a binary world, where there is only male and female, and marriage is defined only as a union between these two. Stepping over the threshold into the unknown space— where gender is a spectrum and love has no limitations—feels like giving up your caterpillar skin without knowing that butterfly wings are possible.

No, surrender is not easy. It can be a time of chaos and conflict, shock and grief. We risk a great deal of loss when we surrender. We may lose important relationships with people who don't want to see us change. We may lose status and position within our community. We might have to walk away from jobs that no longer feel right, or we might even get fired for no longer accepting the status quo.

I once listened to a podcast where a few pastors who'd lost their faith were being interviewed. At the time of the interview, these pastors (who were speaking under cover of anonymity) were still leading their faith communities but speaking from the pulpit of things in which they no longer believed. They'd entered their own personal liminal space but hadn't yet "come out of the closet" with their truth, because the people they led expected them to stay where they were and offer a comfortable, familiar faith.

These pastors expressed the anguish of the positions they were in. They loved the work of leading and counselling their communities—it was the only work they were trained to do—but they were no longer teaching from a place of integrity.

Those of us who've stepped over the threshold into liminal space can understand some of the anguish these pastors must have experienced. It's hard to speak of your experience to those who've not yet found themselves in the chrysalis. It's hard to accept the risk—and the loss—that can come of that.

The time we spend in liminal space can also be much longer than we expect or want. We want to rush through it, to get back to a place where the ground feels solid under our feet. But rushing through will only short-circuit the process. If you try to force a butterfly to emerge before it's ready, it will die and never discover the beauty of flight.

• • •

We have to allow ourselves to be drawn out of business as usual and remain patiently on the "threshold" (limen, in Latin) where we are betwixt and between the familiar and the completely unknown. There alone is our old world left behind, while we are not yet sure of the new existence. That's a good space where genuine newness can begin. Get there often and stay as long as you can by whatever means possible.[7]

RICHARD ROHR

• • •

My most significant period of liminal space came after I lost my stillborn son. Before that time, I had a stable, rather predictable life. I had a good job and was rising through the ranks of the federal government, on track to eventually reach the highest level of public service as an executive director. I had two young children, a house in the suburbs, a church community, and a trailer that we parked by the lake each summer. I had all the things that feel solid and comfortable. I was in the "caterpillar on the ground" portion of life.

But then my life was thrown into chaos when my third pregnancy was suddenly at risk. I had to spend three weeks in the hospital trying to prolong it so that my child would have a better chance of survival. During that time in the hospital, my faith— and everything I believed in—underwent dramatic and irreversible change. I emerged three weeks later with no baby and a huge question mark where my belief system had once been.

Those three weeks were hard, but they taught me so much about surrender, trust, and stillness. And in that time I was offered a hint of a different kind of life, a life based on open-heartedness and purpose. Though I didn't call it that at the time, it was in my hospital room that I first became a life coach and spiritual guide. I sat and listened to people in a different way than I ever had before. And while I was listening, I was learning to hold space.

I spent the next ten years trying to find solid ground again, trying to find the life's purpose that I'd glimpsed in the hospital.

I left the government and took a non-profit job that sent me to some of the poorest parts of the world. I began exploring different spiritual teachings and discovered the labyrinth, meditation, mandalas, and The Circle Way. I eventually left the church that had once sustained me and, at the end of those ten years, finally walked away from the marriage that hadn't evolved enough to fit into the new paradigm in which I was now living.

I lost relationships, left communities, spent a great deal of time in loneliness. It was painful and chaotic and scary. But once I started down the path, I knew I couldn't go back. And something that was both deep inside and far ahead of me kept telling me it would all be worth it.

Though I've offered the above diagram to describe the path through liminal space, it's important to note that its complexity goes far beyond what any diagram can offer. If it were completely accurate, the diagram would include many smaller liminal space journeys layered overtop of the larger one. For example, while many of us find ourselves in a significant transition at mid-life, there are often multiple journeys under way, each of which qualifies as its own liminal space within that larger period of transition.

In my ten-year spiritual quest after losing Matthew, for example, I went through multiple transitions. Two years after Matthew died, my dad died very suddenly in a farm accident. Two weeks later, my uncle died. And two months after that, my grandma (and last remaining grandparent) died. It felt as though my family was going through a season of death. Each time we caught our breath, the phone would ring, and we'd learn of another passing.

My work also transitioned during this time. The year after my dad died, I left the federal government and started my work in non-profit. Six and a half years later, I left that job to start my own business. Each of these experiences represented another journey through liminal space, overlaid on a more extensive ten-year quest.

Perhaps we go through some version of the liminal space journey—both personally and in our communities and families—throughout our lives. And in the end, there is one inescapable journey we must all take: the journey from life to death.

•   •   •

Most of us arrive at a sense of self and vocation only after a long journey through alien lands. But this journey bears no resemblance to the trouble-free "travel packages" sold by the tourism industry. It is more akin to the ancient tradition of pilgrimage—"a transformative journey to a sacred centre" full of hardships, darkness, and peril.[8]

PARKER PALMER

3

the essential elements
of holding space

NOW THAT WE have a clearer understanding of liminal
space, let's talk about what it means to **hold space**
for the liminal journey of others.

When we hold space for another person's path through liminal space, we essentially serve as a container—like the shell of
the chrysalis—offering and creating a safe place for the chaos,
the mess, the fear, the grief, the rage, and the ecstasy (and
everything in between) to take place. This container does not
direct or control the transformation; it simply provides a safe
and contained vessel where it can happen without irreversible
destruction. The container is protection, support, and safety.

As I mentioned in chapter 1, consider how Lego pieces, after
deconstruction, represent the messiness of liminal space. If
you've lived in a house with small children, you probably know
what happens when someone deconstructs a Lego structure
and the bricks are not contained. There is Lego everywhere,
sure to cause pain for the unsuspecting, barefooted person
making their way to the bathroom in the middle of the night.

The bowl that holds the Lego does not change the process or shape the destruction, nor does it direct the creation of what's to come. It simply *contains*, offering safety, boundaries, and support so that nobody is inadvertently wounded in the process. It also ensures all the pieces remain available for rebuilding.

In the transformation process between caterpillar and butterfly, there are cells in the chrysalis called "imaginal cells." These are the cells that hold within them the DNA—the essence—of the butterfly. While other cells are dying, the imaginal cells begin to direct the process toward emergence. They hold hope for the future within the chaos. The chrysalis, like the bowl, holds the space so that those imaginal cells are not lost and remain available to do the work of providing the building blocks of the new, future butterfly from the disintegration/destruction of the caterpillar.

Thus, the person (or people) holding space for someone undergoing personal deconstruction becomes like the bowl, holding a space so the imaginal cells within that person can do the transformational work they need to do. "Being the bowl" is *how* you serve when you hold space for others.

Let's consider what that bowl is made of. I imagine it to be composed of three layers: **what you offer** to another when you hold space; **what guides you** as you make that offering; and **what supports you**.

What You Offer: The Inner Layer of the Bowl

The inside layer of the bowl is *what you offer*, based on the needs of the person or people for whom you're holding space (Figure 2). It's the lining of the bowl, those aspects that will be experienced by the person in the midst of the liminal journey.

(Note: not all of the properties below are necessary every time you hold space; there will be ebb and flow depending on the circumstances.)

You offer:

1 Witness
2 Containment
3 Compassion
4 Selective Non-Judgment
5 Selective Guidance
6 Space for Complexity
7 Autonomy
8 Flexibility
9 Connection
10 Allyship

FIGURE 2. THE INNER LAYER OF THE BOWL

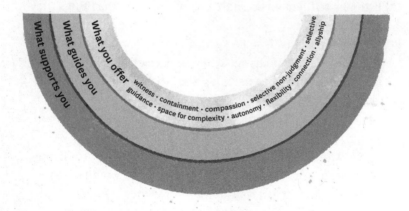

LET'S BREAK down these properties:

1. *Witness*

A person in liminal space can feel invisible, as if they've dropped out of sight and no longer have value in the world. When they're in the middle of a period of grief, for example, or they're adapting to a disability that has changed the way they function in the world, they may not operate in the way that once gave them value and made people notice them.

In those times, they need people to see them, honour them, and pay attention to what they're going through. Holding space is about **bearing witness**. It's about showing up for a person we care about even when they have nothing to offer us in return. It's about noticing the little things that make them who they are and showing up in a way that lets them know they are still seen—such as bringing them a cup of coffee with just the right amount of cream, showing up at the funeral of their parent (even though you didn't know the deceased), or listening to them go through a checklist of all the things they have lost.

Bearing witness is *showing up without answers*. It's listening without needing to change the narrative or the situation. It's hearing the things in a person's story that others overlook. It's letting them know they still have value, even in those moments when they are unable to do the things that once helped them assign value to themselves.

We often underestimate the power of simply seeing and being seen. I once had a coaching client who would occasionally say, "Can you just sit and look at me for a moment? It just means so much to be truly seen by someone who has no judgment in their eyes."

In my experience, there are various levels of "being seen," but we can't assume that everyone is capable of all levels or has done the spiritual work required to be present at all depths. Most of us have only a few select people in our lives who can bear witness to the deepest, messiest, most spiritual parts of us. While other friends may hold space for portions of us, we may be reluctant to trust the whole of who we are to their container. To be truly seen by someone is to know they can look into your deepest soul without backing away, that they hold your soul with reverence and delight.

I have a dear friend, Beth, who meets me in that holy and raw place more or less weekly on a Zoom call. We often start our conversations with five to ten minutes of silence in which we simply look into each other's eyes and witness each other (a practice we learned from the book *Evolutionary Relationships*). Occasionally, our eyes well up with tears while we look at each other, because there is something so sacred about being seen in this way.

The act of bearing witness is the act of inviting the sacred into the space. When we can lower our defences, show up with vulnerability and trust, and look deeply into each other's soul, something mystical can show up that is beyond words. It's here that we are on holy ground.

• • •

Here's the deal. The human soul doesn't want to be advised or fixed or saved. It simply wants to be witnessed—to be seen, heard, and companioned exactly as it is. When we make that kind of deep bow to the soul of a suffering person, our respect reinforces the soul's healing resources, the only resources that can help the sufferer make it through.[9]

PARKER PALMER

2. Containment

Liminal space is primal space, where we often find ourselves returning to our most basic needs. One of those most primal needs—a need that shows itself in our first hours of life (and even earlier, inside the womb)—is the need for containment, safety, and protection. The chrysalis is a little like returning to the womb. While we are in it, we are tender and raw and may experience a need for the same kind of containment and protection as an infant.

We will do a great deal to feel safe, even if it means harming ourselves or the people around us if necessary. Imagine, for example, an addict in the liminal space of recovery. They may have intense moments when they need someone with a clearer mind than theirs to contain their actions and help keep them safe.

Liminal space can be a frightening place if there is no protective containment. Those who hold space can help keep those in liminal space from further damage while they deconstruct and rebuild. This may not always feel like kindness. Sometimes, in fact, it can feel like rigidity. Sometimes when we're holding space, we must be firm with the person, holding their best interests in our heart. That might mean checking an addict into rehab, for example, or keeping a child in a confined space while they're having a temper tantrum. I have seen parents of children with autism or sensory issues wrap their children in tight bear hugs when they begin to spin out of control, offering the kind of containment that helps them ground themselves and feel safe.

One of my daughters went through a rough period a few years ago when she was non-communicative and pushing against my boundaries. Not surprisingly, she was angry at me for separating from her dad and was occasionally deliberately disobedient as a result. I was lenient with her at first, hoping it would help heal the divide between us, but one day I couldn't ignore her belligerence anymore. I laid down the house rules and took her cellphone away. After her initial anger, a surprising thing happened: she softened. She became more compliant and co-operative and treated me with more kindness than she had before. It seems my discipline served to keep her safe, reminding her that she could fall apart while not worrying that I would fall apart in the process of supporting her through it. She was both contained and protected by my firmer way of holding space for her.

Occasionally, containment also means erecting and/or holding boundaries on behalf of someone who is vulnerable, oppressed, or too deep in grief or trauma to care for their own needs. When my former husband spent time in a psychiatric ward, for example, holding space for him sometimes meant erecting boundaries on his behalf and letting friends know when it wasn't a good time to visit.

Sometimes when I host retreats, people go through fairly intense personal transformation. I've seen participants fall apart emotionally, sobbing uncontrollably as they let go of an old story or process a key realization. For these situations, I've adopted a version of a practice that I learned from my teacher, Christina Baldwin. After I ask the person to nod if they're okay with being touched, I silently kneel in front of them and hold their feet to the floor. I speak no words, simply kneeling there for as long as they need, holding them energetically to the Source of their grounding. Alternatively, I'll place a blanket around their shoulders so that they feel the containment that a weighted blanket can give a person with nervous system overload.

It's a powerful thing to offer, a powerful thing to witness, and—what I've heard from those who've experienced it—a powerful thing to receive. The earthing/grounding aspect tethers them to a primal form of protection and connection in their moment of falling apart. I've witnessed the person come back from their momentary liminal space with a light in their eyes that wasn't there before.

Containment is also about offering a sense of tethering to "home." As I write a portion of this book, for example, I am in the warm and welcoming backyard cottage of my dear friends Lorraine and TuBears. I'm in a city far from my home, but in a home that grounds and supports me. It's a special space, full of sacred objects and infused with energy from the spiritual work TuBears does, far enough removed from my day-to-day life that I can write without distraction. By offering me containment, these friends hold space while this book emerges.

On the reverse side of this attribute, we must recognize the difference between providing containment and protection and interfering with a person's process. Sometimes our own stories, issues, and interpretations of what a person needs get in the way, and sometimes a safe place becomes too much of an escape that lets them avoid the work they must do. Other times our offer of protection feels more like control and judgment.

Consider a toddler who's learning to walk. If you surround the child with so much protection that they can never hurt themselves, they will never learn to walk. Imagine wrapping a child in one of those inflatable sumo wrestling suits; they'd be so off balance they'd simply roll across the floor. Instead, you need to sit vigilantly a few feet away, encouraging the child to take that first step while offering the safety of your arms should they fall.

Like the shell of an egg, though, containment is always meant to be temporary. An eggshell is just strong enough to contain the embryo, but not so strong that the fully developed chick can't peck its way out when the time comes. Once the chick is ready, it must trust its instinct to start pecking. The eggshell cracks open and is discarded so the chick can step into the big, beautiful world.

When you hold space, you provide a container that's both firm and enclosed enough to allow for protection and development, but flexible enough to avoid becoming a trap. A person needs the freedom to fly from the nest. As the one holding space, we must allow them this freedom, even though it means they may no longer need us or might leave us behind. It may hurt when they do, but our work is to let them go.

3. Compassion

As mentioned earlier, liminal space can be a lonely, isolated place. Some of the connections we had before might be lost when we begin the liminal journey. We can become unmoored from our communities and possibly even our families. In this time, we need tenderness, compassion, and a soft place to land that doesn't make us feel anxious or afraid.

Compassion can take many forms. It might be the casserole we bring after a funeral, the babysitting we do for a recently divorced single mom, or the listening ear we offer when the person needs to rant. Parker Palmer, who's been through several bouts of depression, once shared a story of a friend who showed up at his house every day during his depression simply to rub his feet and sit with him in silence.

When my sister-in-law lost her dad to a sudden heart attack and had to fly back to the city where I live, I was there at the airport waiting to drive her to the town where her mom lived. She told me she was getting a ride with her brother's friend, but I knew she needed someone familiar and safe waiting for her. It didn't feel like much for me to show up, but she has since remarked what a relief it was to see me at the airport waiting for her. She knew she was with someone who would be compassionate and safe to be with while she fell apart.

It's important to note that, when holding space, compassion must be offered in a non-patronizing way. Once we bring sympathy—rather than empathy—into the picture, we're offering compassion from a position of superiority, making the person feel judged and inferior. With empathy, we try to see the world through the other person's eyes, recognizing that it could just as easily be us in the situation they're in. Empathy assumes equality, while sympathy (or pity) tends to create inequality in a relationship.

• • •

If I dare to hear you
I will feel you like the sun
And grow in your direction.[10]

MARK NEPO

• • •

4. Selective Non-Judgment

When I first started teaching about holding space, I used the term "non-judgment" to describe what we do when we support people without judging their experience or making them feel shame for their choices. After working with the term, however, I've adjusted my thoughts on this. There are times when we *do* indeed need to use our best judgment. If a person is doing things that hurt, oppress, or marginalize other people, for example, we need to let them know that we can't support their choices.

In the book *Letters to a Young Therapist*, Mary Pipher says that we still need to hold on to our own values while doing this work and make judgments from that place. For example, she told one client that she could no longer work with him as long as he remained in a white supremacist group. In another situation, she wouldn't support a client's goal of breaking up the marriage and family of the wealthy man with whom her client was having an affair. A third client dealt with her anger and sadness by shopping, and Pipher did her best to steer her toward a healthier outlet for her emotions.

> In spite of what some theorists suggest, we can't claim to be and we shouldn't be value neutral. Our responsibility is to be honest with our clients about our values.
> Therapists are sometimes naive about evil. I remember one therapist who dated a convicted murderer recently released from our state prison. He was clearly a jerk, interested only in her body and her apartment, but she claimed she could see the good in him. Well maybe... but I felt she was so nonjudgmental as to have virtually no common sense.[11]

Instead of non-judgment, we should use our discernment to determine when it's best to withhold judgment and when it's best to use our judgment in the interests of the person for whom we're holding space (or, if applicable, for the person they're hurting), to stand up for our values or steer the other person in a less destructive direction.

Most of the time, we should do our best to withhold judgment and avoid imposing shame on the person. Shame is counterproductive to the transformation process. It will cause that person to contract rather than expand, to shrink rather than grow.

As people who hold space, we can't project our own choices and experiences onto others, though that's often tempting. Someone else's falling apart doesn't look like our falling apart. For example, they may need a longer time than we would need to navigate their liminal space, or they may need therapy while we might work through a similar situation in our journal or in our personal support circles.

When I was raped several years ago, some people insisted that I should go for therapy, but when I tried it, I didn't find it helpful. (Side note: I do sometimes regret not looking harder for the *right* kind of therapy after my rape. It can be difficult, in a time of crisis, to find the right person who can hold space in the way that you need.) I've since gone for therapy for other things, however, so I'm not saying it's universally unhelpful for me. Instead, I did a lot of writing and talked to supportive friends and eventually wrote a play about the experience. Seeing that play produced onstage was an unconventional way of healing. My theatre instructor was worried that it might reopen the wound, but it worked for me. I can't, however, expect another person to process their pain in the same way. Instead, I withhold my judgment while they find the therapeutic and spiritual practices that work for them.

After writing publicly about my divorce, I had a number of people come to me for coaching to help them decide whether or not to pursue a divorce. At first, I thought I could help them because I had empathy for their situation, but then I realized how difficult it was to refrain from projecting my own story onto theirs and how tempted I was to assume I knew things about their situation that I didn't. I stopped accepting those clients and sent them elsewhere because I was not able to be sufficiently non-judgmental in those situations.

If you find yourself in a place of judgment while holding space for someone, it might be helpful to stop and find an objective outsider with whom you can work, someone who's not in relationship with the person you're holding space for. That person can help you process when you become frustrated, or help you discern whether or not you should step out of the holding space role if your judgment is getting in the way. It can also be helpful to use a mindfulness approach in response, i.e., notice it, label it, get curious, and let it pass without attachment (more on this in chapter 16). Curiosity also helps: ask a question that lets you see the situation through a new perspective.

5. Selective Guidance

Offering guidance is probably the trickiest aspect of holding space, because it's the place where we most often get things wrong. The temptation for many of us is to offer assistance each time we see someone faltering. But that can be more damaging than supportive. Often tremendous struggle can precede a tremendous breaking-through point; if we interfere with that necessary process, we can hinder it and rob the person of its potential. Also, as we learn from those who study intrinsic motivation, people have a much greater chance of long-term success and growth if they are able to find their own solutions and learn to motivate themselves rather than rely on external sources. Too much advice or guidance leads to dependence rather than growth.

However, when a person feels lost and alone in the middle of their liminal journey, they may need some gentle guidance to help them travel safely through the darkness. Consider the thread that Ariadne offered Theseus for his labyrinth journey to slay the Minotaur. She didn't try to control the journey, nor did she take Theseus's autonomy away. She simply provided a thread that would help him find his way back out.

How can you offer a "thread" of guidance to help someone through their own labyrinth without interfering? For this I return to the story of Mom's palliative care nurse, Anne. She didn't hand us an onerous medical textbook on *The Hundred Things You Need to Know about Dying*, nor did she stay at the house with us to fix all our problems. Instead, she gave us little bits of information that would help us get through each of the stages we experienced with Mom. More importantly, she made it safe for us to ask questions when we needed more.

One of the most important pieces of guidance Anne gave us was this simple sentence: "You don't have to call the funeral home right away." She gave us permission to spend as much time with Mom as we needed, and to find our own rhythm and rituals for releasing Mom's body. The hours we spent while those who were important to Mom came to say their goodbyes to her body were wrenching and painful, but also healing and beautiful. We would have missed that if Anne hadn't given us her gentle, non-judgmental guidance. I remember, for example, how poignant it was to see my aunt sit beside the body of her baby sister, the last of her siblings to die.

Sometimes guidance is just that—giving someone permission to do something their own way when they might not otherwise know they're allowed to do so. So many of us are wrapped up in cultural and familial expectations that we have a hard time imagining how to function outside them. But when you give a person permission to shake off those expectations and trust their own intuition, it can offer a great release.

To hold space well in these situations, we should offer only *judicious* guidance, waiting for the right time, and then only offering the right amount (based on our intuitive sense, or what the person actually tells us they want or need). We should always pause to ask ourselves whether our guidance is really in the best interest of the other person or if we're offering it from a place of ego, pride, insecurity, or jealousy. My friend Jo Ann Unger, a psychologist, tells her clients that there are two kinds of conversations: listening ones and problem-solving ones. "I then encourage people, particularly couples or parents of teenagers, to assume all conversations are listening ones unless someone asks for your guidance or wisdom. That leads to another thought that can help discern whether to offer guidance: do I actually have *wisdom* in this area? We all have opinions about things, but this is not the same as guidance or wisdom. We may also have some experience of our own, but each of our journeys, our values and needs, is so different."

When we DO discern that our wisdom and guidance may be of value, then it must be provided without attachment to the outcome, always remembering that the other person has the choice whether or not to use that guidance. If we become offended when someone doesn't follow our advice, we're not truly supporting them; we're only looking after our own ego. Provide advice and guidance only if you can do so with no strings attached.

● ● ●

We're here for a reason. I believe a bit of the reason is to throw little torches out to lead people through the dark.

WHOOPI GOLDBERG

● ● ●

6. Space for Complexity

Sometimes people came to me for coaching because they wanted support for a specific decision, but by the second or third session they realized that what they *really* wanted was much more complex than that. The original question only scratched the surface of what was transitioning in their life; it was simply a doorway into the much deeper question or longing.

One person started out asking herself whether she wanted to pursue a PhD and found out she was really on a quest for a deeper spirituality, one that embraced the feminine Divine. Another person was looking for support as she considered a job change and discovered in her third session that she really didn't want either job, but instead was longing for a sabbatical that would allow her to reimagine her whole life. In both cases, the right questions led them to probe a deeper level of exploration and complexity.

When we hold space for a person initially, it may seem like a simple matter of sitting and listening to them over a cup of coffee. But when trust is built, and safety established, the heart can take a person to a much deeper place than first imagined.

I've seen it happen in retreats many times. We start out at a surface level and move into something much more profound, after we've tested the walls of the container and found them strong enough to hold us. Once, for example, on the third day of a retreat, a man revealed that he had been the victim of childhood sexual abuse, something he'd never spoken of before.

Complexity can show up in many ways. Sometimes it's complex emotions, i.e., two seemingly contradictory feelings that manifest simultaneously. Sometimes there's complexity in the stories, i.e., a person uncovers a history of abuse or trauma that they didn't initially anticipate. Other times there's complex morality or ethics in the decisions that need to be made, i.e., should they risk losing their job to blow the whistle on a situation, or allow the unethical/destructive/damaging situation to continue? Sometimes a person's response to a situation is made more complex by unresolved and/or unrecognized trauma or injustices.

In group processes, complexity can show up as conflict, power imbalance, oppression, or divergent purposes. Imagine, for example, holding space for a church community where there is a mix of races, genders, and socio-economic backgrounds. If you treat that community as a homogeneous group with a common purpose, you will only ever attain the level of "pseudocommunity" that M. Scott Peck talks about in the book *The Different Drum*. But when you instead hold space for complexity, understanding that each person brings unique wounds, fears, and other experiences to the circle, you'll be better able to get through the chaos to true community.

When we hold space for someone, we need to be prepared to hold space for the *whole* of them, not just the parts that seem easy and straightforward (or that are easy to understand because they resemble aspects of ourselves). We need to be prepared for the deeper layers that will be revealed once the other person has found a safe place to be vulnerable—layers that might not always make us (or them) feel comfortable, and layers that might not present themselves without tremendous patience and the safety of the container.

Remember the whirlwind of complex emotions and chaos included in the typical liminal journey. When we hold space, we must be willing to engage these potential complexities so that the opportunity for resolution is not lost. If we shy away from complexity as space-holders, we potentially encourage the other person to bypass complexity instead of truly engaging in their journey through liminal space.

      • • •

Abandon the urge to simplify everything, to look for formulas and easy answers, and begin to think multidimensionally, to glory in the mystery and paradoxes of life, not to be dismayed by the multitude of causes and consequences that are inherent in each experience—to appreciate the fact that life is complex.[12]

M. SCOTT PECK

      • • •

In early 2017, my friend Saleha attended the Women's March with me and my three daughters. She was excited to attend, but had no idea how the event would affect her. Suddenly, complexity showed up for her. Here's what she shared afterwards: "Little did I know that all of that screaming and the energy would open an old wound, terror, and tremendous fear in me. In that moment, I couldn't speak and I lost my voice completely. My life experience as an Arab Muslim woman in the part of the world where I grew up was all brought up by that scene. The Arab Spring was just over psychologically and it ended with a deep pain you see in every refugee's eyes, and in every person who was forced to choose another land and call it home. It was so hard for me to see the police trying to protect the women in the march while the picture in my head was for the police to kill people who spoke against their dictators. Heather was there, she *was there*! It might be confusing for her and her daughters at that time to see all those emotions of fear and terror coming out of me, but she *was there*, she held me! She asked me if I wanted to leave. She was so content that I felt safe with her. And that was my first event to accept the complexity and the package I came with. That event was the beginning for me to see things differently and dig deeper for different meanings of things around me. I'm still working on that!" (A couple of years later, I was delighted to attend Saleha's citizenship ceremony when she became a Canadian citizen. We continue to hold space for each other's complexity.)

Complexity can show up unexpectedly, but it's often not the end of the journey. I believe, as Oliver Wendell Holmes Jr. did, that there is usually something on the other side. "I would not give a fig for the simplicity this side of complexity, but I would give my life for the simplicity on the other side of complexity." When we hold space for complexity, a person or group can often find themselves emerging on the other side into a space of simplicity, clarity, and peace.

7. *Autonomy*

Autonomy is defined as "the quality or state of being self-governing; self-directing freedom and especially moral independence." When we allow for the autonomy of those for whom we hold space, we allow them to govern their own lives and make their own decisions. We need to *trust* in their ability to find solutions for themselves.

When I was writing the original version of this text, I was away from home at a cabin that afforded me the kind of quiet time to concentrate that I don't always get as a single mom in a home with three daughters. However, a series of text messages from home made me aware that one of my daughters was having an anxiety crisis. If I were an overprotective "helicopter" parent, I would have packed my bags and rushed back home to support her. Instead, I trusted she had the tools to cope with her anxiety herself and to ask for the help she needed. Her sisters were there to support her, and her dad was not far away if she needed him. So, I didn't rush home. Instead, I sent her text messages to check in regularly and offered one suggestion I learned from a therapist friend, which she agreed to try.

At this stage of her life, I knew she was better served if I allowed her the autonomy to find her own way through her anxiety. I probably would have returned home if she had asked me directly, but since she wasn't asking, I trusted she would find ways to cope. She is learning self-reliance and reliance on individuals and communities beyond her mom (her sisters, teachers, guidance counsellor, etc.). This, I trust, will enable her to grow into adulthood with more self-confidence than if I were to rush in to rescue her each time she became anxious.

Sometimes (especially when it's our children) it can be extremely difficult not to rush in and offer the solution to another person's problem. We want to see them whole and happy again, and we're often quite certain that our solution will bring them back to that state. But if we fix what's not ours to fix, we take away their power and autonomy instead of supporting their growth and transformation.

When it comes to autonomy, there is a fine line between empowering and overwhelming. When a person is in the midst of grief, for example, they may be grateful for someone being willing to step in and make decisions for them. But if another person continues to make decisions on their behalf, it can become stifling and controlling.

When my dad died very suddenly and left behind a farm to manage, there were several people who held space for us in just the right way, leaving us our autonomy in the places that mattered while taking away some of the decision-making that threatened to overwhelm us. One of Dad's friends, a quiet man who never got in anyone's way, simply showed up on the yard and started feeding Dad's animals while making some of the farm decisions that he knew were beyond our capacity. Another friend brought over a basket of things she knew we would need, including a notebook that she handed to my brother, saying, "When you're planning a funeral, you need to keep track of a lot of details. You'll want to know that everyone in the family has access to that information. Keep it all in here." That notebook was a godsend, as was the woman who brought it. She offered both selective guidance *and* autonomy.

• • •

Not I, nor anyone else can travel that road for you.
You must travel it by yourself.
It is not far. It is within reach.
Perhaps you have been on it since you were born,
and did not know.
Perhaps it is everywhere—on water and land.

WALT WHITMAN, *LEAVES OF GRASS*

• • •

8. Flexibility

Much of what we've talked about so far relates to holding space for the difficult complexities of the journey through liminal space—the fear, rage, loss, despair, and disillusionment. But we can't ignore the more "positive" aspects of the spiral, such as joy, elation, relief, and satisfaction.

This is not a simple, linear journey, and the person for whom we're holding space will spiral through all types of emotion. We need to be flexible and prepare ourselves to hold space for the heights of ecstasy in the same way we hold space for the darker aspects. Though we should limit our positive/negative binary thinking in this work, the more "positive" aspects can sometimes be just as challenging to support as the others.

Often a person's emotions won't be what we expect them to be. For example, when I told my friends that I had separated from my husband, they were prepared to hold space for my grief, fear, and loneliness. But that's not how I felt much of the time. I felt a huge sense of relief because it had taken me *years* to make this difficult decision and I was finally emerging on the other side. I wasn't lonely at all, because I realized I preferred solitude to the conflict I had before. Sure, I went through grief and fear, but what I often wanted was someone to hold space for celebration as well. That request confused some friends, but most adapted to my needs.

While we were planning the funeral in the days after my dad died, my siblings and I found ourselves giggling over something very silly (it had to do with the cheese being served at the funeral, but you'd have to be there to understand the strange humour in it). The laughter was like a release valve, giving us momentary relief from the pressure cooker of intense grief. If anyone had walked into the house at that moment intending to support us in our grief, they would have been very confused. But laughter is a part of grief just as tears are. Shutting down either, because they don't make sense to us, would be a tremendous disservice.

I love what Mary Pipher says about the complexity of emotions and how our language can be so limited in defining them:

Years ago I made a speech in Japan. I was impressed that in the Japanese language there are many words that describe having two or even three feelings at once. English has only a few such words, "bittersweet," maybe "poignant." But in fact, most of the time we are feeling more than one thing. When I leave a family reunion, I am relieved to be in my quiet car and sad to be saying good-bye. When I am angry with my husband, I am also sympathetic that he may be doing his best. Watching a sunset, my heart can break two ways at the same time: joy at its beauty and sorrow at the shortness of life.[13]

When we are holding space, the best that we can do is to release our expectations of what emotional states a person is going through and try to show up with the flexibility to support them all. This can put us through an emotional blender ourselves; we'll need to ensure that we have our own avenues— and people—available to hold space where we can process as necessary.

9. *Connection*

One of the most challenging things about the journey through liminal space is the way in which it leaves us feeling disconnected, lost, and often very lonely. In the quest for greater authenticity and meaning, we may leave behind relationships that once felt important to us and find ourselves growing away from others. "It feels like nobody understands me anymore," is a phrase I often hear from people in this unfamiliar space, and "I'm not even sure I understand myself anymore."

I went through my own deep loneliness in my ten-year liminal space. I longed for someone to talk to about what I was going through, to help me make sense of the journey. But almost every time I tried to talk to friends or family about it, I was met with puzzlement or even outright abandonment.

Some days it felt as though I were suddenly speaking a foreign language that nobody could understand. Much of the time, I didn't know if I understood it myself.

One of the greatest gifts you can offer to someone for whom you're holding space is connection. You can go a long way in making them feel less alone by simply showing up, not giving them puzzled looks, and not abandoning them when they talk about strange things. You can let them know that even though they are going through a transition you might not understand, you don't intend to abandon them. Sometimes this includes physical touch, so that they can feel physically as well as emotionally connected to at least one other person. A hug (if they give consent) can go a long way.

Connection in the midst of liminal space can feel like dropping anchor into a solid seabed when the storm is tossing your ship around on the waves. As a space-holder, you can't make the other person's storm go away, but you can help their anchor find solid ground.

Attachment Theory teaches us that a baby who has a secure attachment—commonly defined as a safe haven and secure base from which to explore the world—will have a much greater chance of developing into an emotionally mature, resilient, and socially competent adult. (The safe haven is the place to come home to where we can receive comfort and share successes. The secure base is the launching pad—the encouragement and cheerleading that allows us to take risks, explore, learn, and grow.) Our attachment needs do not go away when we grow up. Everyone is better able to weather the storms that life brings if they have the kind of safe haven and secure base that the act of holding space can offer.

In addition to offering connection with ourselves as space-holders, we can support the deepening of the other person's connections with themselves, the sacred, and the earth.

Offer to book a reiki session for them, or a visit to a health spa or meditation retreat, to help them connect more deeply with their own body and heart. If they follow a spiritual tradition with a particular sanctuary space, go with them to a church, synagogue, mosque, dojo, or sweat lodge. Accompany them on walks in the woods or along the beach to help them connect more deeply with the earth. Help them connect to their sacred source, but be cautious not to impose your own spiritual beliefs or take away their autonomy. Again, you can offer selective guidance, but don't take it personally if they choose another path.

• • •

I define connection as the energy that exists between people when they feel seen, heard, and valued; when they can give and receive without judgment; and when they derive sustenance and strength from the relationship.[14]

BRENÉ BROWN

• • •

10. Allyship

It's impossible to hold space from a pedestal. It's also extremely difficult to hold space from a place of unacknowledged privilege or from a place of sympathy or superiority. Instead, we must step into the messy, complex spaces where we're willing to do our own work in order to truly recognize and centre the value and rights of the person in front of us.

Holding space from this place means that we commit to a practice of "allyship." The Anti-Oppression Network defines allyship as "an active, consistent, and arduous practice of unlearning and re-evaluating, in which a person in a position of privilege and power seeks to operate in solidarity with a marginalized group."[15]

Being an ally means choosing to walk alongside another person (or group of people) in a way that witnesses them as whole and seeks to minimize the harm done to them by oppressive systems (and/or individuals) and by our own blind spots and unconscious biases. This means choosing solidarity over our own comfort. It means we listen more and speak less. It means we commit to continuous learning about the ways in which they've been impacted by unfairness, abuse, oppression, and marginalization. It also means making repairs and changing our behaviour when we make mistakes.

The topic of allyship (especially when holding space in anti-oppression spaces) is multifaceted, and later chapters in this book are dedicated to deeper inquiry into this as it relates to holding space.

Let's look at it from the viewpoint of a parent–child relationship. One of my daughters recently let me know that she was holding some resentment toward me for what happened to her when she was in high school. She was experiencing emotional abuse from her father at the time (he was struggling with how to parent teenaged girls and his unhealed wounds added to the complexity), and she didn't believe that I had done a sufficient job serving as her ally. At that time, I saw my role in the family as that of peacemaker, trying to help her and her dad resolve their arguments so there was peace in the home. What I didn't sufficiently consider, however, was how much she—as the person with little power—was feeling abused by him and abandoned by me when I didn't do enough to challenge his unhealthy behaviour and protect her from the impact of it.

Had I practised effective allyship in holding space for her at the time, I would have spent more time listening and less time trying to make peace. I would have walked alongside her more effectively, putting my own comfort on the line, advocating for her, erecting boundaries on her behalf, and taking ownership of my own blind spots that were getting in the way.

In another example, one of my clients, who works in the prison system, recently shared a story of how she supported inmates in a goal-setting exercise. Two of the men shared that their goals when they got out of prison were to make money from criminal activities. As she reflected on what she was learning in our Holding Space Practitioner Program, she said, "In the past I thought my job was to correct them or to help them develop more productive goals. Instead, I decided to listen without judgment and to ask questions that showed genuine respect and interest in the complexities and barriers in their lives. They responded to me quite differently than they once would have." In that moment, she was practising allyship.

There's a reason why allyship is a practice rather than an identity. We are *always* in practice, trying to unlearn the ways we've been taught to show up, trying to challenge our biases, and trying to show up with greater and greater humility and solidarity.

Conclusion

My own understanding is continuously evolving as I teach about holding space, but I believe this list covers the essential elements you'll offer as a space-holder. This is not an exhaustive list of the inner-bowl properties that come into play when you hold space. There are others—including patience, kindness, justice, and fairness—but trying to include everything makes the list too cumbersome. Plus, all of these properties are embedded in the ones we've discussed above. Not all of the properties are simultaneously necessary, and some might occasionally feel contradictory, as in the case of autonomy and containment.

It's also true that each element you offer when holding space can have a shadow side. Containment, for example, can become "entrapment." Selective non-judgment can turn into "allowing bad behaviour." Flexibility can manifest as "being wishy-washy." Connection can slide into "enmeshment." Selective guidance can emerge as "bossiness." When you hold space, you will need to check in with yourself regularly, examine your ego, motivation, bias, and baggage, to ensure you consistently choose the light and make corrections when the shadow takes over.

In the next chapter, we'll explore the other two layers of the bowl.

4

what guides and supports you

THE INNER LAYER of the bowl (**what you offer** to the person for whom you're holding space) is held in place and guided by the outer two layers: **what guides you** and **what supports you** as you hold space for others. All the layers are necessary to hold space in a healthy, consistent manner.

What Guides You: The Middle Layer of the Bowl

The middle layer of the bowl contains five properties that you, as the space-holder, must strengthen in order to hold space well (Figure 3). Think of the properties in this middle layer as the "muscles" necessary to hold space, muscles you build with years and years of practice—skills that help you be effective and make good decisions about what you offer. The strength of this middle layer is rooted in the space-holder's capacity, personal development, and emotional intelligence.

THE PROPERTIES that guide you are:

1 Intuition
2 Discernment
3 Humility
4 Courage
5 Curiosity

FIGURE 3. THE MIDDLE LAYER OF THE BOWL

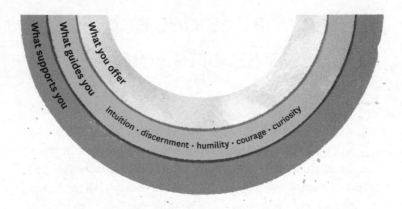

1. Intuition

When holding space, intuition is one of the things you rely on to understand a person's needs in any given moment. Your intuition or "gut feeling" is a sensation of enhanced under-standing that appears quickly in your consciousness. Often very quickly, your brain scans the signs in front of you, sifts through the lessons of past experience, and then incorporates your relationship with the person to help interpret their needs.

Through this process, your mind, body, and heart collectively offer up knowledge to help you know what to offer from moment to moment. This intuition tells you when to be quiet and when to speak, when to share a story, when to let them fall apart, or when to offer the other components of the inner layer of your bowl.

The practice of holding space is essentially a practice of sharpening your intuition. Though these intuitive hunches might seem to show up without rational explanation at first, they become more accurate as you build up years of experience and learning. The more you practise, the better you get at reading the signs and recognizing the needs as they appear. In the beginning, when your intuition is less fine-tuned, you might read the signs incorrectly or act on the wrong gut feeling. Don't let these "mistakes" hinder you, but rather consider them to be learning opportunities that help you fine-tune your intuition. When you're committed to being a lifelong learner in this practice, your intuition will develop into an essential tool. Ideally, you'll learn to trust and utilize this intuition when it appears.

Look for practices that help you sharpen your intuitive senses. Mindfulness practices help you stay present in the moment, journal or art practices help you to process what you're learning, solitude practices help you to be more present for and more trusting of your own thoughts, and body practices help you to tune in to your deeper resources. Your intuition will serve you well if you foster it, trust it, and fine-tune it.

It's worth mentioning, though, that sometimes trauma gets in the way of intuition. Some of us have had such difficult experiences that our intuition cannot always be trusted and we may confuse trauma triggers with intuition. We may have become overly sensitized to signs of danger or rejection when, for example, we grew up with substance abuse in the home. In that case, it might be necessary to seek treatment such as dialectical behaviour therapy (DBT), which helps a person discern when they are responding only to "emotion mind" and are not balancing it with "reasonable mind." With therapy, one can learn to hold both together and get in touch with "wise mind," another way of understanding "intuition."[16]

2. Discernment

Discernment is the ability to make good judgment calls. Add discernment to intuition and knowledge and you get wisdom.

To become practised at discernment and good decision-making, one must rely on intuition along with information, analysis, a strong sense of self-trust, and the support of wise advisers and supporters. Accurate discernment often requires testing the information or asking good questions of trusted advisers to increase the analysis.

For example, when I'm in a coaching conversation, intuition might tell me there's something the client is not telling me (based on their body signals, voice changes, etc.) but which I think might be meaningful in helping them. I use discernment to guide me in deciding what questions to ask next. Sometimes it feels a little magical; sometimes the person looks at me in amazement and marvels that I've asked *exactly* the right question to uncover some stubborn, hidden aspect.

Like intuition, discernment is based on many years of having such conversations, studying coaching practices, learning from other people, and exploring ways of revealing the invisible barriers that get in people's way. It's a well-practised muscle I've learned to trust.

Discernment isn't necessarily something you fine-tune on your own; you also need to surround yourself with a community of discerning people so that your own discernment grows. It can include drawing on the expertise of others in order to see what you are missing—gathering people to serve as a sounding board of witnesses and coaches.

3. Humility

Humility is a willingness to recognize and take responsibility for your mistakes and weaknesses. It's a choice to be honest and authentic, to apologize when you fumble, and to make repairs when necessary. Humility allows you to be in equitable relationship with people rather than seeing yourself as superior. Unless you are willing to approach this work with humility, you will likely find yourself hijacking space instead of holding it.

I'm not talking about false humility or humility rooted in insecurity, where you're inclined to be overly apologetic or self-deprecating, beating yourself up for every mistake. No, that behaviour gets in the way of holding space because it leads you to centre *yourself* in the story rather than the other person.

Rather, I'm talking about the humility that allows you to be a lifelong learner, recognizing that holding space is a practice you will never have mastery over. Humility consistently reminds you that your role is not to *control or direct* but to *hold* the space for another person's discovery, to acknowledge their capacity to find their own solutions in the process.

Humility helps you recognize that the other person is usually better served if you *listen* rather than talk; that in helping them to figure out their own answers, sometimes even all your years of expertise may not be of use. Humility also lets you know when you're the wrong person to hold space for someone, that there may be another person better suited to the task.

4. Courage

It takes courage to show up in a way that allows us to hold space for another person. It takes courage to hold them in their messy liminal space. It takes courage simply to *be with the mess* when much of the world is wired for productivity and shininess.

Courage is a heart word. The root of the word courage *is* cor— *the Latin word for heart. In one of its earliest forms, the word* courage *meant "To speak one's mind by telling all one's heart." Over time, this definition has changed, and today, we typically associate courage with heroic and brave deeds. But in my opinion, this definition fails to recognize the inner strength and level of commitment required for us to actually speak honestly and openly about who we are and about our experiences— good and bad. Speaking from our hearts is what I think of as "ordinary courage."*[17]

BRENÉ BROWN

• • •

Sometimes, when you're holding space, things will get so messy and complex that you'll want to run and hide. Sometimes the person you're holding space for will need to release a great deal of emotion. They may project all of their anger and pain onto you, blaming you for what they can't control. Sometimes (as when the situation calls for allyship) you may even find yourself in a precarious position, where your own sense of self is questioned (which may be when you return to discernment to help you decide whether to stay in the situation or remove yourself). It may not be easy, and you might feel quite vulnerable holding space in those situations, but with courage guiding you (along with discernment and intuition) you'll find your capacity to be bold on other people's behalf.

5. Curiosity

The best antidote for judgment is curiosity. The two cannot comfortably coexist. Judgment closes us off, while curiosity opens us up. Judgment sees the other person as flawed and in need of fixing, while curiosity is willing to look beyond what seems obvious to witness the complexity underneath. Judgment closes your heart and mind, while curiosity opens them.

When you find yourself slipping into judgment, wanting to fix someone, give them advice, remove an obstacle for them, or shame them for the state they're in, you can make a choice to bring curiosity to the situation instead. Curiosity asks meaningful, open-hearted questions and doesn't assume it already knows the answers. Curiosity is willing to have its opinions changed. Curiosity doesn't assume its own stories and answers apply to other people's lives.

The kind of curiosity I'm talking about here is not the same as nosiness or a quest for information to feed the gossip mill or to justify your own position. When curiosity partners with discernment, it is balanced and not invasive. It creates openness and possibility. It holds space for potential and does not assume it already knows the answers.

To check in with yourself about whether you're allowing curiosity to guide you, ask yourself whether a quest for information is in service to the other person's need for support or to your own need for information.

● ● ●

For to listen is to continually give up all expectation and to give our attention, completely and freshly to what is before us, not really knowing what we will hear or what that will mean. In the practice of our days, to listen is to lean in, softly, with a willingness to be changed by what we hear.[18]

MARK NEPO

What Supports You: The Outer Layer of the Bowl

The outer layer shapes and supports the entire container (Figure 4). It includes:

1 Mystery
2 Community

FIGURE 4. THE OUTER LAYER OF THE BOWL

FIGURE 4. THE OUTER LAYER OF THE BOWL

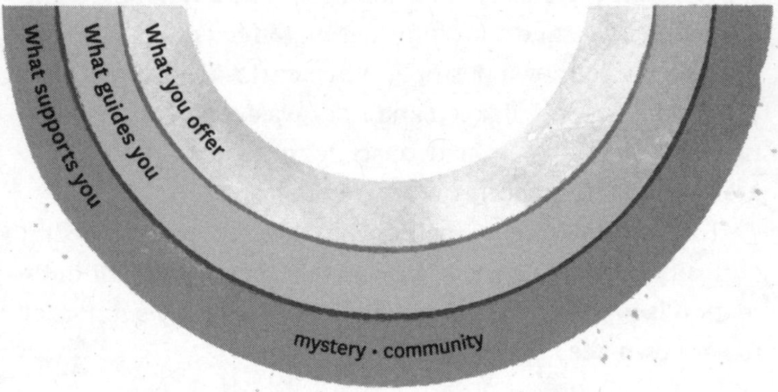

1. Mystery

After years of doing this work, I am convinced that holding space is a spiritual act and that what holds it all together is something bigger than any of us. While we hold space, there is a greater essence that we can lean into, especially when we need courage, strength, and wisdom.

I am intentionally not going to try to define this Mystery for you; your version of the Mystery might be different from mine. It's something meant to be just outside our human reach and understanding.

When we hold space, we do so in a way that invites Mystery into the process. That means that you, as the space-holder, open yourself to the spiritual and take cues from a Source far larger than you. It means that you trust the person for whom you are holding space to also be held by the same Source.

You don't need a specific spiritual belief system to accommodate this mystical element of holding space. If you're Muslim, it may be Allah you trust to work with you. If you are Hindu, you might invite Shiva, Kali, or Ganesha into the space. If you are agnostic or animist, you might simply believe that the Earth or the Universe or Love is holding the space with you. If you are Christian or Jewish, call it God or Yahweh. If you are Indigenous, call it Creator, Mother Earth, animal spirit guides, or the ancestors. Whatever the case, the work deepens when you open yourself to Mystery and acknowledge and invite a sense of the Great Unknown into the work.

When you do open yourself to Mystery, prepare for the unexpected. Prepare to be humbled and awed by what is beyond your control. I have witnessed some of the most magical things when holding space in this capacity.

Sometimes, for example, animals will appear. Once, after a shamanic womb healing ceremony at the edge of the ocean, our circle of women was visited by a dolphin, a manatee, a seal, and several birds. My friend TuBears, an elder in the Choctaw nation, was with us for the ceremony and said, "Of course! They want to be part of the healing energy in this space."

Another time, at the end of a retreat in which we discussed transformation and liminal space, we came out of the centre to be surrounded by millions of migrating butterflies. At other retreats, bears or coyotes have shown up at auspicious moments. Other times the weather shifts, and a clap of thunder accentuates something profound that was just expressed in the space. I've witnessed this magic so often, in fact, that I often send people out into the natural world at retreats to explore what nature may want to teach them about holding space. At a place where I teach in the Netherlands, people often gain insight from the ocean that is near our gathering place.

Some of the work of holding space is about paying attention to, and working with, the energy in the space you're holding. Sometimes that energy can simply be attributed to someone's mood (sadness or anger, for example) and sometimes there's a deeper Mystery at work. It may not be possible to fully explain that Mystery or how it changes the energy in the room (though you may find ways of framing it within your own belief system), but it's worth paying attention to, nonetheless.

Each of us has a different way of connecting to Spirit and understanding energetics, so I will not be prescriptive in telling you how to do this. But I will say your work will deepen when you silence the skeptic in your mind and open yourself to your own version of Mystery.

2. Community

Holding space does not happen in a vacuum; it's an act of Community at its finest. Even when I hold space for a dear friend and we are sitting alone in a coffee shop, there is rootedness in Community that we can access, a much bigger love than either of us can muster, alone or together.

For me as a space-holder, Community looks like the close friends who listen when I'm struggling, the people on my team who help teach my courses, the business manager who makes sure all of the pieces fit together, my siblings, my therapist, my teachers, my women's circle, my daughters, my colleagues around the world, my ancestral lineage, and you, my reader. Community also includes the trees in my backyard, the river by my house, and the wild birds that fly over my head. All of these and more have woven their threads together to form a giant bowl that holds *me* so that I can trust my inner guidance, lean into the Mystery, and hold space for the people who show up.

Like Mystery, Community is not a single, easily identified thing. For one person, it might appear to be very small and include only one or two friends and a cat or dog. (I say "appear to be" because there are aspects of Community that are beyond what we have a physical experience of.) For another person, it might be quite large and include global connections with people they've never met in person. Whatever it is, embrace it, nurture it, and lean into it.

An aspect of the Community that may be invisible to you is your lineage and the family system you were born into. Your parents, their parents, their parents' parents, and so on and so on—all of these are part of the vast container in which you are held and supported as you hold space for others. You may never have a conscious experience of them, but they have influenced you, they have passed their DNA on to you, and they have helped to shape who you've become. If you are in conflict with your family, or have chosen to break ties because of abuse, this may feel painful for you to consider, but even in families where there is considerable inherited trauma, there is also inherited goodness, strength, resilience, and a desire to thrive. You can honour the container they created for you to be born into even as you work to heal whatever may be broken in the lineage.

Mystery and Community are intricately intertwined and hard to separate; it's all those things that you connect to and lean on when you need strength, guidance, and resilience in the work of holding space. When you lean on Mystery, your Community often shows up in support. When you lean on Community, Mystery often makes an appearance. They both function most beautifully when they are in relationship with, and in service to, the whole.

I considered including Love in this outer layer as well, but I believe that Love is part of Mystery and Community and therefore requires no separate naming. It is, perhaps, the essence of both. Neither can exist without it or outside it.

The Glue between the Layers

There is one more property that bears mentioning, one that doesn't necessarily fit into a specific layer. Instead, it's the glue that holds all the layers of the bowl together. That property is **trust.**

For the practice of holding space to happen, everyone involved must lean into trust. The person for whom you're holding space will need to trust you. You will need to trust them, trust yourself, and trust Mystery and Community.

Trust building is one of the most crucial aspects of holding space. Without trust, it's much more difficult for transformation to happen. Without trust, the person might not surrender enough to the journey through liminal space to allow evolution and transformation to take place.

As I write this, I'm watching a bird outside my window. The bird is resting on a thin branch that looks as if it would easily snap in my hands. But the bird has experience with branches like this. It has enough knowledge and instinct to know what's safe so that it can sit there without worrying the branch will give way beneath it. That branch could not hold space for me, but it can hold space for the bird.

The bird trusts the branch, the branch trusts the tree trunk, the tree trunk trusts the roots, and the roots trust the earth.

When we hold space for someone, the person might not know their "branch" is safe enough to hold them. We must establish enough trust so they know they've found the right branch on which to rest, one that can support their needs. We do that partly by leaning into that which holds us: Mystery and Community. We can also learn to trust the process itself, knowing that the act of holding space will serve all involved.

Trust building can happen slowly or in an instant. Sometimes trust relies on the credentials we know the person has, or the patterns we've witnessed in their relationships. Have they proven they can keep things confidential? Do they refrain from giving me unsolicited advice? In a friendship, it might take a few years of trust building before I share what's going on in my life. With a therapist or coach, on the other hand, I may show up in the room (or on the phone) with enough trust to start sharing deeply right away.

If you are holding space for someone, you build trust by being dependable, consistent, available, respectful, non-judgmental, reliably confidential, and self-aware. On the other hand, you destroy trust by controlling the other person and insisting they do things *your* way, by breaking confidence and telling others about what they're going through, and by judging or shaming them. You can also destroy trust by consistently putting your needs ahead of theirs or by refusing to acknowledge the way your own biases get in the way.

I am often amazed at how quickly trust is built within an intentional circle gathering. Sit down in the right container, be intentional about how you create a safe and supportive space, offer deep and uninterrupted listening, and people very quickly begin to share from a vulnerable and authentic place. The intention and care you put into how you hold the space greatly influence what shows up in the space.

Some of the best conversations with my teenage and early-adult daughters happen around fires when we are camping or hanging out in our backyard. There's something about removing ourselves from our typical spaces and sitting in a circle around a fire that's conducive to slower, deeper conversations. It might also help that it's usually dark outside and nobody is looking directly at each other.

There is no guarantee in trust building, though; you cannot impose trust. You can do everything just right, and a person may still not trust you to hold space for them. They may have been deeply wounded in other relationships, they may have trauma in their past and be easily triggered, or something about you might represent the source of their oppression or abuse. The best thing you can do is recognize the dynamic and allow that person the autonomy to find the people they *can* trust.

WHEN ALL three layers of the bowl come together and are held together by trust, it's a thing of beauty to witness, to practise, and to receive. As practitioners of this sacred act, we know the beauty of the gift and know that we are held by something greater than ourselves, even when we fumble.

5

refining your container

AS YOU BECOME comfortable with the qualities necessary to hold space, there are three additional considerations that are key to shaping the container you hold for others.

Recognize the Shape of the Space

A few years ago, when I was visiting Oregon, a couple of friends gave me a beautiful raw crystal with a lot of jagged edges and sharp points that project in all directions. It's intricate and fragile, and when it came time to pack my suitcase, I wasn't sure how to pack the crystal securely enough to get it home in one piece. I ended up wrapping it in multiple layers of scarves and, fortunately, it arrived home without mishap.

I contemplated that crystal a few months later as I prepared for another trip. For me, it had become a metaphor of a person on a liminal journey who's fragile, with a lot of rough edges. I decided to bring it along as a teaching tool for my retreat that week and set out to create just the right container to hold it.

At the local craft store, I found a circular box made of heavy cardboard that was just the right size. It was rigid, though, and needed some softness to cushion the sharp edges of the crystal. I cut layers of soft foam to fit the negative space between the crystal and the container and glued them inside the box, covering it all with fabric. I lined the inside of the lid in a similar manner. When I was done, the crystal could nestle inside a custom-made container, one with an inner softness to weather any jostling and an outer hardness to protect the crystal from outside force.

Every person or group for whom you hold space is like this crystal—fragile, intricate, and unique. Their sharp edges can hurt people and can easily be broken. They need to be cared for appropriately.

To effectively hold space for someone, consider what kind of customization their space might need. Where do they need extra cushioning to soften the raw places? Where do they need rigidity to protect them from outside forces?

Not only does each person need to be uniquely held, but each stage of the liminal space journey may require a different kind of holding. In the depths of the chrysalis stage, they may need secure containment and protection, but when they are ready to emerge, they'll need to be more lightly held, with freedom to grow and evolve.

Being pregnant with and then raising babies provided some of the most valuable lessons I've learned in holding space. When the embryo was first planted, my womb provided a highly controlled and well-protected space with lots of nourishment from me. My womb was a fully enclosed container, just right for the early stages of growth.

When my baby was fully gestated, it was time for the membrane to rupture so the baby could be released from the womb's safety. The baby began breathing on their own, no longer needing to be as well protected from outside forces. I needed to adapt as well, providing a different form of protection along with nourishment from my breast milk.

As each baby grew, they needed less and less protection, and more and more autonomy. From the moment each baby left my womb, they started a journey of increasing independence, learning at each stage of growth to meet their own needs, and eventually looking to people other than Mom to have those needs met.

For me, it was a constant process of adapting the space I held for them. My babies are grown now, and though I still hold space for them, the container is loose and open. They are nearly fully autonomous. They still like it when I cook meals for them. They come to me with their problems now and then, but I avoid getting too involved unless they are in crisis mode.

I don't have to tell you how problematic it would be if I held space for my grown daughters the same way I held it for them when they were infants. People evolve, their needs change, and the container that holds them needs to change too. Paying attention to those needs is crucial if we really do have their best interests at heart.

Not only do the needs of each person vary, but it's important to recognize that our capacity to hold space also varies. Some of us provide pretty but fragile bowls, while others offer sturdy and functional bowls that are less aesthetically pleasing. Some of us can withstand heat while others can handle a lot of chaos or pressure. Each bowl is different, and no single bowl serves all purposes.

In the same way, we are each different in our strengths, how we hold space, and under what conditions we best function. Some of us hold space well for young children in a classroom, while others serve well at hospital bedsides. Some of us function well in crisis, while others fare better under more predictable circumstances.

Recognize Who Is at the Centre

One of the most valuable questions you can ask when holding space for other people is, "Who is at the centre?"

The person at the centre is the person for whom space is held and whose needs are placed at the top of the priority list. In that position, it is *their* stories, *their* emotions, *their* transformation, and *their* pain that is central. That doesn't mean that you need to withdraw yourself entirely from the situation, or that you shouldn't seek out other places where you can be centred. It simply means that you make a choice to honour their needs at this particular time. You can turn to other people (or yourself, nature, or the Divine) to get your own needs met.

A simple diagram (Figure 5) by Susan Silk and Barry Goldman is helpful in understanding this distinction. In an article in the *Los Angeles Times*, they shared their concept, called Ring Theory, using Katie, a woman recovering from a brain aneurysm, as an example:

> *Draw a circle. This is the center ring. In it, put the name of the person at the center of the current trauma. For Katie's aneurysm, that's Katie. Now draw a larger circle around the first one. In that ring put the name of the person next closest to the trauma. In the case of Katie's aneurysm, that was Katie's husband, Pat. Repeat the process as many times as you need to. In each larger ring put the next closest people. Parents and children before more distant relatives. Intimate friends in smaller rings, less intimate friends in larger ones. When you are done you have a Kvetching Order.*
>
> *Here are the rules. The person in the center ring can say anything she wants to anyone, anywhere. She can kvetch and complain and whine and moan and curse the heavens and say, "Life is unfair" and "Why me?" That's the one payoff for being in the center ring.*

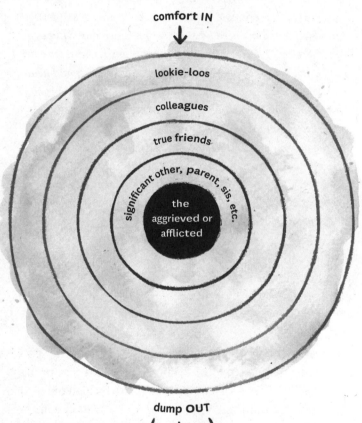

FIGURE 5. RING THEORY
by Susan Silk and Barry Goldman

comfort *IN*

lookie-loos

colleagues

true friends.

significant other, parent, sis, etc.

the aggrieved or afflicted

dump **OUT**

Everyone else can say those things too, but only to people in larger rings.

When you are talking to a person in a ring smaller than yours, someone closer to the center of the crisis, the goal is to help. Listening is often more helpful than talking. But if you're going to open your mouth, ask yourself if what you are about to say is likely to provide comfort and support. If it isn't, don't say it. Don't, for example, give advice. People who are suffering from trauma don't need advice. They need comfort and support. So say, "I'm sorry," or "This must really be hard for you" or "Can I bring you a pot roast?" Don't say, "You should hear what happened to me" or "Here's what I would do if I were you." And don't say, "This is really bringing me down."

If you want to scream or cry or complain, if you want to tell someone how shocked you are or how icky you feel, or whine about how it reminds you of all the terrible things that have happened to you lately, that's fine. It's a perfectly normal response. Just do it to someone in a bigger ring.

Comfort IN, dump OUT.[19]

When you have not had your own emotional needs met as a space-holder, it can be tempting to move yourself closer to the centre circle of the "Kvetching Order" relationship dynamic. When you feel that temptation, first look at where your own needs are coming from. Are you feeling taken advantage of (in which case perhaps you need to step back from holding space)? Are you being triggered by old trauma (in which case perhaps you should walk away for a while so as not to burden the people more wounded than you)? Do you need to work on your own healing first before you can adequately hold space for the people in the centre? Do you resent the person at the centre because they always manage to draw the attention to themselves?

After my dad died and my mom moved to the city where I lived, my sister and I became Mom's primary sources of support.

She was feeling completely lost, not only having become a widow very suddenly but also having uprooted herself almost immediately and moved from the farm to a city. She had to find a new community and make new friends, figure out how to navigate the city, and take stock of her new financial reality, among other things—all while in the middle of the most debilitating grief and loneliness she'd ever experienced. She was more needy than I'd ever seen her, and both my sister and I (and my brothers, though they both lived farther away and did not support her immediate needs as much) were exhausted with the emotional labour of trying to support her.

In the middle of my own grief, I found it difficult to hold space for her with compassion and without judgment. Losing my dad had sent me into my own emotional tailspin, and I had young children and a busy career to juggle as well. I wanted desperately to centre *myself* in my own grief narrative, but hers kept taking precedence over mine. It was overwhelming and exhausting, and I know I made many mistakes. I remember, for example, when she started crying in the hairdresser's chair when I took her for a haircut. I found myself shutting down emotionally, unable to have compassion for her and judging her for unloading her grief on a hairdresser she'd never met before. I am sure, in that moment, that I came across as cold and lacking in compassion, but I simply didn't have the energy to be her bowl at that moment.

Sometimes (as we'll discuss in chapter 7) we are not the right ones to hold space in a particular situation or for particular people. Sometimes walking away, or suggesting they reach out to someone more objective about the situation, may be the best thing we can do for all parties involved.

It's often the hardest to hold space for the people with whom we're in the most intimate relationships; we are directly impacted by whatever they're going through and so the stakes are high. For example, when an intimate partner is going through a liminal journey, we often experience our own fear, along with the realization that our own life might also be turned upside down. We don't know how they are going to change, which puts our own safety and comfort at risk. We have a vested interest in maintaining the status quo, in having them stay the same, or at least in minimizing the potential disruption.

If, while holding space, you experience the need to be at the centre—or you're resentful of the person or people at the centre—it may be a signpost that you're not meant to be the bowl for them at that time. Perhaps, after stepping away to do some personal work or self-care, you'll be strong enough to return and put the other person back in the centre.

Recognize the Expenditure of Emotional Labour

It requires a great deal of *emotional labour* to hold space for another person. This is not something we should take lightly, because it can drain our energy much more significantly than we might expect. Sometimes, emotional labour requires more energy than physical labour.

"Emotional labour," a term coined by Arlie Russell Hochschild in her 1983 book on the topic, *The Managed Heart*, was first used to define what is required of people in the workplace. Wikipedia defines it this way:

> *Emotional labor is the process of managing feelings and expressions to fulfill the emotional requirements of a job. More specifically, workers are expected to regulate their emotions during interactions with customers, co-workers and superiors. This includes analysis and decision making in terms of*

the expression of emotion, whether actually felt or not, as well as its opposite: the suppression of emotions that are felt but not expressed.[20]

Some of us do a great deal of emotional labour in our places of work. Whether we are nurses expected to support people in the midst of their greatest fear or grief, servers expected to remain cheerful even when diners are grumpy or demanding, or pastors managing conflict in our congregation, we are doing emotional labour on behalf of those we serve.

Many of us have been in jobs where the emotional labour was taken for granted, where we weren't paid in a way that reflected the true value we offered to the organization. Take a receptionist, for example. Often among the lowest paid in an organization, they're expected to do a great deal of emotional labour, staying pleasant and managing the emotions of disgruntled clients regardless of how they feel personally. My oldest daughter worked in accounts receivable at a water company not long ago, and she came home every day with tales of the abuse she would take from customers who hadn't paid their bills, or who weren't satisfied with the service. In my opinion, they weren't paying her well enough for the emotional labour required for the job. (And then there's the emotional labour I put in on a regular basis listening to her vent about the customers— but I haven't yet found a way to get paid for being a mom!)

Consider the effort you must continually put into your own personal healing and growth so that you are strong enough to hold space for others. That alone is a *lot* of emotional labour. Add to that the emotional labour you are now doing on other people's behalf, supporting them while they fall apart, guiding them when they're lost, and listening when their emotions overflow. That's like running an emotional marathon nearly every time you hold space.

A few years ago I had the privilege of creating a "liminal space" ceremony for a couple of people who were about to launch a business together. It was one of the most beautiful—and yet energetically draining—things I've done in a long time. I created a metaphoric journey that invited them, over the course of a couple of hours, to peer into both their shadow and their light. When they dove into their own darkness, I held them both physically and emotionally. When they stepped into the light, I was there to steady them. At the end of the ceremony, we celebrated what they were about to birth.

The ceremony itself took only a couple of hours, but the emotional labour required meant that my personal restoration afterwards took a lot longer. After the ceremony, I had a pounding headache. That night I had frightening and disorienting dreams. It took me a few days of intentional self-care and gentleness to shake off the weariness. While it was an amazing experience for all of us, it took a lot out of me both physically and emotionally. (Note: In the pagan world, it's customary to do some sort of "grounding" after a ritual experience like this—siphoning the excess energy away and sending it back into the earth so that we don't continue to carry it. You may want to look into some version of this if you find yourself doing similar work.)

I've developed a fondness for slow modes of transportation after intense work; it gives me time to process and release whatever happened. A few years ago, after facilitating two retreats plus a one-day workshop in Australia, I took the train from Brisbane to Sydney. I planned to read or watch a movie on that fifteen-hour train ride, but instead I stared out the window the whole time. The retreats had required so much emotional labour that all I could do was zone out and breathe. Afterwards, I spent a week wandering around Sydney to further replenish my energy.

Don't ever underestimate how much the work of holding space requires of you. We need strong boundaries and good self-care. We need to check in regularly with our capacity and be honest about how much we can manage.

Many people, especially those in crisis mode, are unaware of how much emotional labour they ask of others. Other people might have a propensity to take advantage of our willingness to hold space for them and will usurp our capacity for emotional labour. When this happens, it becomes an unhealthy balance that is difficult to sustain. In situations like this, we'll need to consider how to erect healthy boundaries that help us maintain our energy (more on this in chapter 10).

One of the ways I have learned to better manage the emotional labour required in the work of holding space is to invite people to do some of that emotional labour alongside me. In my Holding Space Practitioner Program, for example, I have a team of people who help me hold the space. They are people who've already been through the program and demonstrate a high level of capacity. Often, they are people who bring unique capacity that fills in the gaps where my capacity might be lacking. For example, some of the people I've brought onto the team have somatic understanding of how we hold space with our bodies, some help to make the space more equitable for marginalized individuals, and some bring skills in hosting in online spaces. It's amazing how much difference it can make to have someone else noticing and responding to the needs and energetics of the group.

It serves us well to become more attuned to the amount of emotional labour we expend, and to what we have available in our reserves. Consider the gas tank in your car: you wouldn't set out on a long journey without filling your tank, especially if you're travelling to a remote area where there may not be many service stations. It's the same when you hold space for someone's journey through liminal space: fill up your tank so you have what it takes to do the emotional labour. (Note: Each of us may have different ways of filling our "gas tanks" and different ways that our tanks are depleted. Extroverts, for example, may not be as depleted by emotional labour as introverts are, so it's important to pay attention to yourself and not assume that you're the same as everyone else.)

TOGETHER WITH the qualities of the bowl outlined in the previous two chapters, these considerations should heighten your discernment and intuition about when and how to hold space. Let's switch gears now and talk about the *opposite* of holding space...

6

hijacking space

A FEW MONTHS AFTER I wrote the original blog post about holding space, I was asked a provocative question during an interview: "What's the opposite of holding space?" It was the first time I considered that question, and it cracked open months' worth of thought. What I finally came up with, after searching for a term that satisfied me (and trying out a few versions), was this:

| **The opposite of holding space is hijacking space.**

When you hijack a vehicle (a plane, train, ship, etc.), you illegally seize it for your own purposes and force it to a different destination.

While *holding space* involves supporting without judging, fixing, or controlling the outcome, *hijacking space* involves manipulating, disempowering, and imposing various forms of judgment and control.

When we hold space, we *liberate*. We give someone the freedom to be who they are, to make sovereign choices, and to control their own outcome. When we hold space, we leave the person feeling supported and empowered.

When we hijack space, we *violate*. We take away a person's freedom, limit their ability to make choices, and take control of the outcome. When we hijack space, we leave the person disenfranchised and weakened.

While holding space offers people an open bowl for their journey through liminal space, hijacking space puts a lid on that bowl (see Figure 6).

FIGURE 6. HIJACKING SPACE

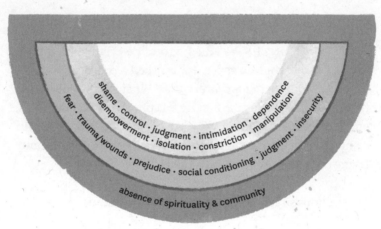

Some forms of hijacking space are obvious and intentional (such as violence, abuse, overpowering, or bullying), but other forms are much more subtle and inadvertent. Many of these more subtle forms of hijacking space include the kinds of behaviour of which we are all guilty—and usually more frequently than we care to admit.

WE HIJACK space when we:

1 Expect another person to experience or interpret a situation the same way we do. For example, when someone is afraid to try something, we dismiss their feelings by saying, "It doesn't scare me, so why are you being such a chicken?"

2 Act as the "tone police" when someone's emotions are stronger than we're comfortable with. For example, when someone is expressing rage, we admonish them with, "Calm down! You're too angry!" This implies their emotions are unmerited or that our comfort has more value than their feelings.

3 One-up another person's story with a better one of our own. For example, when someone tells us how frustrated they are with bureaucratic red tape while applying for insurance benefits after an injury, we respond with something like, "Oh, that's *nothing*. I went through a lot more frustration when I was going through my divorce." This can place higher value on our story, potentially leaving the other person feeling shame for taking their problems too seriously.

4 Imply that our emotional response is more important than theirs. For example, when a mutual friend has died and we act as though our grief is worse and we need more attention because we were closer to that person, thereby shutting down our friend's equally valid emotional response.

5 Don't allow a person to trust their intuition and insist they do things our way. If, for example, they decide to cancel a trip to visit a family member because it will require more emotional labour than they have the capacity for, we insist, "It will be fine. You should go anyway. Otherwise, people will think you're unreliable." This dismisses their intuition and imposes our beliefs and fears on them.

6 Interrupt. When a person tells us about how lost they feel, for example, we interrupt instead of listening to the whole story, leaving them feeling invisible and unvalued.

7 Act dismissively when someone shares a personal experience. This can be as subtle as not looking at them when they're talking (being distracted by our phone, for example) or as obvious as making dismissive comments about how we don't believe their story or think they're "making a mountain out of a molehill."

8 Ignore a boundary or a request for behaviour change. If a friend tells us, for example, that they're not comfortable being in the same room as their ex-husband, and we invite them to the same event anyway, we're disregarding their requested boundary.

9 Break trust. If, for example, someone shares a personal story with us and we pass that story on without their permission, we have violated the trust they placed in us.

10 Fix a problem for someone or take away their power to fix it themselves. For example, if a friend shares that they've had a disagreement with a family member and we later phone that family member without permission, trying to resolve the issue on our friend's behalf, we are disempowering them. In addition to violating their trust, this can leave them feeling incapable of handling their own problems.

11 Show up with fragility that puts focus on our own emotions in a situation where someone else is more directly impacted. If, in a mixed-race situation, a white person weeps over the injustice of a young Black man killed by the police, the people of colour in the group can find themselves providing the white person with support and care while their feelings are ignored.

12 Apologize excessively so that the other person becomes responsible for making us feel better. For example, instead of holding space for a friend when we show up at their house, we spend the first hour repeatedly apologizing for not attending their mother's funeral, shifting the focus to us and sidelining the other person's grief.

13 Expect them to feed our ego with praise and appreciation, etc. When we refuse to hold space for a friend because they neglected to shower us with thanks for the last time we supported them, for example, we make it about us and ignore the fact that they may have been too overwhelmed by their situation to remember.

14 Treat them passive-aggressively and cause shame. If a friend shares a heartbreak over a fight she's had with her husband and we say, "Well, at least you *have* a husband," we make her feel ashamed for complaining while we have no partner.

15 Gaslight them by calling into question their memory, perception, or sanity. When, for example, a person tells us that they are being emotionally abused by their partner and we say something like, "You're just imagining things. Your partner is really nice and wouldn't ever do those things," our response makes them doubt their interpretation of the experience.

16 Over-explain things or re-explain what someone has already said. Terms like "whitesplaining" or "mansplaining" have become common ways of identifying this behaviour based in a (likely subconscious) belief that people of colour or women are less intelligent and less understandable. When a person is treated as though they lack intelligence or their way of explaining things is insufficient for the larger population, they're left feeling marginalized and devalued.

17 Worry about someone excessively. While people appreciate our concern, they rarely appreciate hovering or excessive worrying. If we check on them constantly or say things like, "I'm worried that you won't be able to get over this," then we're implying that they don't have the capacity, strength, or intelligence to survive on their own. We also risk fostering codependency in both ourselves and the other person.

As illustrated in the above diagram, the bowl that hijacks now offers shame, control, judgment, intimidation, dependence, disempowerment, isolation, constriction, and manipulation. People who've been treated that way have trouble developing positive self-esteem and healthy coping mechanisms. They will likely doubt their own capacity, worry that they're not good enough, and feel that they need to rely too heavily on other people's intelligence and strength. When they've had their space hijacked, it will undermine their trust in themselves and others.

Hijacking space is not just something "bad" people do; we *all* do it sometimes. We do it to our children, our friends, our spouses, our employees, and even our parents. Sometimes we do it because we're tired or overwhelmed. Sometimes it's because the situation has triggered an old trauma we may not be aware of. Sometimes we do it because we have no idea how to express unconditional love (maybe because we've never experienced it in our lives) or we have never learned the skills of holding space. Other reasons might be that we're feeling insecure, we think that offering solutions is the only way to contribute something of value, we're behaving in alignment with family patterns and dynamics, we've learned unhealthy ways of getting our needs met, or because certain emotional states may not have been permitted for us growing up and so they elicit a fear reaction in us.

What guides us when we hijack space (the middle layer of the bowl) is fear, trauma, our wounds, prejudice, social conditioning, our judgment, and our insecurity. When we hold space, we are grounded in Mystery and Community, but when we hijack space, we are disconnected from those sources of support.

We often hijack space to assert our own power in ways both subtle and overt. Not long ago, for example, my teenaged daughter came home from film camp complaining about a girl in her group who annoyed her. I nearly jumped in to assure her that it wasn't really as bad as she claimed, and that she needed to be kind to people no matter what. If I'd done that (gaslighting!), I would have immediately disempowered and shamed her. Instead, I tried to listen without judgment and speak with compassionate, selective guidance. The next day, she figured out how to deal with this person on her own, without me needing to intervene.

We also hijack space in situations where we're trying to increase our power in a relationship. Consider a time, for example, when you felt intimidated by someone, and consequently interrupted them, dismissed their emotions, gaslit them, and/or tried to control the outcome of the conversation. While upsetting the power imbalance may have felt good in the moment, it's not the most effective way to transform a relationship.

Most of the time, we hijack space unintentionally because of our own unconscious baggage and bias. In rare situations, hijacking becomes something more deliberate and intentionally oppressive or manipulative, but the people guilty of that type of hijacking wouldn't likely be reading this book.

While the hijacking may be unintentional, there will be times when we need to take responsibility not only for our *intention* but for the *impact* of our actions and/or words. For example, when we fix someone's problem for them, our *intention* may be to make things easier for them, but the *impact* will be to make them feel disempowered. It is tempting to hide behind our intentions, but if we value the relationship, we'll want to make repairs based on the way the other person experienced the situation.

Not long ago, for example, my daughter pointed out that I'd said something in a passive-aggressive tone. My reaction was to jump to my own defence and say that I hadn't intended it that way, but then she challenged me on my defensiveness. Finally recognizing that my relationship with my daughter was more valuable than my need to be right, I paused, took a few deep breaths, and said, "Yes, I understand how that sounded passive-aggressive and defensive. I apologize. Let me try again." I then restated what I'd originally said with less attitude. We shared a good laugh afterwards and she offered to go grocery shopping for me. Now that's a *real* win!

When we serve as the space-holding bowl, we don't intervene, control, or need to be right; we simply hold, protect, and create safe space for the deconstruction, liminality, and emergence of another person. When we hijack space, we put a lid on that bowl and attempt to mould the outcome. Instead of liberating, we entrap. Instead of empowering, we weaken. Instead of creating safe space for emergence, we force another person into the shape of our choosing. We manipulate, direct, and judge.

It takes a lot of emotional maturity to be the bowl instead of the mould. We need to do our own work to dismantle our inner hijacker and to look deeply into our shadows. We need to address our shame and our fear. We need to practise releasing control and sharing power.

7

when close is
too close

TWO DAYS BEFORE his first suicide attempt, I threw a phone at my then husband. I was desperate and afraid.

We were standing on the lawn beside our house. I was about to get into our vehicle and drive away with the cordless phone. It was in the days before cellphones; if I took the phone, there was no other way to make a phone call. Marcel, my then husband, was standing next to the house begging me to give it back.

"Fine!" I screamed as the phone sailed across the lawn. "Have it! Just go ahead and give up. Make the fucking phone call."

I had taken the phone away from him out of some misguided (and fearful) attempt at tough love. The day before—after weeks of depression, panic attacks, and missed work—he'd finally decided he was ready to go back to work. But then panic consumed him once again and he couldn't do it. He was about to call his boss to say he couldn't return. After arguing with him, I took the phone away and ran out of the house in an attempt to keep him from what I thought was a terrible mistake.

I was sure he needed to face his ghosts and get back to work. I was sure I knew how to get through this better than he did.

Those were some of the hardest, darkest days of my life. For weeks we'd been living under the shadow of his depression. I was overwhelmed and really, really scared. We'd been married for three years and I was five months pregnant with our first child. We were both in over our heads. He'd never been through such a deep depression before and I had no experience supporting anyone in that place.

I tried to get him help, but I was at a loss to figure out the mental health system. The only psychologist I could find who'd see him urgently only made him feel worse when he implied that Marcel just needed to grow up. And one overnight stay at a temporary mental health care facility made him even more afraid of his own darkness.

I was scared he would never get better. I was scared I'd have to support a mentally unstable person all my life. I was scared of raising our child alone. I was scared he'd never go back to work and we'd be poor. I was scared of this bottomless neediness that showed up in him when he was depressed. I was scared I'd never be in a "real" marriage partnership and would forever have to be the strong one.

I was scared I wasn't enough.

I just wanted everything to go back to "normal." Maybe if he went back to work, we'd get back to normal more quickly.

He didn't go to work that day, and we weathered the storm. But two days later, he got up in the morning, kissed me goodbye, told me to take care of our unborn child, and let me believe he was finally heading to work. I got up a little later and went to my office, happy that things had shifted.

When I phoned his office halfway through the morning to check how his day was going, they told me he'd never showed up. Terrified, I ran out of the office and somehow, in a blur of tears, found my way back home. He wasn't there. I started making phone calls, but nobody—his brother, his mom, his cousin, my mom—had seen or heard from him.

We spent the day looking for him. His cousin and brother looked in some of his childhood haunts. My mom drove in from the farm and we went to his favourite fishing spot. The search was fruitless.

My mom tried to care for me, insisting I needed to rest and look after myself and my unborn child. I couldn't rest. I paced the house and made more phone calls. The police told me they couldn't start looking for him until he was gone at least twenty-four hours. He was an adult, they said, so he probably didn't want to be found.

Finally, after an impossibly long day faded into darkness, the phone rang and it was Marcel's brother. He was at the hospital with Marcel. "He's alive," he said, "but he's in rough shape. He'll need surgery."

Marcel had made repeated attempts to end his life, first with pills and then with a knife. He needed multiple surgeries to repair damage to his wrists, throat, and chest.

I rushed to the hospital and found him before they took him in to surgery. My first words to him were desperate and not kind. "How could you *do* this?" I pleaded. "Didn't you know what it would do to all of the people who love you? Didn't you know what it would do to *me*?"

One of the nurses suggested I not say too much, that it would be better to wait until both of us were in better frames of mind before looking for answers. So I whispered, "I love you. I don't want you to die."

Surgeons did what they could to repair the physical wounds, but the emotional wounds ran much deeper. Staff at the hospital said they would transfer him to the psychiatric ward for care after he was in better shape physically, but then, after a week on the regular ward with no psychiatric support, they changed their minds and released him into my care.

Once again, I was terrified. How could I take him home? What if he did it again? How would I support him when I'd already made so many mistakes? What did I know about helping someone heal from that?

We stayed with his parents for a week, and gradually settled into a new (though anxious) normal. He started seeing a therapist and went to group sessions at the Anxiety Disorders Association. I hovered less and stopped trying to fix everything for him. I gradually started to trust that we could have a more balanced, reciprocal relationship again. In a few months, he went back to work and our first daughter was born.

We had lots of good years together after that, but we weathered a lot of storms. One baby quickly led to two, and then our third pregnancy ended in a stillbirth. Surprisingly, our grief in that time didn't weaken our relationship but seemed to deepen it, at least for a time. Less than two years after that, another baby arrived, this time healthy and strong.

When our third and final daughter was born, he quit his job to be a stay-at-home dad and attend university. His work in the transportation industry no longer fulfilled him and he wanted to become a teacher. I became the primary income-earner and supported him both financially and emotionally as he navigated this new territory. I edited a lot of his university papers during those years. He rarely had the confidence to turn anything in without letting me see it first.

Despite the outward appearance of coherence and partnership, there was a troubling pattern in our relationship that I kept trying to ignore. We were unbalanced. I treated him as though he was incapable of carrying half of the emotional burden of a marriage, and he lived up to my expectations. When he was weak, I tried to make him stronger. When he was lost, I tried to point him in the right direction. When he was broken, I tried to fix him. Sometimes I did it with anger and sometimes I did it with compassion. Sometimes I was therapist, sometimes I was parent, but rarely was I partner. I kept trying to mould him into the man I wanted to be married to, but he kept falling short of my expectations. In retrospect, I see the trauma caused by his first suicide attempt that left me forever trying to keep him from falling apart.

He did some work in self-improvement, but much of the time he did it primarily to keep me happy. I bought him books on self-confidence, anxiety, and personality disorder. Each time, he would read a few chapters and try some of the exercises, then lose interest.

When he went to university, I was hopeful that it would be the catalyst for him to become more confident, self-aware, and emotionally stable. I once again projected my expectations and need for stability onto him, rather than being fully present for, and accepting of, who he was and what he was capable of.

We agreed that after he finished university and found work, it would be my turn to step away from my job and pursue my dream of self-employment. However, when he finished, he couldn't find full-time work. As a substitute teacher, he wasn't making enough money to support our family. I had to stay at my job, still the primary income-earner.

In 2010 he finally found a fairly stable term position, and I thought it was a good time to launch my business. I flew to Chicago to attend a conference, planning to give my notice at my job once I got back home.

Just before I left for Chicago, however, things started falling apart at his new job. Panic attacks returned, as did some of the old patterns of depression. I left for my trip anyway, hopeful that he would work through it without me, but mostly in denial that this was happening again.

Things deteriorated while I was gone. He dropped our daughters off at his sister's place and checked himself into a mental health facility overnight. In my hotel in Chicago, I grew more and more afraid, and more and more angry.

The anger surprised me. I hadn't experienced it when he spiralled into the depths fifteen years earlier. This time, however, I felt as if I was being cheated. He fell apart just when I needed him to support me. His emotional needs, once again, took priority over mine. As much as I tried to convince myself that my thoughts were unfair—that he couldn't be blamed for his mental illness—the anger still surfaced.

A few days after I returned home, his mom phoned my office. "Marcel is here. He took a lot of pills. What should I do?" Oh wow, another suicide attempt. Would this be the time I lost him? Would this be the time our daughters became fatherless?

I rushed home and met my mother-in-law as she drove into the driveway. She stayed at our house to meet our girls after school and I climbed into her van and raced with Marcel to the hospital. "Stay awake!" I kept shouting at him as we drove. Once in the hospital, I had to fight to be taken seriously. Finally, he got a bed in the emergency room, where he was monitored to see if he needed his stomach pumped.

This time, he was transferred to a psychiatric ward after a couple of days in the emergency room. That turned out to be rather disastrous, however. Nobody paid much attention to him, and the psychiatrists who came to see him (a different one each day) barely gave him fifteen minutes of their time—just enough to prescribe stronger medications.

The anger I felt the week before dissipated, replaced by desperation, fear, and surprisingly fierce loyalty. I fought like a warrior to get him the right kind of help. When I became convinced he wasn't receiving appropriate care, I snuck him out of the psychiatric ward to see a psychologist a friend had recommended. I was desperate to help him, to fix him, to make things normal again. More than anything, I needed safety and security, and I was terrified of losing that. We had three children to care for; I didn't want to be a single parent, or even a parent whose partner was incapable of carrying at least some of the emotional load.

Again, I wanted him to be different from what he was. I fought to make it so.

He gradually got better, and a few months later he received another short-term teaching contract. Things were stable enough that we felt relatively confident he would find full-time work, enabling us to survive financially while I built my business. I quit my job, cashed in some of my retirement savings, accepted a contract to teach a few courses at the university, and started to grow my business.

The point in telling this story is that it reflects some fundamental principles about holding space and the challenges of effectively holding space for those closest to us.

When I teach about holding space, people often ask me why it seems so much harder to do it for family members or people we're in intimate relationships with. It's harder for a simple reason: because there is greater risk. The closer we are to the person, the more our lives overlap, and the harder it is to let go of the outcome—because the outcome has a direct impact on us.

It's much more difficult to allow someone space to do their own work and take responsibility for their own outcome when that person is your partner whose suicide attempts disrupt your life and your children's lives. I couldn't hold space for my husband during those desperate times because whatever happened to him had a significant direct impact on our family. That's not to say that one can't love someone through all of that—but sometimes love and holding space are separate things. Sometimes love causes us to hijack space instead of hold it.

Considerations

If you find yourself in a difficult position trying to hold space for someone close to you, consider how much capacity you have, how much you're directly impacted by the outcome, how much they're prepared to receive your support, which historic patterns of the relationship might get in the way, and who else could be available to hold space for them.

A friend or client might come to me with the same depression and anxiety Marcel experienced and—though it might trigger some fear in me—I could probably remove myself from the story enough to hold space for them during their struggle. (In fact, that scenario happened when I was a manager and one of my employees threatened suicide before disappearing from the office.) But when you are so close to the story that it triggers your trauma, desperation, and fear, it may be time to remove yourself or at least find someone else who can do the holding. You can continue to love without being the one holding space.

Could I have done anything differently when faced with the situation I had with my husband? That's a difficult question to answer, one I wrestled with repeatedly over the years. It's difficult to answer partly because it was part of a much larger pattern in my marriage, a pattern in which I was (as a marriage therapist once reflected to us) the "over-functioning" person in the relationship.

My over-functioning showed up in the way I tried to resolve too many problems for him, teach him how to handle things that overwhelmed him, and serve as his advocate when he should have been figuring out how to navigate the system on his own. Most of the time, he wanted me to do it because he felt safer that way—and so *neither* of us was really doing any favours for the other. We had no idea how to truly hold space for each other. We tried, through repeated marriage therapy attempts, to shift those patterns, but we never succeeded. Ultimately, I chose to end the marriage believing it was in the best interest of both of us.

Your story might be different, however, and so I won't project my narrative onto yours. Your intimate relationships might have the capacity to evolve and meet the changing needs of the individuals involved. Or if your capacity is low at the beginning of the relationship, you might, through practice and perseverance and a lot of honesty about your needs and feelings, learn to hold space for each other. Perhaps you'll arrive at an agreement that you can hold space for some things but not others (when you are at risk along with the other person, for example). In those cases, maybe the partner agrees to seek out someone more objective and less impacted by the outcome—an outside therapist, a coach, or even a friend who can hold a more detached space.

As I write this, one of my daughters is participating in a support group for anxiety and depression, and I am happy that she has found this space. I recognize I have limited capacity for holding space for what she goes through. Though we have a good relationship, I'm not always the right person for her to talk to because I am directly impacted by her emotional journey. As her mom, I have too much of a desire to see her whole and "fixed" and so I offer too much advice. I noticed this even during the intake meeting for the support group: the intake worker got through to her in ways that I wasn't able to because of my proximity, both to the situation and to the outcome. I could take that personally and assume I must be failing as a parent, but I'd much rather receive it as a positive thing and release some of the holding I do to someone with more detachment.

Questions to Ask Yourself

When you're in an intimate relationship with someone and wondering if you're the right person to hold space for them, here are some key questions to help clarify whether or not doing so is healthy:

- How impacted would I be by the outcome? Can I be effective despite this?

- If I hold space for that person, to what extent are we both able to maintain healthy boundaries?

- What are the unmet needs in this person that are beyond my capacity to hold space?

- What are *my* unmet needs? Would my help entail trying too hard to get that person to fill those needs?

- How much of a need do I feel to protect or fix this person?

- What unhealed wounds (if any) does that person trigger in me?

- Are there patterns of either of us hijacking space in the relationship? Is there potential to change this?

- Can I truly remain detached and compassionate when this person struggles?

As we were about to separate, Marcel and I were in a therapist's office together. He talked about the arrangements he needed to make to move out of our house. I started giving him advice about finding a place to live. The therapist jumped in and said, "You're going to let him figure that out himself." It didn't take her long to recognize one of the most well-established, stuck patterns of ours: I felt safer when I could control things, and he felt safer when he could relinquish control to someone else. The therapist's simple words served as a mirror, reflecting back the ways I tended to hijack space rather than hold it (especially when triggered).

Stuck patterns, flimsy boundaries, unhealed hurts, and the subtle ways we control and influence each other can be insidious and hard to identify, making holding space for those close to us a difficult, tangled proposition. Being clear and asking hard questions ahead of time can make this a healthier process.

And yet, holding space for each other is part of what we do as family members and friends. What I learned from my past situation now helps me be more effective in how I hold space for my daughters, how much I trust them and expect them to make their own decisions, and when I support them in seeking out others who can hold space for them. We are learning together, sometimes getting it right and sometimes getting it wrong. Intimate relationships provide us with endless opportunities to practise.

8

problematic behaviours

I N THE FALL of 2012, I taught a six-month course at the university during which I spent a full day in the classroom with the students each week. At the beginning of the term, one student seemed determined to become attached to me. She chatted with me during breaks and lunches, asked my opinion about everything, and contributed to every discussion she could. I didn't mind at first, when my emotional gas tank was full. Halfway through the term, however, my mom's cancer became progressively worse and I had increasingly less capacity for emotional labour on behalf of anyone outside my family.

I returned to the classroom a few weeks after Mom died, but it required a lot of strength to get through six hours of teaching. I had little left to give and needed stronger boundaries than before, and so I found excuses to be out of the classroom at lunchtime or during breaks. Doing my best to hold it together in front of the class, I was admittedly rather short when some students interrupted or asked too much from me.

A couple of months later, before the class ended, I got an email from the student who'd attached herself to me. She was angry and needed me to know it. She shared with me how disappointed she was that I had acted so nice at the beginning of the term and then behaved so differently after a few months. "For someone who makes a big deal about being authentic, and who writes about it on your blog," she said, "you're showing a very different side of you. You're not as authentic or compassionate as you pretend to be."

The email hurt—a lot. As a recovering people-pleaser, my first reaction was, "How do I make this right? How do I prove to her that I'm a nice person? How do I convince her I'm not a fraud?" My second reaction was, "How *dare* she accuse me of this so soon after I lost my mother? What does she know about the grief I've been through?"

I took a few days to respond to the email. What I finally sent back was a simple, straightforward note (i.e., not loaded with any of the emotion I'd managed to work through), inviting her to consider what it had been like for me in recent months, how the grief took so much energy that I had very little extra to give. She apologized and said she'd try to be more understanding. We ended the term on a fairly positive note.

A year after I finished teaching that class, I got another email from that student. She was in a rough place and needed some support and hoped I would take her on as a coaching client. But because she had no money to pay me, she asked if I'd do it for free.

My answer to her was a clear no. I knew I was not the right person to serve as her coach. The history between us made me certain we wouldn't have a successful coach–client relationship because it would be difficult to erect and maintain healthy coach–client boundaries. Plus, I was just growing my business and couldn't afford to give my labour away for free.

There are some people for whom we need a clear no. There are other people for whom we might be able to hold space in a limited fashion, but only with firm boundaries and clear limitations—and at possible great cost to ourselves. For example, you might hold space for an ailing parent, but need to communicate a clear boundary with that parent that they can only call you once a day and/or that you will only visit once a week.

It's helpful to consider the energetic ways in which people show up in our lives and respond to our efforts to hold space for them. Below is a list of some behavioural "archetypes" that may be red flags indicating where you should proceed with caution. I don't suggest using this as a way of defining people (especially not as a weapon against them), simply as a tool for understanding what can happen when you try to hold space for someone. Remember that this is a list of *behaviours*, not *people*.

It should be noted that some of the behaviours below could be the result of mental illness or personality disorder (many, for example, can be found in the description of narcissistic personality disorder), so I'm not suggesting you should categorically write these people off if they are important to you. Sometimes it works to challenge their behaviour, and sometimes an understanding of their disorder/illness helps you to adapt how you show up for them and what boundaries you set. Instead, what I'm offering is a way for you to identify a potential problem, consider the impact their behaviour could have on you, and how you might need to protect yourself from harm in these situations. (It's also possible that some of these behaviours don't bother you at all, in which case you can hold space without concern.)

Keep in mind also that there is a very good chance some of these archetypes might reflect how *you* tend to show up, or how you have shown up in particular periods of your life. They may be aspects of your shadow self that show up when you feel unsafe, ungrounded, or overlooked. Personally, I could give multiple examples where I've shown up in ways that reflect one or another of these archetypes, so I offer them with compassion and without dismissal.

When we are wounded, when we haven't done our own personal reflection work, or when we find ourselves in abusive situations from which we don't know how to extract ourselves, any one of us could slip into unhealthy patterns we might later regret. (Note: There is overlap between these archetypes and the behaviours listed in the chapter on hijacking space.)

The Bulldozer: This archetype consistently crashes over your boundaries, regardless of how carefully you erect and/or communicate them. They don't seem to hear when you ask them to stop a behaviour that feels uncomfortable to you, and they usually won't take no for an answer, choosing instead to pester you until you give in.

The Leech: This archetype attaches to you and sucks out every ounce of energy they can get. They are bottomless pits of neediness, always wanting more from you than you want to give. They usually don't apologize for their behaviour, and when they *do* apologize, it's usually done in a passive-aggressive way to manipulate you into giving them more.

The Chameleon: This archetype will show you the colours they choose to show you, flip-flopping between needy/emotional and angry/demanding in their effort to manipulate and control the relationship. You never know who's going to greet you when you encounter them, so you are always on guard and somewhat edgy in their presence. Your efforts are rarely the right ones because they keep changing the game.

The Over-Emoter: This archetype uses their tears as a weapon, turning on the faucet any time they want to draw the attention back to themselves. They're the people who often, in group settings, have everyone fussing over them because they are having such an emotionally difficult time and need to be noticed. You leave every encounter with them feeling drained from the emotional charge.

The Complainer: This archetype is never satisfied with anything you do to support them. If you bring them a casserole, they complain there are too many onions. If you sit and listen to them, they'll complain that you didn't come last week. Even if you give up everything, they'll still find some flaw in what you offer.

The Space Hog: This archetype will take up all the space they can, monopolize conversations, claim the best seat in the restaurant, and interrupt people—all while ignoring their impact on everyone else in the room. They have little self-awareness of how much space they take up and little sense of anyone else's need for space. When confronted, they often respond with fragility.

The Thrasher: This archetype erupts into anger very easily and lashes out at people, thrashing around like an out-of-control water sprinkler. They make little effort to control their emotions and pay no attention to the damage they do to other people.

The Peacock: This archetype puts on a great show of being loving and kind and building trust, but when your back is turned, they behave in very different ways. They malign and spread harmful gossip. They catch you by surprise because they're so convincing when spreading their pretty tail feathers.

The Scorekeeper: This archetype keeps a mental account of who owes what to whom. When you do something nice for them, they aren't satisfied until they pay you back, and vice versa. They have trouble receiving, and only give gifts as a way of gaining credit that they expect to one day be paid back.

The Apologizer: This archetype makes a great show of apologizing profusely whenever they let someone down, but those apologies are designed to manipulate the situation and draw attention to themselves. You find yourself managing *their* emotions rather than looking after your own.

The Con Artist: It's hard to build trust with this archetype because you're never quite sure if what they say is truthful. They play with the truth so that it's just believable enough to be convincing. When you're with them, you often have the feeling you're getting played.

The Projector: This archetype isn't self-aware enough to deal with their own fears, anxieties, anger, or frustration, so they project it onto other people. They try to convince you to be as afraid or angry as they are and won't be satisfied until they've altered or controlled your emotional response to the situation.

The Joker: This archetype uses inappropriate humour to avoid feeling or addressing the deeper emotions of a situation. They have trouble treating anything seriously and would rather deflect with jokes than have a heart-to-heart conversation. They often sabotage your efforts with their jokes.

This is not an exhaustive list, and sometimes people display multiple behaviours at once, but it identifies the types of energy you should pay attention to when trying to hold space for a person or group.

People operating with these behaviours probably don't mean any harm. In fact, their behaviour emerges out of their own unmet needs. And often, when/if those needs are met, you will see their behaviour change, sometimes dramatically.

Sometimes all they need is to feel listened to. If you have it in you to provide what they need, by all means do so. But be wary of how much emotional labour is required of you and don't hesitate to protect yourself from harm.

When I managed a team of seventeen people, I used to have the following quote by Rainer Maria Rilke hanging on my wall. It reminded me to be compassionate with people who showed up in ways that challenged me: "Perhaps all the dragons in our lives are princesses who are only waiting to see us act, just once, with beauty and courage. Perhaps everything that frightens us is, in its deepest essence, something helpless that wants our love."[21] The ideas embodied in this quote helped me approach difficult people with a heart at peace rather than a heart at war, and sometimes that was enough to change the way they behaved toward me. I've also found it helpful to remember that these behaviours are learned in some way and are being used to address unmet needs. They are not adaptive in the long run, but have worked and have been reinforced in the past, and so they continue.

Offering compassion and excusing bad behaviour are two different things, though. We can be compassionate without tolerating harmful behaviour.

Often, people don't reveal these archetypal behaviours when we first enter relationships with them. And sometimes they only show these behaviours when under stress. We are often caught off guard when someone shows up very differently during a crisis or transition. This can make it difficult to walk away or erect boundaries in the relationship moving forward; we want to give them the benefit of the doubt and assume they'll go back to their "old self" afterwards.

The longer we adapt to, and put up with, problem behaviours, the harder it is to challenge them and to extract ourselves from the relationship or situation. The best thing to do is to confront the behaviour as soon as we notice it, letting the person know we witness it and have limited tolerance for it. When boundaries are consistently ignored, we have the right to walk away.

Bill Eddy, who wrote a book called *5 Types of People Who Can Ruin Your Life*, teaches about employing the BIFF response when dealing with challenging people (like the people displaying the above archetypal behaviours). BIFF stands for "brief, informative, friendly, and firm." Keep it short, share straight information rather than opinions or emotions, remain calm and friendly, and be definitive in a way that clearly communicates your position and your boundary.

9

bypassing
liminal space

WHEN THINGS GET messy, as they inevitably will in any person's journey through liminal space, our very human inclination is to clean up the mess or avoid it by turning toward something that provides more pleasure and ease. The attempt to avoid the messiness and discomfort of liminal space is called "bypassing," and it's something to be aware of, both in ourselves and in those for whom we hold space.

This may, in fact, be at the heart of what is revealed in the archetypes mentioned in the previous chapter: underneath each behaviour is a desire to bypass in order to avoid and divert pain.

Bypassing can take many forms (see Figure 7). Some people turn to addictions—alcohol, drugs, work, social media, sex, etc.—to help numb the discomfort of liminal space. Others, myself included, use logic and words to try to reason their way through the emotional messiness. Instead of really *feeling* the discomfort, they read every book they can find on the topic. Still other people attempt to deflect their pain onto others,

117

blaming everyone else for their problems and tossing anger around like a grenade.

There are those who turn toward shallow spirituality in times of darkness and discomfort. Spirituality can be a source of great nourishment and support if it helps them walk through liminal space with grace and acceptance. But spirituality can also become a form of bypassing if it leads to avoidance and a focus on "transcendence" rather than acceptance and growth.

FIGURE 7. BYPASSING LIMINAL SPACE

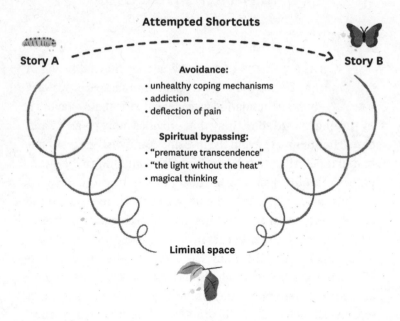

Attempted Shortcuts

Story A

Story B

Avoidance:
• unhealthy coping mechanisms
• addiction
• deflection of pain

Spiritual bypassing:
• "premature transcendence"
• "the light without the heat"
• magical thinking

Liminal space

"Spiritual bypassing," a term coined by John Welwood, is the adoption of spiritual practices, belief systems, and dogma designed to avoid the messiness of liminal space.

. . .

Although most of us were sincerely trying to work on ourselves, I noticed a widespread tendency to use spiritual ideas and practices to sidestep or avoid facing unresolved emotional issues, psychological wounds, and unfinished developmental tasks. When we are spiritually bypassing, we often use the goal of awakening or liberation to rationalize what I call premature transcendence: trying to rise above the raw and messy side of our humanness before we have fully faced and made peace with it. And then we tend to use absolute truth to disparage or dismiss relative human needs, feelings, psychological problems, relational difficulties, and developmental deficits. I see this as an "occupational hazard" of the spiritual path, in that spirituality does involve a vision of going beyond our current karmic situation.[22]

JOHN WELWOOD

. . .

I see this in much of the "love and light" and "thoughts and prayers" spirituality that seems to be ubiquitous in North America: "If I only believe in love and light, if I only have good thoughts, then I will attract good things into my life and avoid the messiness." "Love and light" becomes nothing more than a smokescreen if we're not willing to peer into the shadow and do the hard work.

Once, when I was in the middle of grief from losing my mom, I shared some of that grief on my blog. A reader sent an email admonishing me for being so dark and not thinking more happy thoughts. Influenced by the Law of Attraction, she was convinced that if I filled my blog with light and positivity, I would attract more of those things into my life. She thought it was especially important because of the influence I have over other people—that I should show other people what it's like to walk through grief with "love and light."

"I respectfully disagree," I wrote back to that woman. "This grief is real and if I deny myself the experience of truly feeling it, I will not only diminish the value of my relationship with my mom but short-circuit the growth that comes as a result of my grief. Grief that is not felt now will re-emerge later as addiction, sickness, or bitterness. I choose to feel it now."

In the end, it was that raw and real grief journey that resulted in my viral Holding Space blog post which launched the work that evolved into this book. If I had chosen her version of "love and light" and bypassed the darkness of my experience, I wouldn't have gained the wisdom I found in the dark places. The darkness has much to teach us.

Let me share another example of this from my own experience. A couple of weeks into the hospital stay with my third pregnancy—when I was still hopeful it would end with a successful birth—things got really messy and really scary. I had what the doctors diagnosed as a "psychotic break" due to a combination of the stress I was under and the steroids with which I was being injected to speed up the baby's development.

I wasn't satisfied with the term "psychotic break," because there was an element to it—a spiritual element—that their diagnosis ignored.

My whole time in the hospital was an unusual and unexpected spiritual experience. A few nights before my "psychotic break," I was awake half the night, wrestling with some form of spiritual visitor in my room. It felt like a very physical encounter, not just something inside my mind. I wrestled the way I imagine Jacob wrestled with the angel in the biblical story, a struggle that resulted in him receiving a blessing and a name change. "Your name shall no longer be called Jacob," the angel said to him, "but Israel, for you have striven with God and with men, and have prevailed." (I interpret that night of wrestling from Genesis 32:28 as Jacob's invitation to step into a liminal space journey.)

After my night of wrestling, I woke up with a profound sense of peace—a peace that came as a result of the wrestling experience.

Two days later, that peace was suddenly disrupted when a woman in labour was brought into my room to occupy the extra bed. I wasn't ready to encounter a labouring woman invading my peaceful space (and introducing that element may have been a poor decision on the part of the hospital, considering the precarious state of my own pregnancy). At any rate, I ended up having a full-blown panic attack. As a result, they moved me into the empty private room across the hall.

In a sudden fit of guilt and responsibility, I walked back across the hall to apologize to the labouring woman for my rude exit. As I was standing at the foot of her bed, something came over me, and I was suddenly convinced that I could feel the woman's labour pains in my own body and that, by willingly feeling them with her, I could ease her discomfort.

I heard a voice that I was sure came from inside the room but that I knew nobody else could hear. The voice said, "They will tell you that you've gone crazy, but never doubt that this is from me and that I am with you." And then I fell to the floor, writhing in agony, convinced my body was taking on the labour pains for the woman in the bed.

It took quite some doing, but the nurses and my husband finally got me back across the hall to my new room. For hours, though, I kept insisting I had some responsibility for the woman in labour, and I kept bugging them to check on her.

I was on another plane of existence for the next twenty-four hours, different from anything I had ever experienced before and from anything those around me were experiencing. Some of the voices I heard were prophetic, telling me things that would come to fruition years later. Some of the voices were instructional, giving me clues to the work and life I was being called to (including things that have now made their way into this book).

Sometimes, I found myself living in three separate planes at once—one moving at normal speed, one at hyper-speed, and one in slow motion. I became obsessed with the meaning of these three speeds and what was happening in each. Repeatedly, I asked people if they believed in slow motion, convinced that slow motion was somehow the key to unlocking life's mysteries.

It was scary for everyone watching me, especially my family. They didn't know how long it would go on or what it meant. It was less scary for me. I was confident I was being held by some mysterious force that they couldn't experience or understand. I knew that I was safe.

However, when I finally emerged, I began to take on some of the fear of the people around me and was soon overcome with shame over what had happened. I have always taken pride in my strong mind and my ability to overcome a great deal of stress. Why did my mind—the asset I most valued—slip in this way? And why did I do some of the embarrassing things I'd done (like removing my underwear when I became convinced I was meant to help the woman birth her baby) in such a public way?

People tiptoed around me after that. I was suddenly treated with trepidation by nurses and other medical professionals—with whom I'd developed warm and trusting relationships—as though they might trigger me back to that state. When the psychologist (who was in the room during part of my psychosis) came back to see how I was and to try to figure out what had gone wrong, I became angry and defensive. I didn't want to be treated as though I were crazy or fragile. And I didn't want to be diminished or dismissed as having gone through a weak-minded slide into psychosis for what, to me, was a profound and spiritual experience.

Shame overtook me, and I didn't talk about my experience for many years afterwards. If anyone brought it up, I shut them down very quickly. I didn't even let myself think about it. Whenever it came back into my memory, I distracted myself with activity, food, or sleep.

It was scary for me to think about what had transpired, and so I found ways to bypass the experience: I avoided it. I wrote it off as a reaction to the steroids. I dismissed it with uncomfortable laughter. I was like a caterpillar refusing to surrender to the messiness of the chrysalis.

And yet... as uncomfortable as it was, I knew there was something about this experience that invited me into a deepening quest and a deepening understanding of of who I am (a quest that eventually led me to this work I do). That moment when I slipped down onto the floor in front of the labouring woman felt like an invitation into liminal space.

Before this experience, I had a relatively stable Christian faith in a God I thought was safe and comfortably distant, one who wasn't asking me to wrestle with angels or live in a variable, three-speed world. Afterwards, I had a gaping hole where nothing made sense and the old stories no longer fit.

During the ten years after this experience, I clung desperately to the old shape of my faith, hoping that, in doing so, I could make the uneasiness go away. I committed myself more wholeheartedly to church leadership, even taking a three-year term as an elder. I took a job with a Christian non-profit, hopeful that, by immersing myself in other people's faith, I could revive the old version of my own.

None of it really worked.

What I did in those ten years, while trying to cling to my traditional spirituality and avoid any of the loss, loneliness, or chaos of the liminal space, was what John Welwood refers to as spiritual bypassing. I was avoiding the discomfort and messiness of my liminal space experience.

Eventually, I had to willingly slip fully into the liminal space, embrace my doubts and fears, and admit that my old story didn't fit who I was anymore. I couldn't simply accept the "faith of my fathers," nor could I accept the old narrative of who I was. I had to examine things deeply, accept what felt right, and abandon that which no longer fit. I had to create space for a more mystical spiritual experience, and I had to give up on trying to live up to what others expected of me.

Once, when I was teaching this concept, I made the mistake of referencing a specific spiritual practice as a possible form of spiritual bypassing. I realized this was a mistake when some people in the crowd quickly jumped to defend this particular practice as something that helped them get through liminal space rather than avoid it. I try not to make that mistake anymore, because I believe that nearly every spiritual practice, in any spiritual tradition or belief system, contains both shadow and light. The Christian faith, for example, has great merit and does—when taught with integrity—instruct people not to miss the valuable learning that can be found in liminal space. "Though I walk through the valley of the shadow of death," says Psalm 23, "I will fear no evil."

The flaw in my choice during the grief journey that followed my pregnancy was not about the spiritual path I chose, but the fact that I tried to fall back on an easier and safer spiritual route, one that allowed me to avoid the darkness and the challenges of liminal space but that kept my life small.

What was that spiritual presence that guided me through the strange journey into my subconscious? Was it a guide sent from the Divine? Was it my own "imaginal cells" pointing toward a future I couldn't yet see? Or was it the soul of my unborn son, visiting me briefly before he died? I don't know and I no longer have a need to define it in a way that fits my rational mind. I simply know that I was being invited to a place beyond the limits of my imagination, beyond the confines of the narrative that had defined my life until that point, and into the depths of liminal space. Had I not chosen, eventually, to follow that guide through the darkness and uncertainty, I would have missed the opportunity for this full and beautiful life.

Each person's bypass will look different, just as each person's liminal space will look different. We must each determine for ourselves whether our practices and beliefs help us to avoid or to be present in the chaos of liminal space. It is generally not the practice or belief system itself that is the problem; it's the way we use it.

If you are holding space for someone and suspect that their choices reflect an effort to bypass liminal space, you will need to use discernment in supporting them without judgment or arrogance. This can be tender territory, because they will likely be defensive about their choices. They may even believe their choices are the only ones that can help them survive the messy place in which they find themselves. And you have to consider that these choices may, in fact, offer them much-needed temporary relief. Sometimes, like me in the first few years after losing my son, people aren't quite ready to enter the ambiguity of the liminal space.

If their choices are highly destructive to themselves and/or others (addiction, self-harm, cult membership, etc.), you may need to be direct in how you address the situation. In that case, you can tell them lovingly that you care for them too much to stand by and watch the destruction happen. You might even need to intervene (by removing children from a destructive environment, or helping the person get into rehab, for example).

If, on the other hand, those choices are seemingly valid (i.e., spiritual practices that help them transcend the pain), they may be harder to address. In those situations, the best way to hold space might be to ask meaningful questions that help them recognize their choices as bypassing behaviours. For example: "Does this choice help you cope with the pain or avoid it?" or "I see the grief you need to carry right now, and I'd like to support you. Can you talk to me about it?"

In an interview with Alanis Morissette, developmental psychologist Gordon Neufeld said, "Happiness is on the other side of the tears we haven't shed." [23] In other words, we block our chances of finding our way to true happiness if we block the tears from flowing when they need to flow. He went on to talk about how critical it is for our development that we have people in our lives who can support us in releasing those tears—a parent, for example—who simply holds us when we cry and doesn't rush to fix the source of our tears.

Our human development depends on our ability to shed tears, process pain, and not run from the messiness of liminal space. Bypassing may feel good temporarily, but it will block our long-term growth. When we hold space for each other, we create containers for healthy processing and not for bypassing.

THERE ARE three other essential things worth mentioning on this topic of bypassing:

1 I do not mean to say that you should *always* be willing to feel deep emotions and that you should *never* resort to those things which offer temporary relief. That is simply unrealistic. We must all find ways to cope, especially when we are experiencing great loss, transformation, and disruption. It's okay to seek out those things that help keep us from drowning in the sea of emotions. A long-distance swimmer (someone who swims

across the English Channel, for example) will occasionally take breaks along the journey and simply float on the surface of the water so that they can replenish their energy stores. You're allowed to do that too—choose to float temporarily so that you can continue the work you need to do. For me, that often looks like an evening of Netflix watching. I encourage you, though, to make that a conscious choice and avoid the temptation to stay checked out.

2 Know that there is a fine distinction between "bypassing" and "dissociation." Bypassing is an intentional choice to turn away from the difficult and painful, while dissociation is the way in which some of our brains cope with trauma. Many people who've experienced trauma will shut down when they are triggered (usually associated with the "freeze" trauma response), becoming numb and disconnected. If you find yourself involuntarily going numb and disconnecting from strong emotions when something triggers you, it may be wise to seek professional help. If you *are* dissociating, do not interpret it as your own failure to navigate the liminal space, but rather as your brain's way of trying to protect you from the pain of it.

3 There can be an even darker side to spiritual bypassing, in which it becomes weaponized as a tool of oppression. Those who stay only in the "love and light" version of spirituality too often silence and shame anyone who talks about the darker aspects. They want to believe that "we are all one." When someone experiences intense emotional reactions to dark and difficult issues, these people can gaslight and shame them for not being "spiritual" enough.

  This happens often in discussions around the unfairness of oppressive systems, where people accuse others of not transcending oppression via positivity alone. These are people who try to claim they "don't see colour," for example, and ignore systemic issues. Instead, they shift responsibility onto the shoulders of the oppressed, telling them that their negativity and unhappiness are attracting more negativity. They avoid and/or shut down conflict, because it messes with their fantasy of a peaceful world. They don't want to hold space for the deep brokenness and shadow in the world.

THERE IS something in both our human nature and our culture, especially Western culture, that conditions us to want the path of least resistance. We want to make our way through our liminal experiences without taking the journey through "messy." We search for tools and practices that will help us avoid the darkness, the brokenness, the unpredictability, and the rawness. We are so embedded in the consumer culture of the West that we think we can buy our way to ease. "If I can take one more class, hire the right therapist, or go on the right retreat," we tell ourselves, "I'll be able to avoid all the messy pain and discomfort of transition." Mistakenly, we've bought into the capitalist myth that we are entitled to happiness and ease.

Because the liminal space inside the chrysalis is a scary place, one we are *all* tempted to avoid, we look for shortcuts that will allow us to rush the process and get through the transformation without pain. But in the end, bypassing only lengthens and delays the journey to the other side of transformation.

PART TWO

strengthening
the
container

10

your psychic
membrane

AFTER MY BLOG post went viral in early 2015, my inbox
filled with story after story from people all over the
world. Nearly everyone who emailed wanted to tell
me about the ways in which they held space and how helpful
it was to finally have language that articulated what they intuitively knew how to do. There were stories of people holding
space for parents with Alzheimer's, others with children with
mental illness, and others working in hospices where they
watched people die nearly every day. Still others held space in
prison or in parts of the world surrounded by conflict or poverty.

The stories were endless and varied and came from all manner of people. Together they wove a tapestry of humanity and
showed the boundless capacity we all have for love, compassion, and generosity.

Something disturbed me in the wave of emails, though.
Each one of the people emailing was well versed in how to hold
space for other people, but few mentioned doing the same for
themselves. Hospice workers, teachers, guidance counsellors,

chaplains, managers, parents, community organizers, medical professionals, and more spent much of their lives in service to other people, but few showed evidence that they were inputting enough energy to balance their output. I had a sudden concern that what I offered was missing an important component which they needed in order to survive their emotionally and energetically taxing work.

Fairly quickly, I wrote a follow-up blog post on how to hold space for yourself. This post didn't get as much traction, but there were still many who were grateful that I helped them see how attempting to hold space for others is a recipe for burnout when it isn't balanced with doing it for yourself as well.

Ironically, around the same time, this missing component revealed itself in my own life. I was nearing burnout myself. The demands of a growing business, a sudden increase in readership, and an overflowing inbox full of people who were (intentionally or unintentionally) asking me to hold space for them took its toll.

But that wasn't the sum of everything going on. At the same time, I knew my marriage was ending. It became painfully clear it was no longer nourishing me—and hadn't, in fact, for a very long time. It required a great deal of emotional labour without feeding much back into my own energy stores. Plus my teenaged daughters needed more of my emotional labour than usual because they were being impacted by the instability in our marriage.

I was exhausted. My boundaries were far too porous, and I wasn't reaching out for the kind of help I needed.

Just like the people reading my blog, I was very good at holding space for others but not nearly as good at holding space for myself, or allowing other people to hold space for me. While I was busy helping other people see their blind spots, I was ignoring my own.

The first thing I did was to request a separation, asking my then husband to move out of the house. After that, fairly abruptly, I shut nearly everything down and took a sabbatical. I stepped away from social media, put an auto-responder on my inbox saying that I would be away, and booked appointments for the spa, a body worker, and a therapist. Not long after, I hired an assistant and changed the way I worked so that I had cleaner boundaries and better self-care practices so that I gave less of my energy away.

It was hard work. I had to establish new patterns for myself and change the way I interacted with people. Not everyone appreciated my new boundaries or the fact that I had less time or energy for them. I knew I wouldn't survive any other way, though, so I pushed through. As a result, I came out stronger and more resilient. I strengthened the relationships that mattered most, cleared away those relationships that weren't nourishing, and placed others at arm's length. I found better ways to nourish myself.

In the end, my business thrived, the new family unit (consisting of my daughters and myself) grew stronger, and my understanding of—and capacity to teach—this work deepened.

Since that experience, I've sat with a question that tends to evolve and change shape the longer I hold it: How does a person serve as their own bowl? It seems somewhat counterintuitive to hold your own container for liminal space. How, from inside, can you reach around and hold a bowl for yourself? Is that even possible? And does it diminish the value of other people?

As I talked about it, wrote about it, and researched it, an analogy slowly emerged: when it comes to holding space for ourselves, think less of a "bowl" shape and more of a **psychic membrane** that each of us maintains around ourselves.

In this analogy, a psychic membrane is the invisible, human-sized equivalent of the cellular membrane, the microscopic structure that surrounds each cell in your body. Like the cellular membrane, the psychic membrane protects and nourishes you, yet still connects you to the life and people around you.

Some of you might remember a TV show called *The Magic School Bus*. It was an animated children's program where the teacher, Ms. Frizzle, would take her students on field trips in a magic school bus. They could shrink or expand to any size and enter any space about which they were learning.

Imagine climbing aboard the bus with Ms. Frizzle, shrinking down to the size of a molecule, and zipping along the bloodstream to visit one of the millions of cells in the human body. "Seat belts, everyone!" Ms. Frizzle shouts, just before we shrink and whirl away to explore this inner kingdom of the cell membrane—a fascinating, microscopic structure made up of complex components that include phospholipids, proteins, and cholesterols.

At the cellular level, the membrane separates the contents of the cell (called cytoplasm) from its surrounding environment. The membrane serves as both shield and lifeline for that cell, letting the right things in and keeping the wrong things out while also keeping the cell healthy and strong so it can serve its purpose in the body. It acts as an interpreter for the cell's DNA in its interaction with the outside world.

What's this got to do with holding space? Well, imagine you have an invisible membrane that surrounds you, holds you together, and keeps you safe just like the cellular membrane holds the contents of that cell. Your psychic membrane allows nourishment in and keeps harmful substances out. It works tirelessly to keep you balanced, strong, and vibrant.

This analogy first surfaced when I taught about personal boundaries, which Wikipedia defines as "the guidelines, rules or limits that a person creates to identify reasonable, safe and permissible ways for other people to behave towards them and how they will respond when someone passes those limits."[24]

The term "boundaries" never felt quite right for what I was trying to convey because it seemed too rigid and not reflective of a vibrant, evolving human being. I looked for something more organic and alive, and for a while I used the analogy of a living "hedge" versus a "brick wall"—a hedge being an organic boundary and a brick wall being a hard barrier. The "hedge" analogy was at least permeable and organic, but it still didn't quite fit the way I wanted. Finally, my friend and thinking partner Beth Sanders helped me land on the concept of the "cellular membrane."

Once I started playing with the idea, I realized that a living membrane is so much more than a way to understand personal boundaries; it fits the entire concept of what it means to hold space for ourselves. It's a new way of understanding the bowl, and it's especially applicable to what we do for ourselves. Just as we can "be the bowl" for other people, we need to "maintain a living membrane" for ourselves.

(Note: What follows is only meant to be an analogy and shouldn't be viewed through a scientific lens. There are actually many types of membranes, including plastic ones used to insulate your house. The living cellular membrane is an incredibly complex structure, but its basic function provides the perfect parallel for the following analogy. Just keep in mind I've greatly simplified it for the purpose of our discussion.)

There are many ways the cellular membrane (Figure 8) teaches us about what we need to form our psychic membrane.

1 The cellular membrane is **selectively permeable**. It allows only certain molecules to pass into or out of the cell. The membrane's double layer of phospholipids blocks the entry of most molecules. However, there are doorways (called "channel proteins") along the surface of the membrane that serve as entry points for needed nutrients (oxygen, water, sugar, etc.) and exit points for waste (carbon dioxide, for example). In the

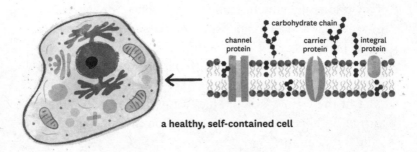

FIGURE 8. THE CELLULAR MEMBRANE

carbohydrate chain

channel
protein

carrier
protein

integral
protein

a healthy, self-contained cell

same way, your psychic membrane has entry and exit points to allow in whatever nourishes you and release whatever does not serve you—all while maintaining the capacity to be rigid when necessary.

2 The cellular membrane has two ways of moving material through it: **active transport** and **passive transport**. Passive transport does not require an energy input; it happens through osmosis. Active transport, on the other hand, requires an input of energy to move material through the membrane (via the channel proteins).

Your psychic membrane acts the same. Sometimes energy and intention are involved in moving material in or out; other times material moves passively and requires no energy. We need to be intentional to *not* allow too much passive transport in (i.e., receiving too many harmful messages via advertising or social media) and instead choose what we will absorb and/ or resist (i.e., turning off the computer and going for a walk).

3 The cellular membrane has **sensors** that distinguish friend from foe. For example, if an approaching object (a molecule,

cell, etc.) is a virus, the sensors work to repel rather than absorb it. When your psychic membrane is healthy, its sensors will signal whether approaching objects are valuable or dangerous for you. Your sensors include intuitive hunches, body signals, past experience, etc. Approaching "objects" can include people, rules, rituals, spiritual teachings, food, jobs, etc., that come from outside yourself.

4 The cellular membrane has **a mechanism that helps it recognize and link up to other cells.** When linked together, these cells help the original cell serve its purpose in the world. A muscle cell recognizes another muscle cell, and they link up to create biceps or deltoids. Fat cells and blood cells do the same. The result is a fully functioning body that can work, play, have sex, laugh, etc. (Imagine the disaster if your cells linked up arbitrarily; there would be no functioning organs in your body!)

In a similar way, a healthy psychic membrane helps you connect and bond with the people and communities that help you serve a greater purpose in the world while disconnecting you from those who don't.

5 The cellular membrane is **fluid.** It is constantly changing: individual phospholipids move about laterally within the same layer but occasionally flip to the other layer. In the same way, your psychic membrane changes and evolves as you grow, responding to your changing needs and capacity.

6 The cellular membrane is **responsive to its environment.** For example, cholesterols increase the membrane's rigidity and firmness to make the membrane less soluble at moderate and higher temperatures (when you develop inflammation and the membrane needs to protect you from infection, for example). At lower temperatures, cholesterols separate phospholipids from one another so the membrane does not become too rigid.

Your psychic membrane should also be responsive to the environment, becoming more rigid and protective when you're at risk and more open and permeable when you're strong and resilient. When you're exposed to "heat" (crisis or grief, for example), your psychic membrane may need to allow fewer things through.

7   The cellular membrane works to maintain **homeostasis**. This allows the cell to keep its state of equilibrium or stability as conditions change (i.e., temperature, nutrients, and salt–water concentration). If homeostasis is not successful, the cell becomes destabilized and disaster—or death—ensues. Homeostasis is a complex, dynamic equilibrium of continuous change, yet it allows relatively uniform conditions to prevail. For example, pressure inside the cell is the same as pressure outside so that the membrane doesn't collapse or explode. Your psychic membrane helps you stay balanced and grounded in the dynamic changes of life. It warns you when you are becoming overwhelmed in your commitments, emotional labour, and other situations. It helps you to release things so that you return to a stable state.

8   The cell membrane interprets your DNA blueprint and **builds the structure** of who you are. According to the study of epigenetics, receptor proteins on the surface of the cell membrane communicate between the outside world and the DNA in the nucleus of the cell. These proteins control which parts of the DNA are transcribed and how that cell is expressed. Who *you* are is a function of how your cells are expressed—for example, whether your eyes are blue, brown, or green. (Although, strictly speaking, your DNA may also contain less desirable aspects that make you prone to diabetes and other conditions—conditions that may or may not ever manifest, depending on diet and other lifestyle circumstances.)

Similarly, your psychic membrane interprets your identity and directs how you show up in the world. It determines what parts of you are expressed or suppressed. When your psychic membrane is healthy, you show up with authenticity, true to your internal blueprint.

Another fascinating addition to this membrane analogy—one I learned from a medical doctor attending one of my New Zealand workshops—concerns mitochondria, organelles housed within the membrane that contains the cell's energy stores. When energy passes through the membrane, it collects in the mitochondrion and is stored for later use. It's like a car battery, gathering the energy stores to keep your engine running and your lights on. When you are well-supported by a healthy psychic membrane, your psychic mitochondrion keeps your energy stores from flagging.

Your goal in holding space for yourself is to keep your psychic membrane healthy and strong so that it can protect and nourish you. When it is tired, overworked, or undervalued, it doesn't function as well, and you are left unprotected and undernourished. As I learned when my blog post went viral and my marriage ended, my capacity for functioning effectively in the world was directly related to the strength of my psychic membrane.

Your psychic membrane is uniquely yours. No two membranes look or function exactly alike. And so it needs nourishment and care unique to you. An unhealthy membrane makes for an unhealthy cell and depleted energy stores in the mitochondrion. An unhealthy cell with no energy reserves does not contribute to the proper functioning of a healthy body, community, or family. (Note: This is not to say that it is your job and yours alone to ensure that you have a healthy membrane and well-resourced mitochondria. It should be the work of a strong community and social network to ensure that all people are resourced and supported. A person with depleted energy stores may be that way because of oppressive systems and because they lack the kind of privilege that allows them access to what they need.)

Your psychic membrane is strengthened when you understand your needs and emotions, your trauma, your authentic identity and personality type, and your social conditioning (as discussed in future chapters). For example, you might be a person who thrives on personal touch and welcomes hugs from anyone. Others are more selective and don't welcome touch. Your membrane might reflect that you are an extrovert who is energized by other people, while an introvert is energized by alone time without a lot of touch.

If you have experienced trauma, it will tend to heighten your sensors, making them more reactive to external stimuli. A personality disorder or mental illness might mean your sensors read stimuli differently. These and other factors have an impact on your psychic membrane; learning to understand them is crucial to holding healthy space for yourself.

Your membrane changes throughout your life, even within each relationship, and nobody but you can decide when you are ready for that change. For example, you might find that something that was acceptable early in a friendship (conversations late into the night) is no longer acceptable now (your health requires you to get more sleep). Or the opposite might be true, and you may have built up trust with a person, therefore giving them more access to your time and attention.

Your psychic membrane can even change overnight. Something that felt good during an intimate moment last night, for example, might not feel good tonight, and you have a right to say no. Or you might even change your mind partway through because your sensors let you know that you don't feel safe. Your body, your choice; your membrane, your choice.

Sometimes the best thing to do is allow your membrane to shut everything down so that you can care for yourself and/or focus on your work. Whenever I work on a large project (like this book, for example), I need to distance myself from social media and the demands of motherhood, so I usually book some type of writing retreat space. I recognize I can focus better on writing when my membrane is firm enough to filter out other voices or distractions. And my membrane is strengthened by the other cells I've connected with that help me fulfill my purpose—reinforcements in the form of an assistant who looks after my inbox while I'm away, and good friends who sometimes host me in their home and tend to my needs while I write.

The healthier the psychic membrane, the healthier the contents of the cell. The better the balance between internal and external pressure, the more the cell thrives. The more the cell connects with other cells that share a similar purpose, the greater the impact.

11

psychic membranes in relationship

EVELOPING THE SKILLS to nurture and strengthen your psychic membrane are key, but before we give those skills more focus, let's talk for a moment about the connection between the bowl metaphor and the psychic membrane—namely, how a strong psychic membrane allows us to "be the bowl" for other people. (Once again, keep in mind that this analogy is not to be viewed through a scientific lens; our living cellular membranes are much more intricate and complex and do not necessarily behave in the ways that I suggest below.)

I kept pondering the relationship between the bowl and the membrane as I taught multiple workshops and retreats on this topic. It seemed that there was an important connection, though at first they simply felt like two separate metaphors.

And then one day the connection became clear.

If we are each within our psychic membranes as space-holders, and those membranes are fluid, flexible, and healthy, then when *your* membrane feels weak and battered, *my* membrane creates a space to hold you. Essentially, my membrane forms a bowl for you.

Imagine that we are two cells which come into contact with each other. We discover (through the sensors on our membranes) that we are like-hearted enough to create connection and begin a relationship. At the beginning, our membranes only lightly touch while adjusting to and assessing the situation (and each other) to see if there's something worth trusting and nurturing (Figure 9). Gradually, as we get to know each other, we allow more of our membrane surfaces to come into contact.

Whether formally or informally, we create some form of social contract between us, expressing our expectations and needs, identifying our boundaries, agreeing on how we'll interact and how much we'll give and receive. If the relationship is largely healthy (recognizing that no relationship is ALWAYS healthy or ALWAYS unhealthy), that social contract might unfold in long conversations between us and in the practice of "asking for what we need and offering what we can." We'll each let the other know what kind of interactions feel comfortable

FIGURE 9. TWO CELLS COME INTO CONTACT WITH EACH OTHER

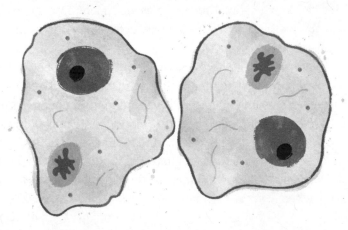

or uncomfortable. We'll be honest about our feelings and respect each other's boundaries.

Perhaps you've already experienced this kind of relationship, where you understand each other to the point where the person doesn't easily get offended when you say something like "Please don't text me after 10 p.m." or "Please stop interrupting me"; where you're both considerate about what the other person has given consent to, or how much emotional labour you're willing to put into the relationship. If you have, you're lucky. This is the sign of an emotionally mature relationship. Both people are intentional about holding space and not hijacking it.

If the relationship is relatively unhealthy, however, the social contract might unfold differently—in small, unspoken transactions that send warning signals letting us know where we're not welcome, in needy requests that we feel obligated to fulfill for each other, or in manipulative techniques that gaslight or shame us into behaving the way the other person wants us to.

Sadly, this kind of relationship, with a lopsided and/or poorly articulated social contract, is much more common, not only in marriages but in extended families, workplaces, and friendships. We settle into patterns of unhealthiness because that's all we know and all we've had modelled for us. Changing these patterns is risky when we don't want to offend or lose the other person. Articulating social contracts where there have been only silent assumptions in the past feels too formal and foreign, and so we live with the little offences, turning a blind eye to the ways that our membranes are being ignored, or even the ways we're disrespecting ourselves by allowing those membranes to be too permeable. We make assumptions that the other person will figure out what we need even though we've never articulated it to them.

It's not impossible, though, to renegotiate a social contract. And in a healthy, thriving relationship, it should be expected. In a documentary about her life, psychologist Marion Woodman described her seventy-plus-year marriage as *four* distinct marriages. Three times in their relationship they found themselves at a place where there was enough growth and change to no longer support the relationship as it existed. Each time, they had to renegotiate their social contract or end the marriage. Each time, they were able to recommit themselves to continued growth alongside each other. Their psychic membranes remained healthy and intact.[25]

When my marriage was struggling, several years before it ended, I was hopeful that we could do just that. As you can guess by the outcome, I was unable to renegotiate the social contract with my then husband. Despite my efforts to communicate how I'd changed and how my needs had evolved, we weren't able to arrive at a place where the relationship could adjust to support the changes.

However, I have since had other relationships in which the social contract was successfully renegotiated. Several years ago, in the early days of our friendship, my friend Saleha was going through some personal challenges and asked if she could hire me to be her life coach. I considered it, but because I was beginning to see Saleha as someone who could equally hold space for me just as I held it for her, I decided to say no. I told her I was afraid that a social contract built around me holding space for her would change the balance of the relationship and I would no longer feel I could rely on her in the same way. I'm very glad I made that choice, because since then our relationship has become one of the deepest I've ever experienced.

Whether healthy or unhealthy, articulated or assumed, formal or informal, there is always some form of social contract that binds two psychic membranes (and the cells within) to each other.

So, how do two "cells" in a social contract effectively hold space for each other?

Well, when one cell begins to struggle and needs more in the relationship, the other creates space within which the wounded/scared/overwhelmed cell can curl up. Like a parent who opens their arms for a frightened child, we set aside our own needs for a moment and stretch our membrane so that there is now a bowl that can hold space. That's what I did for my friend Saleha when she was struggling, but I did it with the understanding that we were friends (and therefore the balance could remain stable) rather than coach and client. It looks a little like Figure 10.

FIGURE 10. ONE CELL HOLDING SPACE FOR ANOTHER

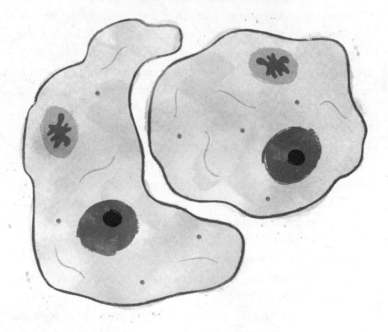

In such a situation, the social contract goes something like this: "I will stretch my membrane in such a way that I can hold space for you. It may cause me some temporary discomfort or require that I make some sacrifices, but I am willing to do this so you have what you need during this challenging time."

When this happens in a healthy situation, the person holding the space still has an intact membrane. They don't become enmeshed with the other person; their membrane remains resilient and selectively permeable, so anything that the struggling person may project outward—such as anger, fear, pain, or confusion—flows around the other's psychic membrane and does not become lodged within.

In strictly scientific terms, a cell doesn't absorb anything that is unnecessary; its lipid bilayer keeps things out unless there is a specific need for transport-mediated entry into the cell. But from a psychological perspective, it would be easy for the one holding space to absorb some of the other person's negative energy, thereby destroying and depleting their own energy in the process. This is where "active transport" is crucial. The one holding space needs to do their own personal work to ensure that what may be projected toward them flows *around* them and is not simply transported into their membrane. There are physical and spiritual practices, for example, that help you release the other person's energy and protect your own.

This act of creating and holding space for each other within our psychic membranes can take a variety of shapes and—at least within a healthy relationship—fluctuate from one shape to another. If I am willing to hold space for you during a time of crisis, the bowl may exist on only one side of the relationship for a period of time. But if I later go through a struggle of my own, we can switch roles and you will hold space for me. Two healthy membranes can fluctuate back and forth, even in the span of a single conversation. Neither gives themselves up to the other; within these exchanges they remain unique and sovereign individuals.

This is how my relationship with Saleha evolved. Not long after she went through her struggle, when I held space for her, I went through a struggle of my own. Because I trusted her to have a strong membrane, she was the first person I turned to. The balance shifted and she held space for me. I received just what I'd given.

Sometimes, though, a relationship is consistently lopsided, with one person always holding space for the other, and the roles are never reversed. This may or may not be okay, depending on the situation. For example, if I am a coach whom you pay for weekly sessions, then this is one type of social contract. It would be inappropriate for me as your coach (as with any coach, therapist, or pastor) to demand that you hold space for me in return. As a space-holder, I would seek out others to hold space for me and ensure the ongoing health of my membrane.

This is what I've learned to put into place whenever I facilitate a retreat or workshop, especially if I expect that the emotional labour required of me will be intense. I reach out to my primary space-holders (my business partner, Krista, for example, who has become very good at anticipating those needs) and let them know that I need them to hold space for me (usually they do it via text or phone, especially if I'm travelling) so that I can maintain a strong psychic membrane and be able to effectively serve the people for whom I'm holding space in the workshop.

Sometimes, though (especially when we're not conscious of our needs and don't put support in place), this lopsided space-holding becomes an oppressive situation where the person holding space is expected to continue doing so but then finds that the space allowed for *them* is diminishing over time (see Figure 11). Imagine, for example, a woman in an abusive

FIGURE 11. LOPSIDED SPACE-HOLDING

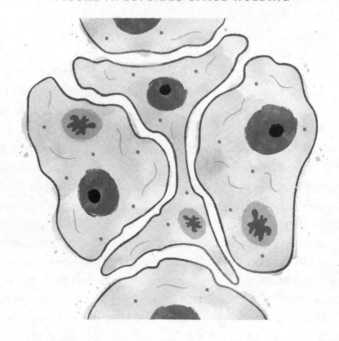

relationship who cares for the needs of both her husband and her children. With no one who ever returns the favour, her psychic membrane becomes distorted into an unrecognizable shape, with nowhere to grow and no energy left in her mito-chondrion to meet her own needs.

Whenever I show Figure 11 to people in workshops, there are a lot of nods and sighs in the room. Most people have experienced this at least once or twice in their life, when they felt so caught within the many expectations placed on them that it was as if they were squished in a Vise-Grip.

My most memorable example of this was when my former husband attempted suicide the second time. Not only was I providing care and advocacy for him while he was in the psychiatric ward, but I had a busy career as the leader of a national team of seventeen people, and was the mother of three children who were relying on me for stability while they dealt with the stress and grief of their dad's near death. I remember times when I would drive from the psych ward, where my role was to be a loving container and fierce advocate, to the soccer field, where I needed to be a stable and supportive mom. In the van between psych ward and soccer field, I shed many tears of rage and fear and exhaustion.

I survived that time, in part, because I started reaching out to the people who knew how to hold space for me. Some of them (like my friend Linda) simply sat and listened while I cried.

If you find yourself similarly squished by the expectations of others, I'm sorry. I wish I could wave a magic wand and make your life better. But I can't, and so I will simply say: *reach out*. Find somebody who knows how to hold the container while you release what you need to release. And find the non-human containers as well: your pets, your garden, the beach, etc. And practise saying no to those people whose needs are not critical right now. I hope and trust that this time will pass.

Ideally, I believe we all seek some form of equilibrium— where we can hold space generously for others and others hold space for us, where there is give-and-take, flexibility and flux, and where no one's needs are overlooked or dismissed (see Figure 12).

It might be tempting to seek this kind of equilibrium in a single relationship, but I think that's highly unrealistic and not even healthy. We are meant to be in community. Relying on only one person to meet all our needs is a sure way of bringing some form of toxicity into the relationship. Nobody can be *everything* to another person. If you try to accomplish that, you risk becoming depleted, anxious, bitter, and/or burnt-out. There was too much expectation of that in my own marriage,

FIGURE 12. TWO CELLS IN EQUILIBRIUM

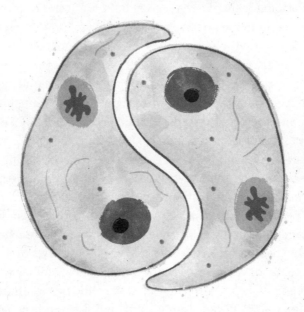

both in the way that he wanted his needs met and in the way I took that on as my duty. This imbalance was a big factor in the marriage's eventual destruction.

Don't rely on only one person, and try not to be jealous when someone with whom you're in close relationship reaches out to someone who's *not* you. In fact, you'd be wise to encourage it; it will help you to stay healthy and not shift into codependency.

I once had a coaching client who was worn out by the expectations of her marriage. Her husband had health concerns and expected her to be his only support. She did all the cooking in the relationship, and always worried whether the food she made was effectively supporting his unique dietary needs, even though he was paying little attention to his doctor's recommendations. She was also his only emotional support, listening daily to his long list of physical complaints. "He doesn't have anyone else," she said. "If I don't listen to him and support him, he'll feel abandoned by the world."

That's not a healthy way to be in relationship. I helped her see that she couldn't be expected to meet *all* his needs; she needed to strengthen her psychic membrane and put up better boundaries. I coached her on what she could say to her husband, asking him to find a therapist or other support person who would listen to his daily worries and concerns, and expecting him to take more responsibility for his own dietary needs.

Their social contract needed to be renegotiated, and other people had to be brought into the situation to ease the pressure on her. His expectation that the marriage would fill all of his needs was unrealistic, unhealthy, and unfair.

A healthy, balanced life looks more like Figure 13. In this configuration, nobody is solely responsible for another person, nobody is isolated, and everybody has the sovereign right to the kind of psychic membrane that supports them uniquely. The social contracts between cells are healthy and can be renegotiated to meet each person's needs. If this diagram were shown three-dimensionally and in a video animation, we'd also see that there is freedom for the cells to move about, change their configuration, or spend time alone when necessary. There is flow, movement, and ease. Each person has their needs met.

This is the configuration I've been working toward developing in my business, thanks in part to the evolution of my relationship with my business partner, Krista (who started as my virtual assistant, four years ago). While she is very good at holding space for me, my work, and the business, we both know that she can't be the only one. She always checks to see what additional supports I've put in place when I teach and/or travel (i.e., people who can hold space from afar or in person),

FIGURE 13. A HEALTHY, BALANCED LIFE

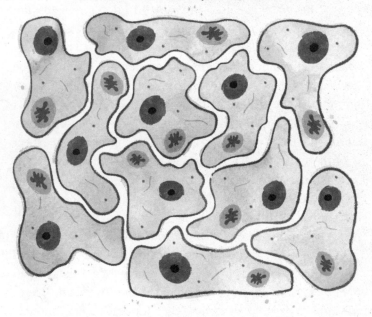

especially for those intense moments when I feel that my bowl is about to crack.

And when I need to go into my "writing cave" to focus on a big project such as this book, she makes sure that there are other people holding space for the parts of my business that need to go on in my absence. For example, at this moment there are three people (two assistant teachers and an apprentice) hosting Zoom calls and tending to the needs of the participants of the Holding Space Practitioner Program.

In the coming chapters, we'll talk more about how to find a similar balance in your life, including how to hold space for yourself while also allowing others to hold space for you so you can maintain a healthy and resilient membrane.

12

circles of trust

LET'S EXPLORE ANOTHER take on the psychic membrane metaphor. Consider that your membrane will fluctuate and change depending on the relationships you're in. A relationship with some people requires a firm membrane that doesn't allow too much of their energy to pass through. Other relationships comfortably allow a more open and fluid membrane because you trust that interactions with them will nourish your energy stores rather than deplete them.

If we stretch the analogy somewhat, we can imagine not just one layer of membrane but multiple layers. Perhaps some things (and people) can be allowed to pass through one layer of our membrane but not through others.

Figure 14 is a simple diagram that examines an ideal way we can manage these multiple layers of psychic membrane in our relationships. I call them Circles of Trust.

The very nucleus of your cell contains the centre of your tender heart, which should be held and protected with care and compassion inside its own membrane (along with the mitochondrion that store its energy). People in this first circle are people with whom you have high intimacy and trust, people who most know how to hold space for you. They're the people with whom you're most vulnerable.

You might automatically expect this circle to include family members, close friends, and people you go to for a fun evening out—but that isn't always the case. While you might spend a lot of time with these people, sometimes these relationships come with too much baggage, complexity, and attachment to outcomes.

People in your intimate, "tender heart" circle are those for whom you are willing to do a considerable amount of emotional labour (outside a therapist–client relationship, of course, where you pay for the service). They are usually at a similar stage of personal growth as you are, and so they know how to show up for you without draining too much of your energy. Your psychic membrane tells you it's safe to connect with these people and keep them close, and so you open up to them. This circle can also include people such as your therapist or coach, or a gender-based circle—people who hold space for the intimate aspects of your life without judgment or control.

With the people in this inner circle, it helps to have a common language and a common understanding about your needs and how you want space held for those needs. Since the people in this inner circle have likely done work on their own personal growth, they will be more inclined to respect your boundaries and not be easily offended or knocked off balance by your articulation of your needs and struggles. My friend Saleha is such a person. Though we come from seemingly vastly different backgrounds (she grew up Muslim in Saudi Arabia while I grew up Mennonite in Canada), we have a lot of shared language around mental health, personal development, and other things. We spend long hours in coffee shops unravelling our old patterns, sharing our relationship struggles, and encouraging each other's growth.

FIGURE 14. CIRCLES OF TRUST

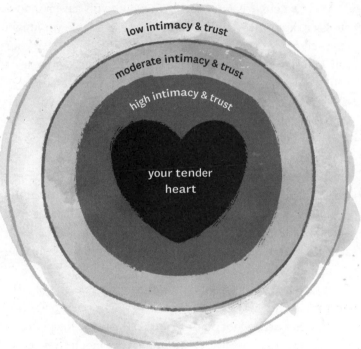

no intimacy & trust

low intimacy & trust

moderate intimacy & trust

high intimacy & trust

your tender
heart

Sometimes people in my Holding Space workshops have encouraged their closest friends, spouses, and family to enrol in my program so they can grow their shared language and deepen their conversations around healing and personal growth. You might want to pass this book along to the people in your inner circle so they have some understanding, for example, when you need to take time away to strengthen your psychic membrane.

The next circle is for those with whom you have a moderate level of intimacy and trust. With these people you might share certain stories while choosing to withhold parts of yourself, knowing they could do some damage to your tender heart. You're only willing to expend moderate emotional labour for these people, and they might only occasionally have capacity to hold space for you—whether it's because they have too much going on in their own lives or because they don't have much depth in their capacity to hold space for others. Others might be less than emotionally healthy, inclined to project their wounds onto you, and therefore less than ideal for the deep intimacy of your inner circle. The sensors on your psychic membrane tell you that, while these people are relatively safe, it's best to maintain a little more distance and keep your membrane a little more rigid.

It's likely that the people in this second circle have not yet undertaken the healing and personal growth work to develop the muscles needed for holding space. It doesn't mean they'll never have this capacity; it might simply mean they're not yet ready or that they haven't had the time or energy to do so. (Keep in mind that those who struggle with poverty or other disadvantages or oppression, for example, may only have energy and capacity to focus on their immediate survival needs or those of their family.) When you feel well resourced and strong, you might be able to hold space for people in this second circle so that they *can* do what's needed to heal and grow. When and if that happens, they might move into your inner circle of high intimacy and trust.

The circle of low intimacy and trust includes people who are in your life but for one reason or another do not have a heart-to-heart connection with you. They may be casual acquaintances, co-workers, or even family members who have not earned your trust. It might be that they have not done enough personal growth work and so feel less trustworthy—or even dangerous—despite being in your life. For them, you'll likely do only a small amount of emotional labour. (Or perhaps you'll do emotional labour on their behalf but not expect it in return—as might be the case with clients if you work in a helping profession.) Your psychic membrane chooses to hold these people at a distance, maintaining some rigidity within the social contract and not linking up with them in an intimate, reciprocal way.

And then there are people with whom you have no intimacy or trust. They may be near strangers—the bus driver who takes you to work or the barista who sells you coffee—or they may be people with whom you've chosen to end or limit a relationship because they consistently break your trust or do damage to your spirit. These people earn little of your emotional labour and being with them risks depleting your psychic mitochondrion. You probably still treat them respectfully when you encounter them, but you likely won't give up a portion of your day to sit and listen to them unburden themselves. Your psychic membrane senses the lack of emotional safety or it hasn't had enough encounters with them to assess their suitability.

The important thing to know about the Circles of Trust concept is that you always have sovereignty to choose how it takes shape in your life. *You* choose whether a person fits in an inner circle or needs to be held at a greater distance. *You* choose whether to move a person closer or further out.

Sometimes—when you've been wounded and need only those people who will support your healing—you can choose to temporarily move people to a circle further out and make your psychic membrane temporarily more rigid. And with some people—your children, for example—you may cultivate high intimacy and trust without expecting them to hold space for your biggest struggles.

Understanding your psychic membrane begins with knowing and trusting yourself while sharpening your intuition (or "wise mind"). The sensors on the psychic membrane around your tender heart recognize which level of intimacy a person should be in. They know when to let someone have maximum (or minimum) access to your heart—but you may need to learn to listen more and to trust those messages. When you trust that you know what you need, you can stand firm in communicating and standing by your convictions. (Note: Once again, it's important to mention that trauma can have an adverse effect on these senses, making it difficult for you to know when you can trust yourself. If this is true for you, treatment may be needed.)

Like your cellular membranes, your psychic membrane is flexible, permeable, and sturdy. As you get to know yourself, you become more and more aware of the signals it sends (for example, telling you when someone crosses a boundary, triggering fear and/or shame, anger, numbing, etc.). You will learn to witness how your body responds when someone breaches your boundaries (for example, how your stomach clenches, throat closes, head begins to ache, etc.). You will pay more and more attention to your needs and how you can meet them (for example, if you're an introvert, recognizing that you need solitude after a public outing, or that you should turn off your phone by 9 p.m. to get the best rest).

Healthy membranes are not selfish and they're not about keeping people out. They're about maintaining the energy, strength, and emotional well-being you need to function in the world. Introverts may need their membranes to be less permeable than extroverts. Traumatized people may need more rigid membranes than those who've never faced trauma. Chronically ill people or those with disabilities may need different membranes than others. People who've experienced abuse or oppression may cultivate different membranes than those who haven't. But all are valid if they help you stay emotionally and physically healthy.

You are not obligated to justify or explain your membrane to anyone; it's yours. You are an autonomous being. When you first communicate a new expectation or restriction in your social contract to someone, more often than not they will resist. They might ignore your new membrane setting because your action may trigger their own needs for safety and belonging. You can do your best to be kind to them, if you care about how they feel. But giving in to demands from them to change your mind, or overlooking their persistent disregard of your membrane, will only do damage in the end.

If they realize that your membrane tending is about you rather than them, over time most people (at least those on their own emotional growth journey) will adapt and learn to treat you the way you've asked to be treated. You may need to move those who refuse to adapt to the outer circles of your Circles of Trust.

Many times, in fact, when people learn to adapt to your membrane, they discover they feel safer with you because they know where you stand. I find that to be the case with clients, for example. If I am unclear about my membrane and what is and is not allowed, they don't know what is safe and are forever anxious about crossing a blurry line (for example, if they email me too often or invite me to social gatherings). But when I am clear, they don't have to worry about whether they're doing the wrong thing.

Just as it wouldn't be acceptable for your next-door neighbour to climb your fence, come into your garage without your permission, take your lawn mower, or start demanding that you paint their house for them, it's not acceptable for someone to push through your psychic membrane, do things to your body or heart for which you haven't given consent, or make demands that you do emotional labour on their behalf. All those things can be freely given, if you so choose. But you are *never* obligated.

You are a sovereign being. You have dominion and power over your body, your time, your energy, and your health. Each person with whom you interact is also a sovereign being. The most successful relationships are those in which the people involved navigate that sovereignty in themselves and each other without jeopardizing it, oppressing it, or being threatened by it.

There are many reasons why people become the kind who "climb over their neighbour's fence." They maybe haven't had good role models with healthy membranes to teach them. They may have personality disorders (and have learned that this is the only way to have their emotional needs met), be on the autism spectrum, or suffer from mental illness. They may have been abused and haven't found healing, and so project those wounds onto other people. And/or they may come from a very different culture where people are used to more communal living and fewer personal boundaries. None of these things make them "bad people." However, if their behaviour is destructive to you, you have a right to protect yourself from that behaviour.

Personally, through a lot of painful missteps, I've come to realize that I have a tendency to look for all the reasons why a person has behaved badly toward me—and then I excuse the behaviour because "they can't help it." I used to think this tendency was about my own grace and compassion, but then I realized I often extend that grace and compassion to everyone but *me*. I am well trained to put myself second on the priority list.

In recent years, I've done work to strengthen my psychic membrane. But the challenge that comes with strengthening one's membrane is that it doesn't always fit the image people want to project onto you. It might mean that, in protecting yourself from what harms you, you now allow yourself to show anger, offend people, look too proud, or become what someone might call "full of yourself"—things a more "polite" version of yourself would never do.

For example, there were several times when I was firm about the behaviour I would no longer tolerate, and other people reacted with some version of the old "you're not being nice" shaming that so triggers me (and was once painfully effective). Every one of these times, my old "be nice or lose everything" trauma (deeply rooted in my religious social conditioning) was triggered and I felt my body respond with a need to "be nice and make it all better," in spite of that person behaving badly.

Fortunately, though, I've learned to hit the pause button when that triggering shows up and do the necessary self-care so that the triggering has less power over me. And then, when the throat-closing-heart-palpitating-brain-spinning reaction has dissipated, I am usually able to respond more clearly in a way that aligns with my values and the way I choose to care for myself.

One more thing: If you find yourself struggling with how permeable or impermeable to make your membrane, take heart. This is a learning process, not something mastered overnight, especially if you're unravelling a lifetime of other conditioning. Psychic membranes are fluid and will adapt as we grow. Begin simply by listening to yourself and paying more careful attention to your needs, what feels safe and unsafe, when you feel coerced or manipulated, when your energy is being sapped, and when you give your energy to people out of a sense of obligation rather than generosity.

You will learn to strengthen your membrane as you learn to know yourself better. And the good news is this: those who spend time strengthening their own membranes begin to attract other people with similarly healthy membranes. You might be surprised how your community of like-minded people grows when you're intentional about who's in your Circles of Trust.

13

the spiral of
authenticity

WHEN YOU WERE a child, you likely had certain subconscious beliefs about what it meant to become a
grown-up. Perhaps you thought it would happen
magically when you graduated from high school or university. Or maybe you thought you'd automatically be handed
your "grown-up" membership card as soon as you got married.
Whatever it was, there's a good chance you saw it as a "once-
and-done" threshold that you'd cross, after which you'd know
everything you needed to get through life. At least, that's the
way I saw it.

Of course, by now you know that real life doesn't work that
way. "Growing up" is a never-ending task. The challenges and
opportunities for learning are endless, and the possibilities for
emotional and spiritual evolution continue until the end of
our days. I had a client once who was in her eighties and said
that was the decade in which she was doing some of her most
remarkable growth, partly because she was finally free of an
abusive marriage.

In recent years, several authors and teachers have attempted to develop models to help us better understand adult emotional and spiritual development. Richard Rohr, for example, talks about the "two halves of life" (based on Jungian concepts). He sees the first half of life as a time of dualism:

> *The dualistic mind is essentially binary, either/or thinking. It knows by comparison, opposition, and differentiation. It uses descriptive words like good/evil, pretty/ugly, smart/stupid, not realizing there may be a hundred degrees between the two ends of each spectrum. Dualistic thinking works well for the sake of simplification and conversation, but not for the sake of truth or the immense subtlety of actual personal experience. Most of us settle for quick and easy answers instead of any deep perception, which we leave to poets, philosophers, and prophets.*[26]

In the first half of life, your psychic membrane may be fairly basic because it seems simple to determine when something is good or bad for you. People in the first half of life can be fairly rigid and closed-minded, shutting out anyone who doesn't agree with them or make them feel safe. For example, I remember a workshop where one woman was baffled by our conversation around the complexity of navigating conflict. "When someone's mean to me," she said, "I just cut them out of my life. I don't have time for that kind of behaviour." She still saw the world through a dualistic lens—good people versus bad people—and was unable to engage in a conversation beyond that.

The second half of life is a time of non-dualism, which Rohr says usually happens after some type of mid-life "fall"—a major failure, a crisis, or perhaps a time of loss and/or deep grief—that causes us to question everything:

Nondual consciousness is about receiving and being present to the moment, to the now, without judgment, analysis, or critique, without your ego deciding whether you like it or not. Reality does not need you to like it in order to be reality. This is a much more holistic knowing, where your mind, heart, soul, and senses are open and receptive to the moment just as it is, which allows you to love things in themselves and as themselves. You learn not to divide the field of the moment or eliminate anything that threatens your ego, but to hold everything— both the attractive and the unpleasant—together in one accepting gaze.[27]

It's challenging to grow a fully functioning psychic membrane in the second half of life. The greater complexities that emerge in this second half lead to a deepening awareness that many things which served us in the first half of life— relationships included—no longer serve us. As a result, we have less clarity about what is good and bad, or right and wrong, and so the sensors and channels on our membrane have to work harder and use greater discernment about what's allowed to pass through.

Rohr's theory on the two halves of life is fairly simplistic, which is probably why it resonated so strongly for me several years ago after my big awakening in the hospital, when I first began to understand this evolutionary process. There are other authors who have put forth more nuanced, multi-layered approaches to understanding psychological development and evolution. These include such writers as Don Beck and Clare Graves (who crafted the theory of Spiral Dynamics), Ken Wilber (who developed Integral Theory), and Mihaly Csikszentmihalyi (who wrote *The Evolving Self: A Psychology for the Third Millennium*). In these theories, our evolution is not a "once-and-done" process but a series of evolutions in which we transform over our lifetime into higher and higher states of consciousness.

Each of these theories has merit, and each has influenced my own thinking on human evolution to varying degrees. They invite an even more complex view into the development of a psychic membrane. For example, a more evolved version of the membrane is required at each stage of Spiral Dynamics. We have to be constantly aware of our evolving needs and challenges, and how that influences what we want to let in, whom we want to link up with, and how we want our membrane "proteins" to interpret and express our DNA blueprint.

I'd like to add my own theory to this growing field, one I refer to as the "Spiral of Authenticity," which provides an additional nuance to the above-mentioned theories. For the sake of simplicity, I present it here as a single spiral, though I see each lifetime as a process of multiple spirals that take us ever deeper into our most actualized and conscious version of ourselves.

Let's go back to the very beginning of our development...

When I first started waking up to a desire to live more authentically, after the disruptive but profound spiritual experience in the hospital when Matthew was born, I found myself wondering, "Where did I go wrong? How did I end up making so many choices that don't align with my real interests, values, and desires? How did I end up a thirty-four-year-old who doesn't know who she is?"

But I hadn't really done anything "wrong." As a child, none of us chooses to live in a way that doesn't align with who we are. Instead, we become separated from our authenticity at an early age because we are busy trying to figure out how to *survive*.

From the moment of birth, each of us starts on a quest to fulfill three core needs: *safety*, *belonging*, and *identity*. We do whatever it takes to meet those needs, and when those needs are threatened, we make hard choices about which ones should take priority.

Somewhere along the line—especially in our formative years—almost all of us sacrifice (though not necessarily through conscious choice) at least some part of our identity to the causes of safety and belonging. **Safety and belonging take precedence over an expression of unique identity.**

This is similar to the "duality phase" of life that Rohr talks about. In the quest for safety and belonging, we make a series of little choices that begin to separate us from who we truly are. There are myriad factors that influence these choices: expectations that we conform to our parents' wishes, even when those wishes go contrary to our true nature; pressures to perform well in school to please our teachers; peer pressures that cause us to give in rather than face the schoolyard bully; and cultural pressures that impose certain actions and choices on us.

These aren't necessarily *wrong* choices; they're choices we make with the wisdom we possess at the time. And yet... perhaps calling these "choices" isn't entirely fair. Is it really a choice when we face harsh consequences for our missteps, perhaps even abuse? Is it really a choice when we're born into circumstances outside our control? Is it really a choice when our brain is not yet fully developed and we're being coerced, disciplined, and shaped by adults whose brains are?

Whatever the case, we slowly but surely lose touch with our identity. We lose our free spirit, our uniqueness, our authenticity. We learn—by careful imitation, by punishment, and by shaming—how to survive the environment into which we've been born. We tame our wildness, our nonconformity, and our defiance. We put on masks to hide aspects of ourselves that we believe are not acceptable to the world. We become the people our parents, teachers, and other influencers expect us to be. We learn to fit the culture into which we've been born.

At that stage of the process, the psychic membrane is fairly simple. Its primary function is to keep us safe from harm and connected to those who give us a sense of belonging. The epigenetics function of the psychic membrane that strives to express our authentic identity takes a back seat to the sensors that work to keep us safe.

And then there is trauma, which further separates us from our identity by putting our perceived safety at even greater risk. No matter its form—childhood sexual abuse, the death of a parent, an unstable home environment, bullying, religious trauma, racism, or others—trauma results in the building of additional defences, especially when we are traumatized as children. These defences, meant to keep us safe at the time, make it tremendously difficult to connect to our identity later on.

At some point—around mid-life, perhaps—we begin waking up to the ways we are disconnected from our identity. For some of us, it's a gradual awakening. For others, it's the result of a crisis that casts us into a liminal space journey. As I mentioned earlier, my awakening began most significantly during the three weeks I spent in the hospital before giving birth to my stillborn son. Before that time, I was busy building a life that was safe, respectable, and comfortable. I tried to hang on to that life after Matthew died, but eventually I couldn't resist the pull toward authenticity, spirituality, and wholeness.

In this process, we could say that our psychic membrane finally begins responding to stimuli that awaken the proteins responsible for interpreting and expressing our DNA blueprint within the cell. When this awakening comes, we face a new choice: return to safety and continue living inauthentically, or risk losing our safety and belonging by stepping into the true expression of our DNA.

Those who choose to return to safety do so at great cost. Many become bitter, addicted, or angry. Some, as Gabor Maté says in *When the Body Says No*, face health concerns when their bodies react to the lack of emotional health in their minds and hearts. They may have safety, but they never find wholeness.

Of course, there is a cost for the other choice too. Those who begin a quest for authenticity may sacrifice jobs, relationships, and perhaps entire ways of life that aren't strong enough to survive the transition. They may face ridicule and abandonment from people confounded by the changes in them. There can be many sacrifices—both large and small—along the way.

If we choose to awaken and accept those sacrifices, we take our first step into the **Spiral of Authenticity**.

The spiral/labyrinth structure once again becomes helpful for understanding because it mirrors the process so well. The Spiral of Authenticity can be overlaid onto the liminal space diagram we considered earlier, but there are distinct qualities that make the Spiral of Authenticity worthy of its own diagram (Figure 15).

When the awakening step happens, we begin to see that the sense of safety and belonging we had before was based on a false construct. We may have *felt* safe and connected, but that was an illusion, because the version of "you" that conformed in order to feel safe and connected wasn't real. It's like the little pig who built his house out of straw in the story of the Three Little Pigs. It may have *looked* like a house, but it was actually a mirage that offered no real security.

When safety is only available to us if we agree never to step out of line, and when we perform and conform in ways that keep those with power happy, it's not real safety; those in power can change the rules at any time.

Consider the patriarchal system, for example: we are taught that if we stand outside the rules the system teaches us, then we put ourselves at risk. But when the system chooses to change the rules, we are forced to conform in *new* ways to avoid risk.

The period of the witch hunts in early modern Europe (approximately 1450 to 1750) is one such example. It wasn't just witches who were burned at the stake; it was *anyone* who

FIGURE 15. THE SPIRAL OF AUTHENTICITY

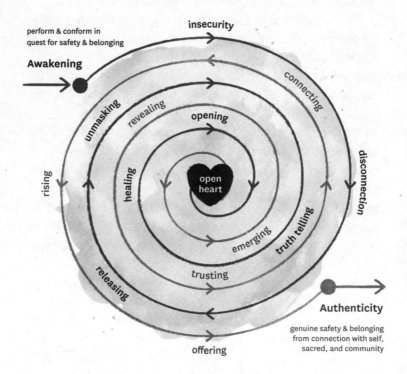

perform & conform in
quest for safety & belonging

insecurity

Awakening

connecting

unmasking

revealing

opening

disconnection

rising

healing

open
heart

truth telling

emerging

releasing

trusting

Authenticity

offering

genuine safety & belonging
from connection with self,
sacred, and community

exhibited an appearance of nonconformity that threatened the dominant culture and political system. In this case, those in power decided it was certain women who posed a threat: women who had their own businesses or substantial sums of money, women who owned property or livestock, women who chose not to marry, or women who were healers in the community. These women were labelled "witches" so that those in authority had an excuse to accuse them of wrongdoing and execute them before seizing their businesses, property, and wealth, taking more power for themselves.

When this movement began, even women who thought they were conscientious about following the cultural and religious rules found themselves targets of persecution. The system and its accusations were arbitrary; the safety they thought they had was an illusion.

When we wake up, we see just how much we have sacrificed to the forces of societal control and influence by submitting to these rules and false promises of safety. We live in houses of straw, and the big bad wolves can come at any time to blow those houses down.

That waking up can feel like a betrayal. We no longer know what's true, what's a mirage, and what/who we can trust. We might discover that those who we thought were keeping us safe were only looking out for their own interests and illusions of safety, and/or reacting from their own trauma. Worse, they may, in fact, have been serving as double agents, destabilizing the environment just enough to keep us turning to them for safety. This is how governments and institutions have wielded power for centuries; it is what the Catholic Church did during the times of the witch burnings. This dynamic creates what has been referred to in Attachment Theory as a "trauma bond," where people find themselves attached to someone who is both their source of safety *and* their greatest threat.

As we grew up, we undoubtedly saw individuals around us who undertook their own journeys—perhaps the adults who broke from conformity but then experienced the inevitable ostracism of the community. Or perhaps the *opposite*: adults who momentarily dared to stand at the precipice of the Spiral of Authenticity but then caved in to their own fear, sense of being overwhelmed, and/or lack of support. (Then, to regain their sense of safety and belonging, they often overcompensated by becoming chaos makers in their own right, hijackers who must draw people into their fear to feel less alone.) And of course there were those who remained forever locked in the system, never making an attempt to break loose.

To find our own open hearts, our lost identities, our DNA in the Spiral of Authenticity, there are two distinct periods: the Inward Journey and the Outward Journey. Though I've listed the steps of the two different diagrams in a somewhat linear fashion, there is no straight line, no "right" way to move through this. The image is an attempt to clarify a process that can be quite muddy and non-linear.

The Inward Journey

After our initial **awakening**, the first stop along the Inward Journey (Figure 16) is **insecurity**. When we've spent much of the first halves of our lives seeking safety, this can be a tremendously unsettling place. It can make us want to rush back to what we knew before. But it is only in *accommodating* insecurity that we can move forward.

How do we learn to accommodate insecurity? By breathing into it. By finding spiritual/body practices that help calm the fears when they arise. By finding other people on similar journeys of authenticity to support and model for us. By holding

FIGURE 16. THE INWARD JOURNEY OF THE SPIRAL OF AUTHENTICITY

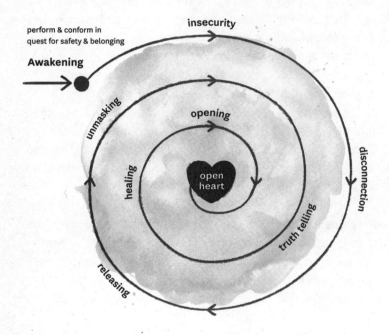

perform & conform in quest for safety & belonging

insecurity

Awakening

unmasking

opening

disconnection

healing

open heart

truth telling

releasing

space for ourselves and strengthening our psychic membranes. And by reminding ourselves that insecurity is part of growth.

The next stop in the journey is **disconnection**. This is where we realize we have to disengage from some of the people, communities, institutions, and systems that once offered belonging but no longer have what we need. Sometimes it's because they are toxic individuals and structures. But more often than not it's because they don't have the emotional/ spiritual maturity to hold space for us at this stage of the journey; they hold us back. They might reject us because they don't understand our growth and are deeply uncomfortable. We might choose to walk away from them entirely or simply find a way to accept that our relationships with them are not as deep as we desire.

This is where we need to trust the sensors on our psychic membranes to tell us who can be allowed into our Circles of Trust and who should be left out. It takes practice to listen to the signals, exercise our intuitive senses, and discern who and what is best for us.

There is often a great loneliness that shows up in the quest for authenticity. As Carl Jung puts it in his writing about the individuation process, we are breaking away from the herd to become true to ourselves. We are in that liminal space where we may have to leave one community without yet finding other communities that match our new, emerging authenticity:

> What is it, in the end, that induces a man to go his own way and to rise out of unconscious identity with the mass as out of a swathing mist? . . . It is what is commonly called vocation: an irrational factor that destines a man to emancipate himself from the herd and from its well-worn paths . . . Anyone with a vocation hears the voice of the inner man: he is called.[28]

Just as we need to learn to be present with insecurity, we need to learn to be present with loneliness and disconnection. We gradually learn to find comfort in being alone. We discover that solitude can be beautiful and meaningful, and that sometimes disconnection from others (especially those who are not supportive) opens opportunity for greater connection with ourselves and with those who enter our lives with greater capacity to hold space for us.

The next step on the spiral inward is **releasing**. In the journey to authenticity there is a releasing of old habits, old belief systems, and old narratives. There is a shedding of all that once kept us propped up and safe and gave us our definitions of who we were. For example, perhaps you were raised, like me, to believe women should not be in leadership. Yet you found yourself shedding that belief to step into your calling as a leader. Maybe you have an old story about your lack of artistic ability, and yet you long to be an artist. Maybe you've been socially conditioned to believe you don't have a right to a position of power due to skin colour, disability, or social standing. Or maybe you have a long-held family narrative that nobody from your lineage is smart enough to make it through university.

These well-ingrained beliefs won't slip out of consciousness without some effort and intention.

Releasing requires the "active transport" function of the psychic membrane: intentionally and actively letting go of that which may be clogging up or hindering your emotional and spiritual health.

There's a reason the path to the centre of the labyrinth is long and circuitous: we can't do all our releasing at once. We need to do it in stages—one story, one belief, one habit, one rule at a time. Sometimes, things we thought we had let go of come back again to haunt us; they might need to be released in small layers, with a little more digging and a little more letting go at each layer. Like the shrub in my backyard that I dug up a few years ago and which still sends up shoots every spring, we get reminders that some stubborn piece of root has been left behind and needs to be dug out a little more.

Then we come to **unmasking**, the stage when we begin to walk away from our old identities and reveal—little by little—who we truly are, first to ourselves and then to others. At this stage, the epigenetic function of our psychic membranes begins to engage, actively interpreting and expressing our DNA. It might be only a whisper at first... but even a whisper can be powerful when it holds truth.

Perhaps it's daring to sign up for a course you've been longing to take. Perhaps it's saying no to something you've always been coerced into saying yes to before. Perhaps it's beginning a job search for something that fits better. Whatever it is, it's likely scary and unsettling, especially if you've faced abuse or bullying in the past or witnessed others being shamed for taking off their masks.

Next on the Inward Journey is **truth telling**, which goes hand in hand with unmasking. As the masks are removed, we begin to reveal the truth about who we are, what we believe in, and what we'll no longer tolerate. At this stage on the inward-moving spiral, it is largely about first telling the truth to *ourselves* and learning to own and celebrate that truth before we begin to speak it aloud.

Years ago, when I was still an active member of a church (not long after my stillbirth, when I was trying to cling to the safety of the old shape of my faith), I was elected to the position of elder because of my leadership skills. I was resistant, because my belief system felt shaky and I wasn't sure I should lead from that position of uncertainty. But the pastor was a dear friend of mine who convinced me that the church would benefit from my leadership—and even my questions and challenges had a place.

About halfway through my three-year term, one of the more conservative members of the church pushed for the elders to issue a statement against same-sex marriage. (It was shortly after Canada had legalized same-sex marriage.) I had come a long way in the evolution of my belief system on that issue but had yet to speak my conviction out loud. In that moment, though, I knew I needed to speak up. I had friends who were members of the LGBTQ+ community and I didn't want to be part of a church that didn't fully embrace them.

I was surprised how scary it was to speak my conviction aloud that first time. The fear of rejection (by my church community and family) consumed me. My safety and belonging were suddenly at risk, and I wasn't certain I was ready to give them up.

But I knew choosing authenticity meant unmasking myself and telling the truth, and so I said, "If you choose to issue a statement against same-sex marriage, then I will no longer be an elder in this church." I was physically shaking as I said it, but I didn't back down. The issue remained unresolved for the remainder of my time on the elder board. I don't believe it has ever come up again, though I am no longer involved in the church, so I don't know.

Scary as it was, that moment was also empowering and life-altering. I learned that my life would not be destroyed if I started telling the truth about what I believed. Fortunately, truth telling gets easier the more you work up the courage to do it. Now, more than a dozen years later, I have no trouble speaking my truth on this issue and am happy to support my daughters, two of whom came out a few years later. (I also recognize I share this story from a place of privilege that allows me to choose whether or not to speak out on this issue. Many people have no choice but to speak in much more dangerous situations, where their own lives are at risk. For them—you?—this truth-telling stage has many more layers of complexity.)

Next on the spiral is **healing**. All of these steps—releasing, unmasking, and truth telling—lead to some deep and powerful healing of the shame, woundedness, and fear carried from the earlier parts of our lives, when we were severed from our true selves. I purposely put this further along the Inward Journey because we can't get to the deepest kind of healing until we've cracked ourselves open, taken off the masks, and started telling the truth. It's like taking a Band-Aid off so the wound can get the air it needs to heal.

As Stephen Levine says: "Simply touching a difficult memory with some slight willingness to heal begins to soften the holding and tension around it."[29] If we don't learn to tell the truth about ourselves and the ways in which we've been silenced and wounded, we keep barriers over the wounds that won't allow them to heal.

The healing process can be long. It can bring up a lot of ugliness that we've become practised at hiding. A family member of mine uncovered repressed memories of childhood sexual abuse, and she's been in therapy for several years because she "touched a difficult memory." The healing process has been long and arduous, but it has also been transformational. When her husband was diagnosed with cancer a few years later, she had more resilience to deal with it because of the healing she'd done.

After healing comes **opening**. At this stage, we willingly become more and more vulnerable, even at the risk of further pain. Though the road is long and often arduous, and we've faced loneliness and disconnection, we've seen enough light at the end of the tunnel to know that the journey is worth it.

Finally, we reach the centre of the Inward Journey, the place of the **open heart**. When we undergo opening, we create space within our psychic membranes to receive what spirit has to offer and to hold space for what is to come. This is a place of deep connection, where we've learned to listen to the whispering of our own souls, where we practise shutting out the noise of the world—and the expectations of others—with a fresh understanding of what it means to be true to ourselves.

It is at the open-hearted centre of the Inward Journey that we begin to recognize not only our identities but our vocations.

• • •

Vocation does not come from a voice "out there" calling me to become something I am not. It comes from a voice "in here" calling me to be the person I was born to be, to fulfill the original selfhood given me at birth by God.[30]

PARKER PALMER

• • •

An open heart is not an unprotected heart—quite the opposite. It requires a stronger and healthier membrane than ever before. True openness is only possible if we are guarded by membranes that honour who we are, that nourish and protect us so we can actively express our authentic DNA.

An open heart is also not the end of the journey to authenticity. The centre is not the final destination of the labyrinth. Rather, it is the midpoint. If we stop at this midway point and stay at the centre, we become self-absorbed and our vocations remain unfulfilled. Our DNA might find expression, but we won't contribute to the functioning of a healthy collective. To be true to that vocation and really *live* authentically, we need to make the Outward Journey and return from the centre.

Self-help books sometimes fall short by encouraging only the Inward Journey to the *self*, and not the Outward Journey back to *community*. This is not a true fulfillment of who we are. This isn't to say we need to rush away from the centre.

Sometimes, in fact, we need to spend a good long time there to prepare ourselves for what is to come. But eventually we must leave the comfort and safety to follow the voice that's beckoning—calling us to connection and service.

The Outward Journey

In the first phase of the Outward Journey (Figure 17) we step into the place of **emerging**. There's an eagerness to share our truest selves and all that we've discovered. And that eagerness comes with some mistakes. Like baby chicks emerging from the eggshell, we might initially stumble over ourselves in an effort to do everything we feel called to do. Stumbling is part of the process.

I see this sometimes in coaching clients, when someone's launching a new business, for example, and becomes obsessed with getting everything—their website, their offerings, and their "elevator pitch"—just right before they send anything out into the world. I always urge them to allow themselves to get it wrong the first time they try. The mistakes are part of the learning and refining process. Imperfection is the best soil for growth.

Revealing comes as we finally allow the world to see *us*, and glimpse the gifts coming from the true expression of our DNA. This is the first expression of our original "medicine," our gifts to the world. As we eventually reveal these gifts—fully and authentically—we find vocations with identities and shapes that go far beyond who we were as individuals.

That leads to **trusting**. The more we practise authenticity and lean into the expression of our gifts and vocations, the more we learn to trust. In trusting, we surrender our egos, fears, and limitations. We learn to lean into the outer rims of our bowls—Community and Mystery—rather than thinking we

FIGURE 17. THE OUTWARD JOURNEY OF
THE SPIRAL OF AUTHENTICITY

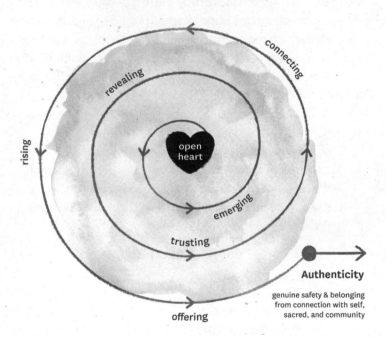

open
heart

connecting

revealing

rising

emerging

trusting

offering

Authenticity

genuine safety & belonging
from connection with self,
sacred, and community

need to figure everything out by ourselves. We allow the path to reveal itself and we let ourselves be held.

And as we share who we are and what we know, our initial stumbling becomes confidence. We let go of much of the fear and are ready to share. We might still be rather self-absorbed in the revealing process, worrying about what others think, wanting to make good impressions, and not wanting to fail. But gradually, if we remain true to ourselves and our sense of calling, we release our ego and move fully into expressing our vocations.

For example, when I first started public speaking, I had a lot of anxiety over my performance. I wanted to get it just right and impress people with my stories and wisdom. But now, after several years of practice, it's far less about me and far more about what I'm teaching.

• • •

Your soul knows the geography of your destiny. Your soul alone has the map of your future, therefore you can trust this indirect, oblique side of yourself. If you do, it will take you where you need to go, but more important it will teach you a kindness of rhythm in your journey.[31]

JOHN O'DONOHUE

• • •

Connecting is the next step of the Outward Journey. When we finally connect to our true selves and live authentically, we begin to find the *community* we've longed for. At this point, our psychic membranes link us up with other "cells," connecting us to communities that truly strengthen us, encourage us, and help us grow into our potential. Collectively, we can serve the greater "body."

We are all longing to go home to some place we have never been—a place half-remembered and half-envisioned we can only catch glimpses of from time to time. Community. Somewhere, there are people to whom we can speak with passion without having the words catch in our throats. Somewhere a circle of hands will open to receive us, eyes will light up as we enter, voices will celebrate with us whenever we come into our own power. Community means strength that joins our strength to do the work that needs to be done. Arms to hold us when we falter. A circle of healing. A circle of friends. Someplace where we can be free.[32]

STARHAWK

• • •

The Inward Journey can feel quite lonely and it can be hard to hold on to hope that we will ever find real connection. But it does happen—perhaps not in big ways, but in small ways, one wholehearted conversation at a time. Authentic people attract other authentic people, and out of that attraction beautiful relationships blossom.

When I wander in the woods, I listen to the great variety of birdsongs, especially when there is a call and response between birds. On one such wander, it occurred to me that in order for birds to find each other, they need their own unique songs. If a crow didn't like the way he sang and tried to be a robin, he would be lonely without the other crows. If a chickadee tried to sing like a loon, she wouldn't find her way to other chickadees.

To connect to the "birds" we're meant to be with, we need to sing in our unique styles. A fake song will lead to a fake community; only authenticity will lead us to real connection. I see this all the time in the retreats that I lead. The community that gathers around this work is, in my opinion, among the most authentic I have ever seen. The people in these spaces almost inevitably show up like birds singing their own songs, and they connect in a deep way to their "flock" when they meet them.

When our psychic membranes are strong and healthy, the antigens on the surface will help us identify others with similar antigens and, in our bonding, beautiful things can unfold. The sense of belonging for which we so hungered earlier—and for which we surrendered so much of our identity—manifests, but it's more genuine and whole than what we once knew.

The next point we reach on the Outward Journey is the **rising**. This is when it all begins to come together. We've revealed who we are and the gifts we bring, learned to trust our vocations, and connected to our communities. And now we rise, like the proverbial phoenix from the ashes, from what once was. We rise as our beauty and strength grow. We rise in authenticity and courage.

The rising may or may not be a big, splashy affair, and it really doesn't matter. Perhaps it is a quiet rising with only a small circle of friends aware of something different about us. Or perhaps we finally have a solo art show that only a handful of people notice. On the other hand, perhaps we gain sudden fame and thousands of people now want something from us. Whatever our rising looks like, it matters. Our gifts matter. Our contribution to the world matters.

This leads to the last spot on the Outward Journey: the **offering** that manifests from our gifts, what some Indigenous cultures refer to as our "original medicine" and other people call "divine assignment," "calling," or "life purpose." No matter its name, our "medicine" becomes our offering, the shape that each of us uniquely provides to the world. Whenever it's found, we need to open our hands and serve it up to the world.

It is only in genuine offering that we find joy in our vocations. If we hold the gifts too tightly, if we refuse to share or let fear control us, we will never be fully aligned and never fully authentic. In the beautiful book *Braiding Sweetgrass*, Indigenous writer Robin Wall Kimmerer talks about how taking responsibility for our gifts—and offering them up in service to the community and the earth—is part of the symbiosis and reciprocity of Creation. Withholding the gift is a violation of our commitment to each other and the land. When speaking of the work of sugaring maples (gathering the tree's sap to convert into sugar), for example, she says:

> *Nanabozho* [the Anishinaabe Original Man] *made certain that the work would never be too easy. His teachings remind us that one half of the truth is that the earth endows us with great gifts, the other half is that the gift is not enough. The responsibility does not lie with the maples alone. The other half belongs to us; we participate in its transformation. It is our work, and our gratitude, that distills the sweetness.*

Later in the book, Kimmerer recounts the lessons she learned from an elder teaching her how to weave black ash baskets:

> *"Just think of the tree and all its hard work before you start,"* he says. *"It gave its life for this basket, so you know your responsibility. Make something beautiful in return."*[33]

Our work may or may not be as tangible or connected to the earth as sugaring maples or weaving baskets, but—no matter the form—it's still part of the larger ecosystem and symbiosis of the universe. Each of us gives something to the greater good, both in gratitude for what we receive and in reciprocity and commitment to the cycle of life.

After we have made the journey to the centre of the spiral and back out again, we reach the point of **authenticity**, where we are in greater alignment with our desires, vocations, giftedness, and longing, and with ourselves. Our psychic membranes are strong; we are more genuinely expressing the blueprints of our DNA and existing in homeostatic balance, giving and receiving, nourishing and being nourished.

This is not the easy path, but the path with meaning, joy, and freedom. Along the way, we gain courage, resilience, and strength.

The place of authenticity is the place of more genuine safety and belonging than we ever knew before. It's not rooted in a mirage, but in our own strength and authentic connection with Community and Mystery. Instead of a house built of straw, we're now like the little pig who chose to build a house of bricks. We've laid foundations in deep connection with our authentic selves, each other, the sacred, and the earth. This foundation cannot be easily toppled by the big bad wolves.

This place of authenticity is *still* not a permanent destination, though. It is simply the doorway to pass through into greater and greater evolution, growth, and understanding. Once in tune with who we are, we have greater capacity for learning, growth, and stretching. We may, in fact, find ourselves travelling in and out of other spirals as we evolve into even truer and wiser versions of ourselves and our potential.

While I have presented this journey to authenticity as a singular pathway (for the sake of illustration), that would be too simplistic an interpretation. It can be an iterative journey, with small spirals occurring again and again throughout our lives (perhaps even in different layers of our lives at different times), bringing us closer and closer to deepening understanding of our authentic selves. However you are making the journey, trust that there is no "wrong" way to do it.

There is no list of rules. There is one rule. The rule is: there are no rules. Happiness comes from living as you need to, as you want to. As your inner voice tells you to. Happiness comes from being who you actually are instead of who you think you are supposed to be. Being traditional is not traditional anymore. It's funny that we still think of it that way. Normalize your lives, people. You don't want a baby? Don't have one. I don't want to get married? I won't. You want to live alone? Enjoy it. You want to love someone? Love someone. Don't apologize. Don't explain. Don't ever feel less than. When you feel the need to apologize or explain who you are, it means the voice in your head is telling you the wrong story. Wipe the slate clean. And rewrite it. No fairy tales. Be your own narrator. And go for a happy ending. One foot in front of the other. You will make it.[34]

SHONDA RHIMES

14

recognizing shock absorbers

I WAS ON MY way to the dentist, feeling anxious because I had a broken tooth and was sure the repair would be expensive and painful. I also assumed I'd be shamed and blamed—for not flossing, for eating hard candy, or clenching my teeth when I sleep. (Plus I felt a little guilty for driving the two blocks to the dentist's office, but didn't want to walk home in the extreme cold with a frozen mouth.)

As I drove slowly through the parking lot, I was hit from behind by another car. In my anxious state of mind, my automatic thought was that I had done something wrong. But then, just as quickly, I realized that there was nothing I could have done in that moment to have caused a bump; it had to be something that hit me.

I turned and processed what had happened. A car was pulling out, hadn't seen me, and hit the back passenger side of my car.

The driver of the other car pulled up beside me and we both rolled down our windows. "I'm sorry," said the guy, looking strangely frantic given how minor the incident was, "but I didn't hit you."

"What do you mean you didn't hit me? My car moved. Clearly you hit me."

"Look," he said, pointing back, "there's a block of ice on the ground. That's probably what you hit."

"What are you talking about?" I said, looking in the mirror at the tiny block of ice. "How could a block of ice have caused my car to move like that?"

And then he just started yelling, "I didn't hit you! I didn't hit you!"

I said, in as calm a voice as I could muster, "Can we just get out of our cars to look and see if there is any damage?"

His voice began to escalate. "But I didn't hit you!"

"Before you drive away, I'm *just* asking you to get out of your car and come with me so we can see if there is damage."

He kept yelling while getting out of his car and we both went to look at the side of my car. Sure enough, there was a small dent on the fender near the wheel (ironically, in the same spot I'd had repaired a few months earlier after backing into a pole).

"I didn't hit you!" he yelled. "How do I know that dent wasn't there before?!" (I knew, because that whole section of the car's body had been repaired and repainted, but I didn't think to say that in the moment.) He started wildly flinging his arms, pointing at other dings and marks on the car. "Next you're going to say I caused that! And that! And that!"

"No, but you DID cause THAT!" I said, pointing at the small dent.

"I DIDN'T HIT YOU! LOOK—THERE'S THE BLOCK OF ICE. AND LOOK AT THE SKID MARKS BY THE BLOCK OF ICE. YOUR CAR WAS HIT BY THAT AND THE DENT WAS ON YOUR CAR ALREADY!"

I glanced toward where he was pointing. In the thin layer of snow on the ground, my tire marks showed clearly where

I'd been travelling in a straight line and then was jolted five inches to the left. Near the zigzag was not a block of ice but a lump of compacted snow that had likely been dislodged from my mud flaps on impact.

As quickly as I'd glanced away, though, I turned back to look into his eyes. Instinctively I knew I couldn't take my eyes off this raging, irrational man or I would not be safe. Behind the anger in his eyes, I could see something else. Fear? Trauma? Shame? Maybe he was driving without a licence? Maybe he'd been traumatized by parents who wouldn't allow him to make mistakes? My mind reeled with the possibilities, wondering what parts of his history and his pain I needed to draw on to defuse this situation.

"Look—I'm not going to take you to court or anything, so please stop overreacting and simply realize that what just happened could only have happened if your car hit mine." My fingers touched the edge of the cellphone in my pocket, wondering whether I should pull it out to record this moment or take a photo of his licence plate.

"I DIDN'T HIT YOU!" Seeing the rage increase in his eyes, I made a split-second decision to let it all go rather than risk being punched in the face. I left the cellphone in my pocket.

"Sir," I said, as calmly and deliberately as I could muster, "the damage is minor enough that I'm not going to report it. Get back in your car now and drive away."

"Okay," he said, getting back into his car. "But I didn't hit you."

I got back into my car and carried on to the dentist. As I sat in front of the dentist's office trembling, I had a flashback, realizing that this wasn't just the story of a five-minute encounter with an irrational man in a parking lot; it was a story of my whole lifetime.

There were two things that were at play in how I responded to that incident, and they were closely intertwined: my social conditioning and my past trauma.

The man's anger instantly triggered the old trauma rooted in my body. I spent my childhood in a home with a father who—though he never hit us—would throw hammers at trees in moments of uncontrolled anger. We learned from a young age to do everything we could not to trigger that anger and to de-escalate it when it happened.

In my marriage, it was similar. I spent many years absorbing the pain of a man who didn't know how to heal his own wounds, and trying to be the buffer so that my children didn't have to absorb it.

And when I was raped as a twenty-two-year-old, much like that moment in the parking lot, I spent two hours trying to de-escalate the situation so that I would not be killed by the blade my attacker held over my head. After he raped me, we sat on my bed while I listened to him talk about his childhood and tried to calm him so that he would leave my home without doing further damage.

Anger, especially in men, triggers my "tend-and-befriend" trauma reaction. Though we have primarily heard of the "fight, flight, or freeze" responses to trauma, researchers have recently added a fourth stress response, considered to be more closely associated with women than men: the **tend-and-befriend** response. (Other versions of this have been referred to as "fawn" and "flock.") This is the trauma response I relate to the most. Here's the definition:

> *Unlike the fight-or-flight response which allows one to fight against a threat if overcoming the threat is likely, or flee if overcoming the threat is unlikely, the tend-and-befriend response is characterized by tending to young in times of stress and befriending those around in times of stress to increase the likelihood of survival. Since a group is more likely than an individual to overcome a threat, this response is a protective*

mechanism for both the female and her offspring. Basically, befriending other females is inherently necessary for the protection of offspring since pregnancy and nursing make a female even more vulnerable to an outside threat. Forming a network not only allows the female to have added protection and help with the raising of offspring, but also serves to secure resources such as housing and food ... Studies even show that females who emigrate and are unable to form a female network, characteristic of female befriending, are more likely to become victims of abuse than women who are able to form these ties.[35]

The amygdala is the part of the brain where our most primitive protection mechanisms live. When it gets hijacked, it takes considerable effort to calm it sufficiently so that the more rational prefrontal cortex can take over. In a situation like the one in the parking lot, my amygdala does its best to protect me from the harm it associates with the trigger.

Researchers have revealed that trauma is rooted in the body as much as it is in the brain. For example, some researchers have found that if the person has not been allowed (or not allowed themselves) to physically shake in the immediate aftermath of trauma, the trauma can become "set" in the body. Like animals whose whole bodies shake when they've faced a fearful situation, we also have a natural tendency to shake. The difference is that humans often deny themselves that trembling.

I remember lying in bed with my entire body shaking after the long, difficult, and traumatic birth of my first daughter. I tried to stop it but couldn't, and I'm glad now that nobody intervened to shut it down. If we *do* shut it down, the trauma cannot be released from our body, and we may find ourselves still dealing with it years later. (For more on this, look into TRE—Tension & Trauma Release Exercises,[36] or read Peter Levine's work on somatic healing of trauma.[37])

One of the additional complexities of trauma is that we not only deal with the trauma in our own lives, but we may also carry *inherited* trauma from our ancestors. The study of epigenetics (mentioned in chapter 10) suggests that trauma alters the way our DNA is expressed. Those altered cells—and the reactivity that comes with them—are passed down to future generations. For example, descendants of Holocaust survivors not only have the same genetic markings of trauma as their ancestors, but respond to trauma triggers in the same way their parents and grandparents did, even without directly facing the trauma themselves.

Our social conditioning is related to trauma as well:

> *Societies have mechanisms designed to train us in our roles as soon as possible after birth. All elements of our environment, family, school, media, peer culture, etc., conspire together to socialize us. This process, socialization, is not free of bias— quite the opposite. We internalize the particular biases of our social context while very young. By the time we are three years old, we demonstrate fluency with social values and norms. Children's play is rich with social roles practice, explicit performance of social norms, and the mechanisms for enforcing them, such as ostracism.*[38]

I have been socially conditioned to be a "nice girl." I've been so well conditioned, in fact, that decades after the training, my body still goes into spasms whenever I deviate from the "nice girl" rule book even slightly.

When you're raised as a pacifist Canadian Mennonite farm girl, that programming runs *deep*. If we didn't "turn the other cheek," we weren't living the way Jesus taught us. If we weren't painfully polite, then we were not only shaming our families, we were jeopardizing our country's reputation for politeness.

If we weren't sacrificing ourselves for other people, we weren't living out our faith.

The list goes on and on: Don't brag about yourself lest you be guilty of the sin of arrogance. Don't stand up for yourself lest you incite an unnecessary conflict. Don't let people know how smart you are lest you make other people (especially men) feel bad about themselves. Don't dress too provocatively lest you lead a man to sin. Don't be angry lest you make other people uncomfortable. Don't be too bold, too confident, too strong, too pretty, too smart, too obstinate, or too aggressive. Don't swear, don't be promiscuous, don't argue, don't dance—oh, and while you're at it, don't say no or be rude to an older adult in the family who wants to kiss you without your permission.

JUST BE NICE. Be agreeable. Be sacrificial. Be supportive. Be demure. Be modest. And... because we're Mennonites... be prepared to be a martyr for your faith.

Our patriarchal society values nice girls, because nice girls don't take up too much space, don't claim too much power, don't challenge authority, and certainly don't threaten to disrupt the system that oppresses them. *And* because nice girls are so co-operative, they police each other so that nobody else has to do the nasty work of keeping them in line. (Note: Our society also puts restrictions on how boys should behave and is even more restrictive when it comes to trans and non-binary people.)

When trauma and social conditioning are so deeply intertwined, they don't respond to logic. They get "stuck" in a person's body, activating fight/flight/freeze/tend-and-befriend behaviour and body signals. For example, my throat often reacts by constricting when I'm triggered.

After the encounter in the parking lot with the angry man, I realized that when my trauma and social conditioning are activated, I become a *shock absorber* rather than a bowl. Instead of holding space for the other person so they can do their own work, I receive their pain, anger, fear, etc., and defuse it for them. My psychic membrane is breached, and I am no longer protected from harm.

A shock absorber becomes responsible for the outcome on the other person's behalf, because if the shock-absorbing person doesn't defuse the situation, they know people will be harmed. Many of us find ourselves serving as shock absorbers not because we want to but because we fear for our safety if we refuse. We absorb the danger and defuse it so that it won't cause further damage, just as I did when I sat on my bed alongside my rapist. Then we pass that trauma response down through the generations; our children learn to be shock absorbers too. (I've seen it in my daughters.)

How do we change these patterns and stop serving as shock absorbers?

There are no easy answers because it's not as simple as changing ourselves; it means changing the very systems in which we exist. Oppressive systems always develop hierarchies that justify some people serving as shock absorbers: men look to women and non-binary folks, colonizers look to those they've colonized, white people look to people of colour, heterosexual and cisgender people look to the LGBTQ+ community, and so on.

The person with more power is more likely to assume that the person with less power will serve as the shock absorber. That doesn't mean that men, white people, and heterosexual people never find themselves serving as shock absorbers, but in a hierarchical system it's always safer to throw your emotional hand grenades downhill.

To stop living as shock absorbers (and/or to stop treating others as our shock absorbers), we need to divest ourselves of these unhealthy systems and put the well-being of those being harmed above those causing the harm. This requires strengthening our internal psychic membranes, paying close attention to the sensors that tell us who is safe and who is not, and connecting with like-minded "cells" that will serve as allies and advocates.

It takes a willingness to disrupt the system and challenge the status quo—an action requiring tremendous bravery, self-love, and self-care. Disrupting any ingrained system will likely result in considerable resistance (and possibly violence) from those used to treating us like their shock absorbers. There's a good chance we'll need to weather significant storms to reach a more equitable and peaceful system.

This is when we need to strengthen our resources: others to hold space for us while we undertake the effort, healthy body and mindfulness practices, and strong psychic membranes. When we disrupt these oppressive systems, we choose to work for healthier ways to coexist. We choose personal sovereignty and we put aside our roles as personal shock absorbers. And if we find ourselves in positions of power and privilege where we take advantage of others as our personal shock absorbers, we seek out healthier ways of having our needs met and make whatever reparations are necessary.

15

holding space and
your unmet needs

NOT LONG AFTER I ended my marriage, I realized there were many things about myself that I simply didn't know. Most notably, I had little idea how to articulate my unmet needs.

For more than twenty years as wife and mother, I focused on everyone else's needs more than my own. I could tell which daughter needed alone time after school, which one needed to figure out new things on her own without intervention, and which one needed a five-minute warning before we left the house. I could tell you which of my family members needed plenty of physical touch and which preferred only rare hugs. I could tell you how long my husband could go without sex before he started getting grumpy.

I could tell you these things more easily than I could tell you what my own needs were.

My husband's mental illness was an added challenge. He was highly reactive, and living with that reactivity meant I spent twenty-two years of marriage in hyper-vigilant mode, always attentive to what might set him off. I knew how to warn him when plans changed, how to tone down my frustration so it didn't result in his anger, and which technique was usually the best to calm him when he got worked up.

In retrospect, though it might sound as though I was being selfless in my attentiveness to his needs, my focus on reducing his reactivity was primarily about protecting my emotional safety and that of our daughters (the tend-and-befriend response I mentioned earlier). Our core needs for safety and belonging were definitely at play here. But mastering his needs and protecting our daughters meant that *my* needs (other than my need for safety) almost always came last.

One of the spiritual practices incorporated into The Circle Way teaching of Christina Baldwin is: **"Ask for what we need and offer what we can."**[39] The concept seems simple and straightforward, yet it contains many layers. It takes self-knowledge to know what you need, self-worth to ask for it, and trust in others that they'll respond accordingly. I have noticed, in fact, when I teach this concept in workshops, that I'm often met with blank stares, because people are not sufficiently in touch with their own needs to know how to articulate them.

It took five years to end my marriage, partly because I had such a hard time identifying, and then asking for, what I needed. When I tried asking for it within my marriage, it resulted in visits to multiple marriage counsellors. But over and over again I abandoned those needs for the sake of my husband and daughters, whose needs I took responsibility for.

After I finally worked up the courage to end the marriage, it took a long time to gain clarity about my own unmet needs. The best exercise for this turned out to be the decluttering and renovation of my home. With each bag I dropped off at the Goodwill store, and with each wall I painted or piece of furniture I refurbished, I asked myself, "What do I need in order to make this home feel like a sanctuary? What do I need to feel safety, comfort, belonging, and ease here? How do I need my physical environment to hold space for me?"

It turns out I needed less clutter, more beauty and spaciousness, and lots of shelves for my books. I needed spaces where I could display items that connected me to my spiritual journey without facing the misguided jokes from someone who didn't understand what they represented or why they were important. I also needed an outdoor sanctuary to feel connected to the soil and the trees.

It wasn't an easy process, and some days I found myself on the floor weeping over all that still required healing. Other days I found myself staring at the shelves in Home Depot, trying to make a decision that overwhelmed me because there were far too many decisions to make and I didn't feel sufficiently in touch with my needs and desires to know how to meet them. Some days my primary need was for fewer decisions—so I occasionally walked out of Home Depot empty-handed.

Little by little, I got better at listening to the quiet voice inside me that had been silenced for so long. Little by little, I found my joy returning. And most importantly, my capacity to hold space for other people—with my own healthy psychic membrane intact—became much greater than it ever was.

Perhaps the most valuable learning from that time was this: *Our unmet needs will get in the way of our ability to hold space for others.*

When we are unable to identify, acknowledge, and ask for what we need, those unmet needs rise up like belligerent children and sabotage our efforts to offer compassion to other people. This sabotage will take many forms, including anger, frustration, depression, guilt, jealousy, and self-deprecation.

And because we're so good at shutting them down, we miss the signs that point to those buried needs.

There may be times—in a crisis, for example—when we have no choice but to ignore an unmet need in the moment. But unless we start making the space for ourselves at some point, the unmet need will continue being an issue. In fact, an unmet need, continually ignored, will grow like a cancer until we're suddenly flattened by it and have no choice but to pay attention. When there are too many unmet needs, our attempts at holding space will likely result in unintentionally hijacking space instead.

So how do you start recognizing the signs of an unmet need? If you start feeling constricted while holding space for others, and notice emotions coming up that clearly want your attention, that's the moment you need to pause and ask yourself, "Is there some unmet need being triggered that requires my attention right now, or am I projecting my own emotions onto the other person? Is there an unmet need at play that is getting in the way of holding space for this person?"

Remember the story I shared about my mom crying in the hairdresser's chair after Dad died, when I found myself becoming increasingly impatient? That impatience was a sign that I wasn't getting my needs met and that I would do well to take some time for myself so that I wouldn't inadvertently do greater harm to my mom's fragile state.

Our needs and emotions go hand in hand. They are intricately linked; one informs the other. Emotions are the sensors on the surface of our psychic membrane, sending us messages when we need nourishment, when we're approaching something dangerous, or when it's safe to bond with other cells. If we ignore them, they will get our attention in increasingly destructive ways.

If you have a hard time identifying your needs, start by taking a look at your relationship with your own emotions. When's the last time you apologized for your emotions? Perhaps you cried in front of people, or got angry, or laughed too loud. Why did you apologize? Because you were afraid of making people uncomfortable? Because you thought your emotions were wrong or too strong?

Let's start here: *Your emotions are not wrong.* They're what make you human and beautiful and interesting. Imagine walking around in the world like a robot without emotions; you'd have no way of making real connections with other people and the world would be rather bland.

For whatever reason, though, our social conditioning has taught us to evaluate emotions, to call some good, some bad, some too strong, etc. I think we're conditioned that way partly because those in power feel threatened by too much emotion. Too much passion can result in the overthrow of power.

When we strengthen our psychic membranes, we create containers within ourselves where *all* emotions are welcome and none are considered wrong. And when emotions are welcome and safe, they help us find truth and clarity about the needs they reveal.

In my coaching work, I use a practice where the client is invited to first express their deepest desires and then their deepest fears. I ask them repeatedly, "What do you want?" followed by, "What are you afraid of?" Once they've answered my repeated questions, they're invited to hold them in their hands, *desire* in one hand and *fear* in the other. I then invite them to place their hands on their heart and imagine themselves having a room in their heart for each of those two things, *desire* and *fear*. In one room, *desire* has spaciousness and comfort and is not chased away or called "bad." In another room, *fear* has the same spaciousness and comfort and does not need to hide. I then encourage the client to promise both *desire* and *fear* that they will visit their rooms regularly, spend time with them, and not shame either of them for needing space. (Go ahead and try this for yourself.)

This is a powerful exercise for many, because they often don't give themselves permission to express either their desire or their fear. Once they give themselves permission to simply want what they want and be afraid of whatever they fear, it's often visibly apparent in their demeanour. I see a new lightness that wasn't there before. They know themselves better and are less reluctant to express who they are.

Imagine that your heart has many rooms. (Call them ventricles, if you will, with the blood flowing freely from one room to the next.) Each room is beautifully designed with comfortable furniture and lots of natural light. In each room is an emotion, and that emotion is made to feel comfortable, never treated like a second-class citizen who doesn't belong. You can visit each emotion and spend time in their room whenever they need attention. And the emotions connect with each other in the flow from one room to the next.

Sometimes the line between emotions is quite blurry. Sometimes, in fact, you can feel two seemingly different emotions (for example, joy and sadness) at once, so you can't pick just one room to visit. For these situations, imagine a common room in the house, where all emotions are welcome to mingle, interact, and live at the intersection.

In that common room, imagine a space big enough to host a circle in which each emotion has a chair—an equal place where nobody feels the need to overpower another. When needed, imagine passing a talking piece around the circle to hear what each emotion has to say. If an emotion has a particular need to be heard, it gets its turn with the talking piece. If it doesn't need to be heard, it can pass the talking piece on to the next emotion. In that way, there is space for all, and none are shamed or excluded.

Your emotions *need* your attention; that's what they're here for. They show up to send you messages—to let you know when you need to rest, when you need to leave a dangerous situation, when you're on the right path, etc. If you ignore them, they will get your attention in much more destructive ways. Sometimes emotions may be stronger than the situation warrants (for example, anxiety that shows up even though the situation is actually safe), and that's when you need to rely on your discernment and "wise mind" to regulate them, but ignoring them completely isn't the solution.

Imagine the opposite of what was just described above. Imagine that all of the emotions—especially ones you don't trust or that you've been taught to believe are "wrong"—have all been banished to the basement. Those emotions will become like monsters, looking for a way out of the basement. They'll try to sneak through the windows or cracks in the walls. Eventually, they'll destroy the foundation and your house will become unstable. At that point, even the "good" emotions that have access to the top floors will start to feel uneasy.

As Gabor Maté says, there are many physical illnesses that can be traced back to repressed emotions. Trauma that disconnected us from emotions in our early years eventually surfaces as physical ailments later on.[40] Being connected to our emotions literally keeps us emotionally and physically healthy.

In the book *The Mindful Path to Self-Compassion*, Christopher Germer talks about how he discovered, in his psychotherapy practice, that people make more progress when they learn to *accept* themselves versus when they attempt to *change* themselves.

> When we fight emotional pain, we get trapped in it. Difficult emotions become destructive and break down the mind, body, and spirit. Feelings get stuck—frozen in time—and we get stuck in them. The happiness we long for in relationships seems to elude us. Satisfaction at work lies just beyond our reach. We drag ourselves through the day, arguing with our physical aches and pains. Usually we're not aware just how

many of these trials have their root in how we relate to the inevitable discomfort of life.

Change comes naturally when we open ourselves up to emotional pain with uncommon kindness. Instead of blaming, criticizing, and trying to fix ourselves (or someone else, or the whole world) when things go wrong and we feel bad, we can start with self-acceptance. Compassion first! This simple shift can make a tremendous difference in your life.[41]

Germer teaches that labelling our emotions mindfully and without judgment can help us practise self-compassion. He suggests that we practise accurate labelling, naming each emotion exactly as we feel it: "I feel fear." "That feels like elation." "That feels like frustration."

According to research he cites, labelling an emotion can calm the brain; it activates the prefrontal cortex. The more active the prefrontal cortex, the less active the amygdala.

The more accurately we label an emotion, the more effectively we become "unstuck" from it. But please don't obsess about finding the perfect label: don't think too much about it. Choose a "good enough" label and return to the breath. Any label will suffice to keep your awareness in the present moment. Perhaps a more accurate label will occur to you later on. If not, don't worry. Let the practice be easy and take your time.[42]

The next time you feel tempted to banish an undesirable emotion from your consciousness, welcome it instead, as you would a guest. Ask it why it has come and what message it brings. How does it work to keep you safe and secure? Paying attention to the emotion—and the need associated with it—will do more good than sending it away.

16

practices that strengthen the container

I F THERE ARE so many things (our unmet needs, our trauma, our social conditioning, etc.) that limit our capacity to hold space, and which often cause us to hijack rather than hold space, then what might we do to be more intentional about growing that capacity and stretching our holding space "muscle"?

There are two concepts I believe are key to the work of holding space: mindfulness and detachment. These concepts are intricately intertwined and both inform the ways we can calm the distractions caused by trauma, unmet needs, and social conditioning.

Mindfulness

The concept of mindfulness has become so intertwined with meditation that we sometimes assume we're only practising mindfulness if we are on the cushion. But when Ellen J. Langer wrote about mindfulness in 1989, she approached it from a

Western scientific/psychological perspective rather than as an Eastern form of meditation. She was talking about *mindfulness* as the antidote to the pervasiveness of *mindlessness*.

"Mindlessness is pervasive," says Langer in her book *Mindfulness*. "In fact, I believe virtually all of our problems—personal, interpersonal, professional, and societal—either directly or indirectly stem from mindlessness."[43]

Mindlessness, Langer says, has three characteristics. The first is "entrapment by category," where we live by relying too rigidly on predetermined categories and distinctions (masculine/feminine, old/young, or success/failure, for example). The second is "automatic behaviour," which is our tendency to continue behaviour we've used repeatedly. The third is "acting from a single perspective," or acting as though there is only one set of rules.

Her definition of mindlessness is quite similar to the way Richard Rohr describes the "first half of life" spirituality: a time when we cling to duality and use simple categories to define the things we encounter, making our decisions simple and rules easy to apply.

Before I entered the hospital during my pregnancy with Matthew, I lived in a fairly mindless state. I did what was expected of me: I got married (to a man, because that's the acceptable norm), bought a house in the suburbs, worked my way into an acceptable and well-paying job, and had babies. I also accepted the belief system that was passed down to me, even though it didn't entirely fit: I went to church every Sunday morning, accepted the doctrine of Christianity, and didn't dabble in paganism, Buddhism, or any of the other things deemed to be "false religions."

I didn't deviate much from the norms of my culture. I was the epitome of someone who is entrapped in old categories, behaving automatically, and acting as though there is only one set of rules. My social conditioning had equipped me well for a mindless journey through life.

It took a significant awakening, through the disruption of my hospital stay and the stillbirth of my son, for me to begin living in a more mindful way.

Part of the problem, says Langer, is that mindlessness is embedded in our education system:

> *From kindergarten on, the focus of schooling is usually on goals rather than on the process by which they are achieved. This single-minded pursuit of one outcome or another, from tying shoelaces to getting into Harvard, makes it difficult to have a mindful attitude about life.*[44]

This affects our ability to hold space. We talked about hijacking space as the opposite of holding space; it is also true that *mindlessness* is the opposite of holding space. We become so habituated to focusing on a goal that it presents a challenge for us to let go of the outcome, both for ourselves and for those for whom we hold space. Automatic behaviour, attachment to old categories, and our tendency to act from a single perspective all get in the way of our ability to let the other person truly navigate liminal space with their own agency.

The three qualities we need to develop for a **mindful** state of being, Langer says, include: the creation of new categories, openness to new information, and awareness of more than one perspective.

This understanding of mindfulness corresponds well with the concept of liminal space. When we enter the chaos and disruption of liminal space mindfully rather than mindlessly, we are able to let go of our former understanding of the way things were and the old tried-and-true categories. We open ourselves to new information and a world that looks different from what we expected. That openness, in turn, allows us to hold more than one perspective. Our comfort with ambiguity increases and our need to know the answers decreases.

When I finally started living more mindfully, I explored my spirituality instead of accepting what was passed down to me. I recognized and eventually left the dysfunctions of my marriage. I found my way into a form of work that felt more purposeful and less automatic. Mindful living finally led me into this work and the writing of this book.

• • •

Regardless of how we get there, either through meditation or more directly by paying attention to novelty and questioning assumptions, to be mindful is to be in the present, noticing all the wonders that we didn't realize were right in front of us.[45]

ELLEN J. LANGER

• • •

The mindfulness practices of Eastern spirituality help us be intentional about living in this mindful way. Mindfulness, in the Buddhist understanding, is about "paying attention to your attention." It's observation and awareness of how you respond to the world. It's noticing when you become mindless, and then finding a path back.

Chögyam Trungpa, a pre-eminent teacher of Shambhala Buddhism (the lineage from which I learned mindfulness meditation), says this:

When you eat with awareness, you find that there is more space, more beauty. You begin to watch yourself, to see yourself, and you notice how clumsy you are or how accurate you are... When you practice awareness, everything becomes majestic

and good. You begin to see that you have been leading a differ-
ent kind of life in the past. You had the essence of mindfulness
already, but you hadn't discovered it.[46]

In the middle of my journey toward more mindful living, I was exposed to Shambhala meditation while attending
Authentic Leadership in Action (ALIA). We started and ended
every day on the meditation cushion at the summer leadership
institute, learning mindfulness meditation from some of the
masters of the Shambhala tradition.

It was also there that I first became attuned to the concept
of holding space. From that moment on, mindfulness and
holding space have gone hand in hand in my mind.

In those sessions, we learned that mindfulness is not
about banishing thoughts or feelings, but rather about noticing, labelling, being curious, and letting them pass through
us without becoming attached to them. In mindfulness, our
intention is not necessarily to empty our minds, but to *release*
our attachment to what enters our minds so that it can exit just
as it entered. In this way, we become less entrapped by those
old categories and automatic behaviours. We can begin to hold
multiple perspectives.

"When the thought comes," the mindfulness teachers said
repeatedly, "don't send it away. Just label it 'thinking' and let
it go. When you wrestle with it, shame it, or try to banish it, it
takes greater hold in your mind."

This releasing is similar to the "passive transport" function of your psychic membrane. Instead of exerting energy
input on your part, you simply open the passageway and allow
thoughts and emotions to pass through the membrane just as
they entered—floating molecules that face no resistance.

The truth is, I haven't become a devoted practitioner of
seated meditation. I've tried to commit myself to it, but it

never seems to last. Perhaps it will someday, but in the meantime I continue to embrace the concept of mindfulness in everything I do: I practise mindfulness when I'm out for a walk in the woods. I practise it when I walk a labyrinth. I practise it when I write in my journal. I practise it when I'm in conversation with my daughters. I even try to practise it when I engage with people on social media.

And I practise it now, as I sit and write this book, paying attention to the way the words flow onto the page, the way my body occasionally gets a little cramped from sitting, and the way I feel as I dig deeper into this exploration.

Noticing, labelling, being curious, and letting it pass: these are what signify mindfulness to me. When I get anxious, I notice, label, get curious, and let it pass. When I get angry, I notice, label, get curious, and let it pass. When I start berating or shaming myself, I notice, label, get curious, and let it pass. When I get frustrated about not finding the right words to explain a concept, I notice the frustration, label it, get curious, and let it pass. When the noticing nudges me to step away from the keyboard for a while, I pay attention so that I don't get stuck in the mindlessness of old categories and automatic behaviour.

I do this with the "positive" emotions as much as the "negative" ones (though mindfulness also invites me to attach less of a binary definition to them). When I get excited about how positively people are responding to something I've written, I also try to notice, label, get curious, and let it pass. In this way, the delight I feel over creating something that people do or don't like does not get attached to my ego. It doesn't end up tripping me up.

Detachment

To hold space effectively, mindfulness and detachment go hand in hand. Mindfulness allows us to notice when we cling, grasp, or try to control the outcome. Detachment helps us loosen our grip.

Not long ago, I was driving with my youngest daughter and we started talking about religion and spirituality. Curious, I asked her, "Do you still believe in God?" She paused for a moment and finally responded, "I don't know." And that was it; from there our conversation wandered off to other things.

When she responded, I had a thought that felt surprisingly refreshing to me: "I am not attached to her answer. If she does believe in God, that's cool, but if she doesn't, that's cool too. I don't *need* her to believe one way or another." I was unattached to the outcome of my question.

This was refreshing, because it was very different from how I grew up. If my mom had asked that question when I was fifteen, I know she would have been attached to the outcome, and that would have influenced my answer. Her own fear of hell meant that she *needed* us to believe in God in order for her world (and that of her children) to feel safe. In fact, that was her last concern before she died—that we all commit ourselves to Christ and someday see her in heaven.

What Mom was doing—though she wouldn't have known how to articulate it—was projecting her fear and trauma (and the old categories and automatic behaviour that comes with it) onto us. It was difficult for her to hold space for our spiritual journeys because she was too attached to the outcome.

Please note: This is not a judgment of anyone's personal belief system, simply a reflection of how we project our fears and trauma, and how we become threatened by other people's beliefs if they don't align with our own. As a Mennonite, I come from a lineage of people who hold generational trauma related to the martyrdom of our ancestors, thousands of whom were slaughtered for their faith. I believe there was tremendous complexity in the fears my mother held that go beyond a fear of hell. She was well trained to believe that non-believers go to hell, and I believe she had ancient trauma rooted in her body that made her reaction primal rather than fully rational. (For more on this, read Marlene Winell's work on Religious Trauma Syndrome.) Mom also lost her own mother when she was six, so she had deep attachment wounds that intensified her fear.

As I received my daughter's answer to my question in the car that day, I realized a key definition of holding space is *being able to ask a question without holding the "right" answer in your heart.*

This is not an easy thing to do, especially when our unmet needs and/or trauma are triggered. It takes a lot of practice and healing to become a person who is both loving and *detached* from the outcome.

When I first encountered the Buddhist concept of detachment (or non-attachment), it confused me because it seemed at odds with my beliefs around the importance of making deep connections and secure attachments in one's life. If I lived a detached life, wouldn't that mean I was cool and aloof and not engaged in interdependent relationships and community? (Note: I use the terms "detachment" and "non-attachment" interchangeably, but some people differentiate between them. Personally, I also wish there were other language to differentiate between "attachment" as it is used in Attachment Theory—a healthy and necessary thing for our emotional and cognitive development—and "attachment" as it is used in this Buddhist understanding, but I haven't found useful alternatives.)

Detachment (in the Buddhist understanding) is *not* about creating distance or separation. Instead, it's about loving with an "open hand." Essentially, it's the same as "being the bowl" versus hijacking the space. It's about making a deep connection without becoming too entangled with, or taking too much responsibility for, the other person's needs or emotions. It's about living alongside people and things in symbiotic relationship without consuming them or losing ourselves in them. It means being able to treat each person as a sovereign individual.

In the book *Let Go Now: Embrace Detachment as a Path to Freedom*, Karen Casey says:

> *Being detached from someone does not mean no longer caring for them. It does not mean pretending they no longer exist. It does not mean avoiding all contact with them. Being detached simply means not letting their behaviour determine our feelings. It means not letting their behaviour determine how we act, how we think, how we pray. Detachment is a loving act for all concerned. No one wants to be the constant centre of someone else's life, at least not for long. Two people lose their lives when either one is constantly focused on the other. That's not why we are here.*[47]

How, then, do we learn to hold space with detachment? I believe that it comes with practice. This is where we return to mindfulness. A mindfulness practice offers us the tools to label and release what's happening.

For example, in the story of my daughter's response to my question, if I noticed myself becoming too attached to her answer, I could label my response "controlling." Or, if I only had enough awareness to recognize how my body responded to her answer, I could bring my mindfulness to an awareness of those physical cues and inquire, "My throat seems to be tightening. I wonder what that's about?"

Then, after I noticed these qualities—controlling and throat closing—I could pause to check what needs, fear, or trauma were being triggered in that moment. Was I controlling because of my abandonment wounds? Was I hoping to control her answer because of my fear of the unknown? Or was I grasping because the situation triggered a trauma memory that sent me into fight, flight, or freeze mode?

Next, I would extend compassion to myself. I could ask myself how I could meet the unmet need being triggered. If I was judging myself for clinging, grasping, or controlling, I could ask myself how to release the judgment and offer kindness instead.

According to Christopher Germer in *The Mindful Path to Self-Compassion*, "self-compassion is simply giving the same kindness to ourselves that we would give to others." If I wouldn't judge someone else for their triggered fear/needs/trauma, then why would I judge myself for it?

Intertwined with these thoughts should also be some self-soothing techniques to regulate my nervous system. A few deep breaths, body tapping, or stretching would be examples of techniques to help bring me back to a calmer state.

Having a controlling-and-throat-closing moment with my daughter wouldn't automatically mean I was unable to hold space for her. Only if I *stayed* in that state would I have insufficient capacity to hold space. If I stayed in that state, I'd hijack the space instead of holding it. But if I paused for mindfulness, non-attachment, and self-soothing, I would be able to detach from her answer and be in a state clear enough to once again hold space.

The more we build our muscles in the practices of mindfulness and detachment—developing awareness to recognize old, stuck patterns and reactivity, and shifting ourselves out of them—the more ready we will be to hold space no matter what comes our way.

17

our bodies and
holding space

NOT LONG AFTER my marriage ended, I found myself in a therapist's office. I talked about how much I was giving away energetically, how much I was still being triggered by some of the trauma from my marriage, and how hard it was for me to develop healthy boundaries.

After we spoke for about forty-five minutes, the therapist said, "I'm going to say something that may sound counterintuitive: I'm not sure it's talk therapy you need. You are really good at articulating everything that's going on in your life, and you're obviously very well read on mental health issues, but my sense is that *you really need to be more connected to your body.*"

I pressed her on what she meant and what she recommended, but she refused to be prescriptive about it. "I think you should ask your body what it needs."

This felt so foreign to me that I nearly burst out laughing. My body? How do I talk to my body? How will I hear when it answers me? What if I don't like what I hear?

Naturally, my next question was, "Can you recommend any books I can read on the topic?"

She smiled. "I'm going to suggest you stop reading books for a while and get out of your head." Again, it sounded as though she was speaking a foreign language. No books?! How could I live? Where would I find the answers?

It was challenging to consider that I needed to turn to my body instead of my mind. How could my body heal what was going on in my life?

But she was right. I'd lived most of my life in my head, disconnected from my body. Whenever I was faced with a challenge, I would always try to *think* my way through it, finding the right books and writing in my journal until I'd processed it nearly to death. A book is often the first place I go when I'm trying to bypass the liminal space.

At the end of the conversation, she pointed something else out to me. "You know how you kept coughing at the beginning of our conversation? Did you happen to notice that you stopped coughing as soon as I suggested asking your body what it needs? Do you suppose your body is already responding?"

I left her office feeling a mixture of relief and frustration. It seemed so simple, and yet it was so foreign. I knew how to talk, write, and read my way through problems. I even knew how to use art journaling, mandalas, and other tools to tap into that which doesn't show up in words. But I didn't know how to get out of my head and into my body.

I spent the next six months trying to figure out how to talk to my body. I tried several body-healing modalities, including reiki, healing touch, body work, and craniosacral therapy. I went for several massages, including one exquisite aqua massage with shower heads sprinkling water on my body while the massage artist worked. I visited an Ayurvedic healer and learned about my body type. I went for long walks and talked to my body along the way. I danced and swam and lay in the grass bathed in sunlight. I experimented with body-related trauma healing practices. I spent a lot of time in water.

While this was happening, I was renovating my house. I pushed my body to its limits, tearing out old flooring, painting walls, and building shelves. I spent more days that summer with a hammer or drill in my hand than a book. Building things with my own hands became an important part of my therapy.

Gradually, I learned to listen to my body in a new way. As I did, I could feel the stress and anxiety leave my body. I was being healed deep in my molecules in a way I'd never experienced before. I had more energy and more emotional lightness than I'd had in years. Some of the physical ailments that troubled me (persistent cough, restless legs syndrome, yeast infections) disappeared. I was also sleeping better than ever.

I learned something critical during that time: To hold space for myself, I cannot only be present for what is in my heart and mind. I need to include my body as well.

Especially when it comes to trauma, many of the emotional issues we need to heal require deeper healing practices beyond what we do with our brains. The body is a key link to processing trauma.

Mental health experts increasingly recognize the value of somatic healing, which focuses on the client's perceived body sensations. This is especially effective for PTSD and other mental health concerns. Modern industrialized medicine separated the mind from the body early on, treating them separately. But new wisdom is emerging that reminds us the two can never be fully separated. What impacts the mind impacts the body, and vice versa.

From the reading I've done and conversations I've had, it seems this disconnect from the body is particularly prevalent among those of us who live in wealthier countries. There are a variety of reasons for this. Access to both financial resources and modern gadgets has separated us from our own indigenous body wisdom. The medical and pharmaceutical industries teach us to hand our bodies over to doctors and lose touch with our own body intuition. Industrialization has further separated us from our bodies by creating more leisure time and less physical labour. Our well-built homes allow us to seal ourselves off from the natural world, and access to nearly anything money can buy allows us to use our bodies very little for growing our own food, protecting our villages, and working our way through trauma.

Religion also plays a role. Many people are socially conditioned to disconnect from their bodies through religious traditions (including Christianity, Judaism, and Islam) that teach us the "sinfulness" of our bodies and bodily functions, and the shame of revealing too much of our bodies. My Mennonite history, in addition to being a lineage of trauma, is also a lineage of body disconnection (and I believe the two things are related). For example, we couldn't dance and were taught that many of our bodily urges were sinful (or at least only acceptable in marriage). To this day, I feel awkward on a dance floor because I didn't learn the rhythm of my own body at an early age.

There are some teachers, like Thomas Ryan, a yoga teacher and priest, who teach body-centred spiritual practices through a Christian lens, but otherwise the resources are few and far between. The only two books Ryan found in his research on the topic were written in the 1960s and are now out of print. In his book *Reclaiming the Body in Christian Spirituality*, he says, "I was amazed to find how little reflection existed from a Christian perspective on the positive role of the body on spiritual life."[48]

Sadly, I fear that body-separation trauma and religious shame have been passed on to people in places Western countries have colonized as well. Western missionaries in Africa, for example, taught people that their tribal dances were demonic. And European colonizers in North America not only forced children into residential schools and separated them from their cultures, they also violated their bodies in all manner of ways, including forcibly cutting their hair (which is considered sacred in many Indigenous traditions). This colonization of bodies has also informed the way we have historically treated gender, namely that there are only the binary forms of male and female and anyone outside that paradigm is deviant.

If we are to hold space for each other in effective ways— whether we are white or people of colour; able-bodied or persons with disabilities; male, female, or non-binary—connection to our own bodies is absolutely necessary. We need to pay attention to when our bodies need rest or movement and ask our bodies what they need when the work is especially taxing. We need to recognize our bodies' signals of safe/unsafe, healthy/unhealthy, and energizing/draining.

I have learned to listen to the signals my body sends me especially after particularly emotional retreats or coaching sessions. When I've held deep space for people's liminal space journeys, facilitated deep conversations, or managed conflict in these situations, I sometimes walk away with a headache, which tells me I need time alone in a quiet, dark place. Sometimes I feel an overall body ache and spend the evening in a warm bath with Epsom salts. Other times I feel restless and go for a walk or ride a bike. I try to book a massage or other body treatment during the week after a retreat.

A few years ago, I taught holding space at a retreat for spouses of trauma-affected veterans and active service personnel. At the retreat, I listened to stories of both trauma and vicarious trauma (the trauma absorbed by the families exposed to the affected person). I heard of the nightmares their spouses had, the way their spouses could only sit still in restaurants if they had their backs to the wall, and the abuse and fear their children lived with when their trauma-affected parent flew into a rage.

On the long drive home, I knew it would be important to listen deeply to my own body in order to release the vicarious trauma I'd absorbed from these stories. I have learned not to underestimate the impact of these stories on my body, and not to short-circuit my body's efforts to discharge them. Just as a trauma victim will often tremble immediately after a trauma, a person who holds space will need to find ways to move this vicarious trauma out of their body. I stopped at a lake, went for a long walk on the beach, gave my body a good shake, took lots of deep breaths, and then sat in the sunlight while writing in my journal. I hope that the participants in the retreat followed up on my encouragement to do the same.

If we don't pay careful attention to our bodies after intense work in holding space, then we run the risk of becoming shock absorbers rather than bowls. As shock absorbers, we hang on to energy rather than allowing it to flow through—and out of—our psychic membranes. This energy can accumulate and become disruptive to our bodies and our lives. Over time, we can break under the pressure of all this accumulated secondary energy.

There are a multitude of helpful practices that facilitate the healthy release of energy after holding space so we don't become stuck. I recommend exploring intuitive dance, yoga, tai chi, reiki, running, somatic healing practices, hiking, and swimming, among others. A new favourite of mine is a practice called havening touch, which soothes your body while you process and release attachment to traumatic memories.

Even though the practice of holding space can seem to lean heavily toward the cerebral (one of the limitations of presenting this in book format), make no mistake that the body is an important part of our work. To keep our bodies strong and resilient, with a healthy psychic membrane, we need to have a host of these body-centric practices available so that we can hold space for other people's "primal scream" without cracking under pressure.

18

allowing others to be your bowl

AS A PERSON who holds space for other people it is crucial that you find someone who has the strength and compassion to hold space for *you* in turn. This is the outer Community rim of the bowl we discussed earlier. Even if it's just one person to start with—a close friend, spouse, therapist, etc.—you need someone supporting your bowl while you offer it to others. If you don't find the right people to support you in your life, your bowl will lose strength and you will eventually burn out or suffer mental or physical illness.

I like to use the visual metaphor of Russian nesting dolls: You hold space for a smaller doll while a larger doll holds space for you. Each doll needs another doll holding it so that it can, in turn, do the same for someone else.

Most of us live in a "post-village" world. At one time, in all cultures and countries, people had no choice but to have their needs met by their communities. Now, we live in a culture where many of us live separate from our families or communities—mostly in big, impersonal cities—and are expected to have our needs met by professionals, institutions, and businesses. We are encouraged to be independent and deny our needs for other people. We are shamed for our neediness if we reach out to others for too much. Reciprocal relationships have been replaced by transactional relationships. We pay for services instead of living in a community where others look after our needs and we look after theirs.

At the end of my visit to a remote region in Uganda, where the village is still a critical part of the culture, my friend Nestar (who grew up there and started the school I support there) said, "It seems to me that what you teach about holding space is what we do very naturally in Uganda. It's not something we need to learn; it's simply the way we coexist." I think she's right. In more Westernized countries, where most of us live quite separately, we have to relearn a skill that's a natural part of more indigenous cultures.

Though I love the type of coaching work I once spent much of my time doing, I sometimes lament the fact that it is even necessary—that we need to pay strangers to listen to us when we struggle because we've removed that kind of deep and intentional support from the way we live. (Granted, there are two sides to this coin: one could argue that we're much healthier now than when people were inclined to ignore their problems and "get on with it.")

· · ·

The things we need most are the things we have become most afraid of, such as adventure, intimacy, and authentic communication. We avert our eyes and stick to comfortable topics. We hold it as a virtue to be private, to be discreet, so that no one sees our dirty laundry. We are uncomfortable with intimacy and connection, which are among the greatest of our unmet

*needs today. To be truly seen and heard, to be truly known,
is a deep human need. Our hunger for it is so omnipresent,
so much a part of our life experience, that we no more know
what is missing than a fish knows it is wet. We need more intimacy than nearly anyone considers normal. Always hungry
for it, we seek solace and sustenance in the closest available
substitutes: television, shopping, pornography, conspicuous
consumption—anything to ease the hurt, to feel connected, or
to project an image by which we might be seen or known, or at
least see and know ourselves.*[49]

CHARLES EISENSTEIN

• • •

I grew up with a sense of the village in the small town where
I spent my first eighteen years, but I moved to a city not long
after high school. Several years later, after having two babies
in quick succession, I was surprised by how lonely and isolated
I felt, and how little community support was readily available
for young moms. My mom lived a couple of hours away, my sister didn't have babies yet and couldn't entirely understand my
reality, and my closest friends had moved away. My full-time
job didn't give me time to connect with other moms on the
playground (or wherever else moms of young children build
community). Social media didn't yet exist, so I couldn't get
support online either. On top of that, my husband worked eve-
nings (so that our children spent less time in daycare), which
meant I spent almost every night alone with my two daughters.

It was the loneliest period of my life. All my self-doubts
around whether I was parenting correctly were amplified by
the fact that nobody was holding space for me.

I'm afraid my experience is far from uncommon. An article
in the *Globe and Mail* calls it an "epidemic of loneliness."

More Canadians than ever live alone, and almost one-quarter describe themselves as lonely. In the United States, two studies showed that 40 per cent of people say they're lonely, a figure that has doubled in 30 years . . . Loneliness has been linked to depression, anxiety, interpersonal hostility, increased vulnerability to health problems, and even to suicide.

Social media doesn't make it any better, unfortunately:

Talk to enough lonely people and you'll find they have one thing in common: They look at Facebook and Twitter the way a hungry child looks through a window at a family feast and wonders, "Why is everyone having a good time except for me?"[50]

It's not a situation that is improving, either. A *Forbes* article entitled "Why Millennials Are Lonely," from a few years after the quote above, says this:

the number of Americans with no close friends has tripled since 1985. "Zero" is the most common number of confidants, reported by almost a quarter of those surveyed. Likewise, the average number of people Americans feel they can talk to about "important matters" has fallen from three to two.[51]

Attachment Theory teaches us that people who grow up with a secure attachment to at least one person have a much greater chance of being emotionally stable and healthy than those who don't.[52] Those without secure attachments are much more likely to develop personality disorders, addictions, and even physical health concerns. Fortunately, many of these conditions can be turned around with healthy connections, even later in life. One of the known successful aspects of Alcoholics Anonymous, for example, is the community factor.

People who have others who care about them are much more likely to successfully deal with their addiction.

An article in *Psychology Today* entitled "The Opposite of Addiction Is Connection" says:

> So it does indeed appear that the opposite of addiction is not sobriety, it's connection. That said, developing healthy interpersonal connections as a part of recovery and healing is not easy. It takes time, effort, and a willing support network. The good news is that we now know for certain that this type of recovery and social connection is possible—even for the most problematic of addicts.[53]

If community connections are so important for our well-being and the ability to hold space for others, then how do we go about finding them? This is a question I am often asked in my work. Not only do we not *have* the connections, but we also don't know how to *find* them. We are living in the midst of a loneliness epidemic without the antidote.

According to Peter Block and John McKnight, we start by shifting our mindset from "consumer" back to "citizen."

> A consumer is one who has surrendered to others the power to provide what is essential for a full and satisfied life. This act of surrender goes by many names: client, patient, student, audience, fan, shopper. A citizen is one who is a participant in a democracy, regardless of their legal status. It is one who chooses to create the life, the neighbourhood, the world from their own gifts and the gifts of others.[54]

When we become engaged in our neighbourhoods and start to ask ourselves, "What is our responsibility as citizens of this place?" then our interactions become less transactional and more communal. We return to what we learned in chapter 15: "Ask for what we need and offer what we can." A citizen lives a reciprocal relationship, both offering and asking, both giving and receiving—not assuming everything will be done for them, but also not trying to do everything alone.

It is not easy to build these kinds of reciprocal relationships that will both nourish us and require something of us. We need to be willing to take risks, be vulnerable, and get hurt.

● ● ●

The practice of love offers no place of safety. We risk loss, hurt, pain. We risk being acted upon by forces outside our control.[55]

BELL HOOKS

● ● ●

It is only with risk that we find the kinds of relationships we are seeking. It is only when we are willing to put our heart on the line that we begin finding the people able to hold space for us.

On my first trip to Africa I travelled with a group of people to villages where there were programs supported by the non-profit organization I worked for at the time. We spent long, hot hours on the bus together, travelling from village to village. It was an intense experience, especially for someone like me, a person who needs solitude on a regular basis to maintain my emotional health.

There was one woman on the bus who, at the beginning, irritated me. I experienced her as a know-it-all who had more knowledge of the world than the rest of us. She intimidated me and triggered my insecurities, so it was really more about my interpretation of her than it was about her actions.

One day, for whatever reason, I was feeling some softness toward this woman, and admitted something really personal to her. I don't remember exactly what it was, but it was related to the fact that I had my period and we were travelling in an area where the only access to restroom facilities was often in the form of dirty outhouses. We had to squat over a hole in the ground and there was no running water to clean ourselves afterwards.

The moment I spoke my vulnerability to her, something shifted between us and she started opening up to me in turn. I soon learned that she was intimidated by *me* as well and felt she needed to prove herself with her knowledge.

This woman and I became tight friends for the rest of the trip, even sharing a very narrow bed in a small hotel room one night when there weren't enough rooms to go around. And when I was sick in the middle of the night at a different hotel and scared I'd pass out (I have a strange tendency to faint when I vomit), it was to her hotel room I went so I wouldn't wake up alone on the cold concrete floor.

In my opinion, *this* is how we connect with people and build communities. We begin by becoming vulnerable and admitting we need them. We let our guards down and embrace the uncertainty of not knowing if we might be wounded. We ask each other for help and express a willingness, in turn, to extend that help to others. We dare to wake people up in the middle of the night when it's risky to be alone. We dare to live in countercultural ways and serve as citizens rather than consumers.

Yes, it will hurt sometimes, when your vulnerability is rejected. But the pain will be worth it because you'll have people in your life who can hold space for you.

Earlier, I shared the story of how I became burnt-out when my blog post went viral because I was giving so much of myself away. After speaking with my therapist, I learned that I not only needed to undertake more intentional body work, I also needed to find a stronger support system that would "be the bowl" for me while I did the same for others.

The first—and best—thing I did was hire an excellent assistant (who's since become my business partner). Krista not only manages how many people have access to me but helps me on a regular basis when my psychic membrane becomes too porous and I risk becoming depleted. While I write this book, for example, Krista is looking after all business matters and ensuring nobody is allowed to interrupt my work.

I also found better ways to do my work, such as working in partnership when I host intense retreats or workshops. For example, when I teach in Australia, I am well-supported by Georgia, the owner of the space where I facilitate retreats. She helps me maintain my psychic membrane and gives me quiet space when I've depleted myself. In my most recent visit to Australia, we co-facilitated a retreat and held the container together, which made it much easier to hold space for the complexity that showed up.

After a recent massage, my intuitive massage therapist told me she experienced the energy of my body as quite guarded. "You need to open yourself up more and let people care for you." I took her words to heart, which is why I went to Reno while I was finishing this book. I stayed in the home of my dear friends Lorraine and TuBears, who provided the kind of exquisite care—good food, a well-tended space, lots of good conversations, and plenty of hugs—that allows me to do the work.

Just a couple of hours before I wrote this paragraph, Lorraine showed up at my door with a protein-rich salad—just what I needed in the middle of my afternoon slump to give me an energy boost so I can continue. The day before, she came with a fruit smoothie. She has an instinctual way of paying attention to my needs and meeting them so that I can work. Again and again, she insists that I simply allow her to do this without protest because she does it out of love and a desire to see my book in print. Because these beloved friends hold space for me, I am better able to hold space for others and for this work.

Being human is about being in the right kind of relationships. I think being human is a process. It's not something that we just are born with. We actually learn to celebrate our connection, learn to celebrate our love... If you suffer, it does not imply love. But if you love, it does imply suffering... To suffer with, though, compassion, not to suffer against... And if we can hold that space big enough, we also have joy and fun even as we suffer. And suffering will no longer divide us. And to me, that's sort of the human journey.[56]

JOHN A. POWELL

• • •

This is not work that you can do alone. If you don't already have people like Krista, Lorraine, and TuBears in your life, then I urge you to seek them out and work hard to foster the relationships that will support you. Remember to always ask for what you need and offer what you can.

19

the shadow

THE SHADOW IS whatever you try to keep out of the light. According to Carl Jung, the shadow is full of *all those things we have no wish to be,* and certainly no wish to present to others: our fears, insecurities, and anxieties. It's the part of ourselves that we are not in touch with or have possibly disowned.

The shadow isn't necessarily your dark side. It's the side of you that is *in the dark.* In other words, it hasn't come into the light yet. It's your personal blind spots. And it can possess both positive qualities—lessons about yourself that you haven't yet found (often called your "gifts")—and negative qualities about yourself that you just don't want to know.

• • •

We have been conditioned to fear the shadow side of life and the shadow side of ourselves. When we catch ourselves thinking a dark thought or acting out in a behavior that we feel is unacceptable, we run, just like a groundhog, back into our hole and hide, hoping, praying, it will disappear before we venture out again. Why do we do this? Because we are afraid that no matter how hard we try, we will never be able to escape from this part of ourselves. And although ignoring or repressing our dark side is the norm, the sobering truth is that running from the shadow only intensifies its power. Denying it only leads to more pain, suffering, regret, and resignation.[57]

DEEPAK CHOPRA

* * *

Our shadows were formed in childhood, when we tried to get our needs (mentioned in the Spiral of Authenticity) met. To get our needs for safety and belonging met, we learned to hide things in the shadows so as to present ourselves as lovable enough for people to accept us and keep us safe. They weren't necessarily bad things; they were simply things we tried to avoid being judged or shamed for.

Sometimes, in fact, they were really good things. For example, I've always had some shadow around my love of public speaking because I was socially conditioned to believe that a) women shouldn't be in leadership, and b) if you love public speaking it means you're arrogant and therefore not very lovable. For me to stay safe and avoid being judged, I had to pretend I didn't enjoy being in the spotlight.

* * *

Maybe another reason we don't take up the gift is because there's a shadow dimension to following our bliss ... Even the word bliss *comes from the French word* blessure, *which means "hurt" or "injury" or "wound." So when we are invited to follow our joy we are also led to an inner wound that our very quest needs to heal.*[58]

MICHAEL JONES

The shadow can show up in many nuanced ways. Think about those little secrets that you hide in your conversations with friends, the things that make you think, "If they knew the truth about me, they wouldn't really like me." Perhaps you're afraid to tell your friends that you're the daughter of an alcoholic. Or you're hoping your co-workers don't find out that you're in counselling because your marriage has hit a rocky spot. Or you're a closet binge-eater or a secret trashy-romance reader. Or you live paycheque to paycheque and never know when the money will run out. Or you hide the things you're really good at because those are the things for which you've been shamed or ostracized.

To be honest, the problem isn't usually the shadow itself but the behaviour it incites in us. When we have shame about something—or we've been hiding it so long we don't even fully acknowledge it as part of ourselves—we often act in ways that are not in alignment with our values in order to defend or deflect attention away from the shadow.

For example, consider a young child whose home is so chaotic that she rarely gets her homework done and never brings the right school supplies for group projects. She will, unsurprisingly, be inclined to do whatever she needs to do—lie, steal, or blame someone else—to hide the fact that her family environment is chaotic. That child will grow up with learned behaviour, which she'll repeat, to hide the things she's ashamed of.

The more we work to keep our secrets in the dark, the larger the shadow grows and the less energy we have to spread light into the world. The only way we can live wholehearted, undivided lives is to address the shadows and to bring them into the light.

It's our *wholeness* in all its complexity that is the gift.

How do we bring our shadows into the light? To start with, we acknowledge that they exist. Once we are honest with ourselves about the things we don't want the world to know, and that we prefer to keep hidden even from ourselves, we can begin allowing the light to shine into these dark places.

· · ·

Your character defects are not where you're bad, but where you're wounded. But no matter who or what causes the wound, it's yours now and you're responsible for it.[59]

MARIANNE WILLIAMSON

· · ·

As Marianne Williamson says, we are not bad, we are simply wounded. When we hide those wounds, we keep them in the shadow where they don't have a chance to heal. They instead fester, get infected, and start taking over our lives.

A few years ago, I facilitated a circle in Sedona when some surprising things came up in the group that brought up some of my own shadow, along with some old stories about my ability to hold space well. As is often the case when we introduce circle work to a group of people unaccustomed to facing each other and the deeper conversations the circle invites, resistance shows up. Sometimes people leave the group, sometimes they sabotage what's going on, and sometimes they simply don't engage and cause the space to feel less safe for others.

When this resistance shows up, it can sometimes trigger *my* old stories of unworthiness as well. The choir in my head begins to repeat some old choruses of, "You don't really know what you're doing," or, "You're an imposter and everyone in the room sees through you," or, "You can't handle conflict."

When these triggers showed up early in my facilitating work, I would do one of three things: consider walking away from this work and leaving it to the "real professionals," get defensive and push back on those who were resisting, or—I hate to say it—sometimes become either downright unkind to the resisters or overly accommodating to make sure everyone was happy.

It's taken a lot of personal work to address this shadow in me, work that isn't, and may never be, finished. (Check back with me when I'm ninety!) I'm gradually learning that other people's resistance is usually not about me, it's about something that person needs to work through. The group may have simply triggered a wound they might not even know they have.

Even when I come home discouraged from a workshop or retreat, I know I am committed to my work and that there are things I need to learn from the rough spots. Every one of those resisters serves as a teacher for me. Each one has helped me see something I need to address in my own shadow so that I can rise stronger than I was before. As I look back at them and recognize what I learned from these interactions, I try to extend gratitude for what they've helped me to learn.

There's a concept (which I believe emerged in the field of Integral Theory) called the "we space," the space that exists uniquely in the relationship between you and me. When the "we space" between us gets cluttered by the shadow of unmet expectations, unspoken hurts, fear of rejection, etc., then it becomes difficult for me to see through it clearly to bear witness to you and hold space effectively.

For example, not long ago I was holding space for a friend and colleague when the "we space" became cluttered by my interpretation of what she was saying. Suddenly I realized I'd shut down and could no longer concentrate on her words; I had deviated from being the kind of container she needed me to be.

It is important for all of us who hold space for other people—whether it's for employees, children, friends, clients, parents, or partner—to spend time looking into our own shadows. Each time we do this, the shadow has less power over us, and we become less triggered when resistance or old stories show up.

We need to find ways to hold space for our shadows. The shadow can't be simply rationalized away or tucked back into hiding to wait for a "better" moment to emerge. And resolving it is not a one-time event. Instead, continual practice in mindfulness, gentle self-care, and self-inquiry (through journaling, art practice, or other methods) helps us detach from the stigma of what others think. We can practise telling new stories that gradually reshape the experience.

Most importantly, we must practise seeing both ourselves and the people who trigger us through the eyes of compassion.

• • •

We can't fight darkness with darkness. We have to find compassion, and embrace the darkness inside of us in order to understand it and, ultimately, to transcend it.[60]

DEBBIE FORD

• • •

When we see through the eyes of compassion, the resister in the circle or the person who is triggering us is transformed. They are no longer a threat to us or "the idiot trying to sabotage our work." Our compassion allows us to see them as someone who might be dealing with something that makes their participation difficult or someone whose background/culture/education/trauma has taught them that this is not a place of safety.

When we see through the eyes of compassion, our own responses to the triggers are not signs of our weakness; they are opportunities to learn about our shadows. This doesn't mean we should tolerate behaviour that harms us, however. We are allowed to protect ourselves from whatever causes us harm.

Holding space within the duality of our light *and* shadow requires two particular skill sets, humility and confidence: confidence to trust our abilities and humility to admit we have shadows. Humility and confidence may seem like opposites, but—like the yin-yang symbol—they work together to keep us grounded.

Keep in mind that humility and confidence also have *their* nuanced shadow sides, shadows that can sabotage things when we don't address them. The shadow side of humility is shame, and the shadow side of confidence is arrogance. The challenging thing about these shadows is they often attempt to masquerade as the light—and so our confidence can slip into arrogance and our humility into shame. Like other forms of our shadows, arrogance and shame hide our true light, crippling and sabotaging our effectiveness.

It's a continual practice, being humble enough to admit when we fall short, apologizing where necessary, and accepting responsibility for the consequences of our actions—all while being confident enough to know that we *do* possess the necessary skills.

More than anything, acknowledging and working with our shadows requires getting our egos out of the way. Engaging our shadows, rather than continually attempting to ignore them, releases their power and *frees* us. When we succeed in doing that, our work can have its greatest impact on others, even when we don't necessarily understand what that impact might be. Sometimes what we call failure is actually success.

A few months after the challenging Sedona experience, I heard from the client who hired me. She let me know that the conflict in Sedona helped her recognize and remove the people who were holding the team back. Though it was an uncomfortable experience, it provided a necessary—though unintended—outcome for which she was grateful. I continue to work with her on other projects.

. . .

If we are living under the assumption that we are only one way or another, inside a limited spectrum of human qualities, then we would have to question why more of us aren't wholly satisfied with our lives right now. Why do we have access to so much wisdom yet fail to have the strength and courage to act upon our good intentions by making powerful choices? And most important, why do we continue to act out in ways that go against our value system and all that we stand for? We will assert that it is because of our unexamined life, our darker self, our shadow self where our unclaimed power lies.[61]

DEEPAK CHOPRA

PART THREE

advanced
concepts

20

from safe spaces
to brave spaces

IN THE EARLY chapters we talked about creating and holding safe spaces, where people can go through their liminal space journey with support and compassion. We create that safety by withholding judgment and honouring their process rather than imposing our wishes on them.

But what happens when safety is not enough? What happens when safety leads to complacency? And what happens when one person's safety infringes upon another person's safety?

When I start working with new clients, I often tell them, "It may get worse before it gets better." I want them to know, before taking the journey with me, that they will need to step into darkness with courage, face their shadows without flinching, possibly disrupt some relationships, and practise staying with discomfort in the messy stages of growth.

I want them to feel safe working with me, but I don't want safety to turn into an excuse to stay stuck. If they aren't prepared to feel the depths of their darkest emotions, they likely won't be able to get through the Spiral of Authenticity and will run back to safety and belonging instead.

It's the same when I work with groups. I encourage respectful conversation, and we use The Circle Way to guide us in how to speak with intention and listen with attention. But sometimes people show up in the circle with a lot of pain, a lot of anger, or a lot of conflict. If we focus only on safety, we might be tempted to avoid tough conversations or shut them down because they make people feel uncomfortable. If we do that, we don't move forward into meaningful change. We stay stuck in the place where we started.

This is especially the case when holding space requires wading into difficult conversations around racial injustice, human rights, colonization, conflict resolution, reconciliation, climate change, and other complex topics. When we invoke the need for safety in these environments, we risk shutting down the voices of those who are most negatively impacted by the systems that oppress and marginalize them. Transformation isn't possible unless they're allowed full expression of their outrage and fear despite the way that it makes some feel uncomfortable.

In a helpful chapter in the edited collection *The Art of Effective Faciliation*, titled "From Safe Spaces to Brave Spaces," Brian Arao and Kristi Clemens say that they "found with increasing regularity that participants [in social justice dialogue] invoke in protest the common ground rules associated with the idea of safe space when the dialogue moves from polite to provocative."

When they dug into this a little deeper, they found a common theme, what they called "a conflation of safety with comfort." In other words, in our efforts to create safe space, we can inadvertently give people an excuse for justifying their comfort and avoiding necessary discomfort.

The writers go on to say the following:

it became increasingly clear to us that our approach to initiating social justice dialogues should not be to convince participants that we can remove the risk from the equation, for this is simply impossible. Rather, we propose revising our language, shifting away from the concept of safety and emphasizing the importance of bravery instead, to help students better understand—and rise to—the challenges of genuine dialogue on diversity and social justice issues.[62]

Since reading that chapter a few years ago, I now work on shifting my own language from offering people comfort to offering a place where they will be invited to be *brave*. This requires a deeper commitment from people and does occasionally scare them away. But I believe it's the better way to support people in seeking meaningful change in their lives and in the systems they are part of rather than running from the hard stuff.

Bravery requires strength and resilience on the part of the person and/or people within the space being held. When you invite people to be brave instead of safe, you need to prepare yourself for their possible resistance, anger, fear, and other difficult emotions. Some of this may be pointed at you; they may blame you for bringing this discomfort into their lives or holding up a mirror to reveal their shadows to them. (A couple of my long-term clients jokingly—and lovingly—give me the middle finger when things get messy and scary. Fortunately, they continue to stay with the work.)

A few years ago I had a client with a lot of anger in her life. She was angry at everyone she knew—her neighbours, her children, her extended family—and blamed them for everything that was wrong with her life. When I held the mirror up to help her see that she was giving away her own power by blaming everyone else, she redirected her anger toward me. She'd expected a safe place to vent, not a look into her shadow. A few years after we were no longer in a coaching relationship, though, she sent a note of appreciation for the brave way I'd held space for her, saying it had helped her make necessary changes.

This isn't the first time a client turned against me when offered something too challenging to face. I've come to accept it as part of the risk of holding brave space. When people take the dangerous journey through liminal space, there are bound to be some complex emotions that need to be projected outward, and the person holding the container will likely be the recipient of at least some of that. That's why we need strong containers.

When I worked in international development several years ago, the education director on my team developed an intense and extremely effective teaching tool that gave students a small taste of what it was like to flee conflict in their country and seek shelter in a refugee camp. It was an elaborate role-playing exercise resembling a live-action video game. The students started in a large gymnasium and received passports identifying which country they were running away from, what conflict was disrupting their nation, and the state of their family situation. After a brief orientation, "rebels" (volunteer actors with fake guns) burst in and told the group they were taking control of the gymnasium. Everyone needed to run for their lives or risk being shot.

The students then climbed onto buses and were brought to the "wilderness," usually a large park or field, where they needed to find their way to a refugee camp. As they made their way down trails, through bushes, and over streams, they were periodically attacked by rebels who intimidated them, took away their backpacks and water bottles, and forced them to do physically difficult things (such as stand on one foot for a long time).

Eventually the group found the refugee camp, where they needed to be processed. They filled out various forms, were interrogated if their passports had been taken by rebels, and went through health inspections. At some point they were offered the same kind of meal they would get in a refugee camp (rice and lentils), but sometimes, just before the meal was served, rebels would burst through the bushes and steal all the food.

I once participated in this exercise and found it to be remarkably effective in expanding my understanding of the insecurities and fear involved in being a refugee. The fear felt real, even though I knew the rebels were holding fake guns and probably weren't nearly as threatening as their voices sounded. At one point, they made my group carry a picnic table over our heads or risk getting shot.

All the students in my group were surprised by how much the exercise impacted them. However, this exercise also faced tremendous opposition and was eventually shut down as a result. Parents regularly wrote to us complaining that their children risked being traumatized by it. Schools were reluctant to host the exercise because of liability issues. Stakeholders pushed back because they thought it was a risk for the organization, and the insurance company didn't want to insure the event. Everyone who opposed the exercise seemed invested in the idea that high school students should only experience comfort in their educational environment, not risk.

It's rather ironic that we, in our comfortable, conflict-free countries, cannot handle *play-acting* the same experience so many people in the world face on a daily basis. I understand the need to respect people who've been traumatized and would not recommend this exercise for anyone who's lived through abuse or war. But I also believe our culture has become overly concerned with safety and comfort, to the point where we are unwilling to experience that which makes us uncomfortable.

This cultural tendency doesn't serve us well; it provides us with an excuse for avoiding hard and uncomfortable work in all areas of our lives. On a bigger scale, it creates the kind of complacency that chooses to avoid the uncomfortable work of dismantling abusive systems, speaking truth to power, and challenging oppressors.

Are we growing resilient, courageous children if we wrap them in comfort? Will they have the capacity to be strong leaders if they are always protected from adversity and discomfort?

What about ourselves? How often do we avoid growth because it feels unsafe? Do we allow those for whom we hold space to remain stuck because challenging them to stretch themselves might risk difficult emotions or cause them to turn on us and resent us as a result?

Is safety serving us, or is it becoming a crutch? How is it hurting our society as whole?

• • •

We argue that authentic learning about social justice often requires the very qualities of risk, difficulty, and controversy that are defined as incompatible with safety.

Learning necessarily involves not merely risk, but the pain of giving up a former condition in favour of a new way of seeing things.

When everyone's voice is accepted and no one's voice can be criticized, then no one can grow... that we need to hear other voices to grow is certainly true, but we also need to be able to respond to those voices, to criticize them, to challenge them, to sharpen our own perspectives through the friction of dialogue. A person can learn, says Socrates, "if he is brave and does not tire of the search." We have to be brave because along the way we are going to be "vulnerable and exposed"; we are going to encounter images that are "alienating and shocking." We are going to be very unsafe.[63]

ROBERT BOOSTROM

Several years ago, in one of my first in-person courses on Creative Writing for Self-Discovery (an eight-week program, one evening a week), I invited people to do any form of writing they chose in order to explore who they were and how they were evolving. Again and again, I reminded them that we were in a safe space and that whatever they wrote would not be judged by the group.

It was one of those times when evoking "safe space" backfired. *What is safe for one person is not necessarily safe for another person.* One woman wrote lesbian love stories to explore her sexuality, and when she asked if she could read them aloud, I said yes, assuring her that it was "safe." However, another woman in the group, who was conservative and religious, sank into silence during the class. The next day I got an email saying she would not be returning to class because she didn't appreciate the fact that I allowed someone to read things that made her feel uncomfortable.

Because I was new to my work at the time, it sent me into a tailspin. What was my role in this situation? Should I beg her to come back and insist that I wouldn't allow the woman to read anything about lesbian sexuality? But if I did that, it would no longer be safe for the other woman and *she* might withdraw.

I desperately wanted everyone to be happy because I thought it would reflect poorly on *me* if people dropped out of my class. To be honest about my own shadow in this, I was possibly less concerned that everyone was safe than that everyone was happy; unhappy students would reflect on my skill as a teacher.

But I couldn't have it both ways: either they were happy but not safe, or safe but not happy. I either had to let one drop out because it wasn't a safe space for her or try to find a middle road that meant that *nobody* was truly safe.

In the end, I decided to let the more conservative woman drop out. I sent her an email wishing her well and telling her I was sorry she chose to leave us.

Did I make the right choice? I think so, but I could be wrong. I chose one person's safety over another's. I chose to go with my personal values—that people of all sexual orientations and gender expressions are welcome in my spaces. Since I wouldn't have found it necessary to censor heterosexual love scenes, it didn't seem fair to censor same-sex love scenes. Also, because the heterosexual woman had access to more "safe" spaces in our culture, I felt it right to prioritize the safety of the more marginalized person. (If I were to do it again, I might encourage the whole group to wrestle with this question together, to help them come up with group agreements about what was acceptable in the class, but at that time I wasn't sure I possessed the facilitation skills needed for that. And I also recognize that might have put the lesbian woman at greater risk.)

Since that happened, I have made some adjustments to how I welcome people into the spaces where I teach and hold space. I state that we'll do our best to help them feel safe, but I offer no guarantees. In fact, I am more inclined to tell people there's a very good chance something will happen during our time together that will make them feel uncomfortable. "When you're doing personal work like this," I say near the beginning, "there is bound to be a moment when you'll feel uncomfortable and want to run. That instinct to run might even be intensified by the fact that we're here in community. Sometimes, in fact, someone in the room will hold up a mirror that you really don't want to look into. Or there may be conflict that feels too hard to work through. This is not easy work and if it's easy the whole time we're together, then I'm probably not doing my job."

I encourage people to sit with that discomfort when they're inclined to run, and to inquire further into it. Why is it coming up? What is it trying to teach them? What shadow might it reveal? What growth opportunity might it hold?

"If the discomfort becomes too much and you need to step out of the circle for a while, that's okay. Do what you need to do," I tell them. "Go for a walk, meditate, take a nap, hug a tree... but then do your best to come back. Challenge yourself to step back into the work, recommit to your own growth, explore your own shadow, or challenge what is going on in the circle if necessary. We will welcome you back and try to work through this if you want us to."

I have said some variation of this at the beginning of many retreats and workshops. Several times, there is someone in the group who comes to me afterwards saying, "I'm glad you warned us about the discomfort and gave us permission to step away. Because you said that, I wasn't as afraid when resistance came up. I was able to work through it and stay in the process."

A couple of times, people accepted my invitation to step away and then found the courage to come back. In both situations, those people told me they wouldn't have come back if I hadn't laid this groundwork.

This adjustment in how I welcome people is a movement from holding "safe space" to holding "brave space." I am much more interested in encouraging bravery than I am in keeping people safe and comfortable. I want people to challenge themselves and move forward rather than staying complacent.

My colleagues (and friends) Ericka Hines[64] and Desiree Adaway[65] (both Black women who've done social and racial justice work for many years) teach courses on diversity and inclusion,[66] and this is their response to the question about providing a "safe place to learn":

> No, we won't provide you a safe place to learn and here is why:
> Our 25+ years of experience has taught us that when people are talking about safety, they are actually talking about having a status quo environment that lets them stay where they are. Specifically, they are actually asking us to make them feel comfortable and being involved with diversity isn't about the status quo and being comfortable.

We are interested in moving you forward because that is what a commitment to this work takes. We realize that this topic may be a sensitive one for you. We appreciate the personal, emotional risks that you are taking when you are working with us.

Our experience has also taught us that "real" learning happens when we are at our learning edge. We will be your guides in exploring that edge. We will have clarifying conversations, we will have openness and we will encourage participation in each class and the forum to levels that allow us all to stretch. We will provide and insist on a RESPECTFUL environment with ground rules on how we treat each other in class and Facebook groups. Together we will create a brave space for learning.

While much of what's been discussed in this chapter focuses on group process, this concept of "brave space" is also important in our one-on-one relationships. Not long ago I had opportunities to hold brave space for two of my daughters. The spaces I needed to hold were vastly different, and each of them taught me something.

First, my youngest daughter, Maddy, ramped up her commitment to climate activism and decided to become part of a lawsuit against the federal government for failing to protect youth from the impacts of climate change. Her commitment meant that she'd need to fly across the country to participate in a large press conference where global activists Greta Thunberg and David Suzuki would be onstage with her and the other plaintiffs.

This was a big and very public move for my daughter, especially since she only recently emerged from an intense year in which her anxiety and depression had nearly crippled her. I was worried about the toll that this would take on her mental health, worried that she'd be attacked on social media, and worried that the pressure would be too much. I knew, though, that this was important to her and I had to trust her to make good decisions on her own behalf.

I flew to Vancouver with her and held space from the sidelines, letting her know that I was her champion, her safe place to fall, and (should she need it) her boundary-keeper and protector. The trip was remarkable. Maddy handled it all beautifully, articulating herself clearly onstage in front of fifteen thousand people and in interviews with national media.

When we got home from that trip, some of the backlash started to show up on social media, and I had to step into the role of advocate and boundary-keeper. In one case, when she was called a "silly girl" in a highly critical private message from a cousin of mine, who's older than I am and doesn't even know Maddy, I wrote a strongly worded message letting him know that he was not allowed to contact my daughter ever again.

A few days later, I found myself holding a very different kind of brave space with my other daughter Julie. I could sense that something was bothering her, and so I knocked on her bedroom door and asked if we could talk. She said yes, and we sat down on the bed together. I could see that she'd been crying. "You probably don't want to hear what I need to say," she said.

I took a deep breath and said, "Whatever you need to say, I will listen."

She began to unload a whole lot of pain and resentment, some of which I'd caused. "I've watched you these past weeks as you've supported Maddy, and while I want to be supportive too, what I feel is a whole lot of resentment. You didn't support *me* the same way when I was in high school. I had mental health issues too, but you didn't work as hard to get me into therapy as you did for Maddy. And worst of all, you didn't protect me the way you're protecting her. Dad was picking fights with me all the time, and you stood by while I was being emotionally abused."

The words coming out of her mouth flooded me with pain and shame. She was right—I *hadn't* done the same things for her as I did for Maddy. I hadn't found her a good therapist, I hadn't taken her on a trip to Vancouver in support of what she was passionate about, and—most importantly—I hadn't found a way to protect her from the chaos that her dad had a tendency to create in our home. Unlike the firm boundaries I erected with the cousin who criticized Maddy, I hadn't erected boundaries that made her feel safe and protected.

My first reaction—rooted in a trauma response that doesn't know how to hold pain or shame—was to deny and defend. I wanted to tell her all of the things I'd done *right*. I also wanted to tell her all of the reasons *why* I hadn't been able to support her the way I should have. (Her high school years happened during the time when my mom died, Marcel attempted suicide, I started my business, and my marriage ended. I was distracted and not well resourced.)

But first, I had to *hear* her. I had to hit my internal pause button and let her feel what she needed to feel without dismissing those feelings or gaslighting her experience of them. It was one of the hardest things I've ever done, but I knew how important it was. I value my relationship with her more than I value being *right*. I leaned into the pain and chose a *brave* space over a *safe* space.

Together, we worked through the pain and resentment. To start with, I apologized and admitted that she was right and justified in her resentment. Then I asked if she'd be willing to hear a little more about what was going on for me during her high school years that had left me feeling under-resourced for the work of being her mom. She was willing, so I told her— not to justify myself, but to be more honest with her about my weaknesses. And then I asked her what I needed to do to make repairs between us and change the patterns for the future.

"Honestly," she said, "just being able to say these things and be heard by you is helping me shift the way they feel." I offered to help her find (and pay for) a therapist to continue to work on healing these wounds with someone outside the family. I asked what I could do to help her erect the boundaries that I should have helped her with in high school.

We've had multiple conversations since then, and our relationship has shifted into a deeper, more honest place. I am grateful I had enough emotional resources—and courage—to take the risk of offering a space in which she could be brave enough to confront me.

(Note: One of the aspects of holding space is honouring people's autonomy and right to their own boundaries and narratives. With this in mind, I only share these stories about my daughters with their permission.)

Brave spaces may hurt sometimes, and there is always the potential that the disruption they cause is drastic, but I remain convinced that they are worth the risk.

You can be intentional about choosing to hold "brave" space over "safe" space, whether you are hosting retreats, running business meetings, hosting church gatherings, parenting your children, or holding space for a friend. Here are things you can do to create brave space:

1   **Encourage and set standards for *civility* rather than *safety*.** In an article in the *Canadian Journal for the Scholarship of Teaching and Learning*, the author, who writes primarily about classrooms, argues that we should set standards for **civil space** rather than trying to enforce safe space. Civility is "a consideration of others in interpersonal relationships, manners, politeness, and proper deportment."[67]

Civility is easier to manage because it's about behaviour rather than personal responses to what happens in the space.

Whereas safety focuses on interpersonal relationships primarily as a means to create a particular psychological experience for the individuals in a given social space (thus, ultimately privileging the individual experience), civility is concerned with both the individual and group experience. In a safe classroom, as it is commonly conceptualized, one person's sense of safety may come at the expense of another's, thus raising concerns as to whether the classroom can indeed be a safe space simultaneously for all students. However, a civil classroom requires no such psychological tradeoffs between students. As the focus of the civil classroom is to engage students as citizens of the space, and to encourage behaviour that promotes the collective good of that space, educators can indeed enforce a code of conduct consistent with civility. They cannot, however, always enforce social conditions that simultaneously result in a sense of psychological safety and comfort among all students in a class. When the focus moves from the psychological experiences of individuals to the collective behaviours and interactions in a social space, civility in the classroom becomes not only desirable, but possible. Safety, no matter how desirable it may be to both educators and students, is not.[68]

A word of caution, though: While civility can be a helpful guideline for difficult conversations in brave space, it can also become a way of hijacking space. To insist on civility in a setting where some of the people are more marginalized than others may result in tone policing and gaslighting. If people who have been oppressed, for example, express their anger and are told by those who feel uncomfortable with that anger to calm down and be civil, it can shut down important conversations. If you are using civility as a guide for your brave conversations, you may want to offer some qualifications of what it means and what it doesn't mean.

2 **Avoid clichés such as "everything will be okay" or "we're all friends here" or "let's all just get along" or "positive thoughts will attract positive outcomes."** These are all platitudes associated with spiritual bypassing. You can guarantee *none* of those things, so don't pretend to. Let people know that you will hold space for them in the difficult work, but don't give them false expectations of ease or comfort. One of the most profound things I experienced with my mom as she was dying was when she leaned toward me and said, "I don't know how to do this." "I don't know how to do this either," I replied. And then we just sat there, bonded by our shared lack of understanding of how the dying process would go. There were no platitudes that would have made that moment easier for either of us. We needed bravery in that moment, not empty promises of safety.

3 **Give people permission to resist and feel uncomfortable.** There are inherent power imbalances in any relationship, and it's quite possible that if you are holding space for someone (especially if you are in a position with more authority, such as a teacher, parent, boss, or facilitator), they might have a subconscious desire to keep you happy and not push back against what's happening.

As discussed earlier, if they are still focused on their primary needs for safety and belonging and look to you to fill those needs in the moment, it may be hard for them even to show discomfort in your presence. If this is the case, they may shut down, lash out in anger, or run away instead of admitting their discomfort. When you give them permission to push back and ensure that you won't abandon them in their darkest moments, they may be freer to express themselves and do their brave work.

For example, when my daughter went through a difficult time after I divorced her father, I said, "I want you to know that you have permission to get angry at me. You can yell at me, if you need to, and I will not run away. I promise I will not abandon you, no matter what emotions you need to express."

4 **Avoid telling people how they should or shouldn't be feeling.** Not everyone will experience things the same way, and that's okay. Especially for those who've experienced trauma, it can be quite triggering to be told to feel a certain way. When we tell people how they should feel, we are hijacking rather than holding the space. In an article on the website Decolonizing Yoga, the author speaks specifically to yoga teachers, but her advice is universal to anyone holding space:

> Consider how using statements like, "This yoga pose alleviates depression," or "This imagery exercise is calming and grounding," may make people feel if they don't experience it as such. A simple language switch like, "This imagery experience can be calming and grounding," or "This yoga pose is known to alleviate depression," can help you use some of your favorite teaching lines in a way that does not demean an individual's experience. [69]

5 **Communicate ground rules and/or acceptable behaviour.** Giving people an expectation of behaviour that is—or is not— acceptable in a space will help prepare them for what they will experience. It will also give them something to fall back on if they experience behaviour that doesn't fit with the ground rules. In "From Safe Spaces to Brave Spaces," Arao and Clemens suggest using the following common rules: agree to disagree, don't take things personally, challenge by choice, show respect, and no attacks. [70]

   If you are holding space in an environment where ground rules don't really fit (for example, if you're holding space for a friend rather than facilitating a group), then be prepared to communicate what behaviour is unacceptable and set boundaries as appropriate. For example, if a friend begins to lash out at you, you could say, "I accept your emotional response to this situation, but I will protect myself from threats or bullying. If you aren't able to speak to me in a less harmful way right now, then we'll need to take a break from this conversation and come back to it when we can meet each other with more respect." In other situations, that may be too many words and all you'll be able to do is walk away.

LIMINAL SPACE is by nature—and probably even necessity—a journey through messy and sometimes unsafe places. We know it can involve discomfort, uncertainty, ambiguity, restlessness, fear, and anguish. An effective space-holder will be prepared to welcome and nurture the bravery that it takes to not only survive it but to thrive in it.

21

understanding power

I F WE WANT to hold brave space—whether for a person or a group—it's wise to understand something about the power structure that may be present, as well as the ways that our cultures (and the social conditioning we received from those cultures) are inclined to uphold that power structure. It's also important to recognize how our own power might impact the people we hold space for and how the power structure at play might trigger our own fears, defensiveness, or insecurity.

Are you intimidated by a person with more wealth than you, for example, or a person with an advanced degree? Are you uncomfortable speaking with a CEO of a large business, or a politician? Do you feel different in a room full of businessmen in suits than you do in a room full of children?

In addition to your own response to power, a person you wish to hold space for may have a different relationship with power, and that could be a barrier in the relationship. If, for example, a person has less culturally sanctioned power than you do, it may be very difficult for them to trust you to hold space for them. Though they may not be able to articulate it, they may be afraid that you'll use your power to cause them harm.

In the story I shared in the last chapter about my daughter confronting me with her resentment and pain, there was a power dynamic at play that I had to remain conscious of. As the mom in the relationship, I have more familial power than she does, so it was a greater risk for her to confront me than it would have been for me to confront her. In that power position, I could have done great harm if I'd defended myself, gaslit her, or punished her for confronting me.

Unacknowledged power imbalance in a relationship can thwart potential. In a group setting, for example, when participants feel marginalized by the imbalances within the group, their silence and discomfort can impede the emergence of possibilities and solutions. The same can be true in one-on-one situations. The power imbalance with my daughter, if not handled with sensitivity, could have done long-term damage to our relationship.

Several years ago, I taught a university course on facilitation to a class filled primarily with international students. There were nine countries represented in the group, and only two students out of twenty-eight were born in Canada. It was a great opportunity to learn more about intercultural communication.

I started by teaching the basics of The Circle Way. In the first class we gathered in a circle and I taught them the basic principles: how to use the "talking piece," how to "speak with intention," how to "listen with attention," and what it means to have a "leader in every chair." Rather than stand at the front of the room, as they were used to their teachers doing, I modelled for them by sitting in the circle with them.

At the end of the class, a student from China came to speak with me. "I love being in the circle, but I don't think it would ever work in my culture," he said. He went on to tell me about how, in Chinese culture, hierarchy is very important and disrespect of it is taken very seriously. "When you walk into a room in China," he said, "you have an expectation that you will know instantly who is in the position of authority in the room. A CEO or other person of authority will always sit at the front of the room, and often up on a small stage to signal to everyone in the room that he is in charge, with his next-in-charge close to him. It's what makes people feel comfortable in China—instantly knowing the hierarchy in the room. You don't ever question or disrespect these people, and they don't ever admit their vulnerability or mistakes."

Other students in the room (particularly from Southeast Asia and the Middle East) said similar things. They were uncomfortable if they didn't know who was in charge. From some of my Indian students, I would sometimes receive emails addressed to "Most Respected Professor" (not something I ever received from my Canadian students). For these students, I was the authority in the room, and they were well trained to treat me with the respect my position warranted. It made them feel safer to understand this.

In a different class, a student from Saudi Arabia was once having a conversation with me as we walked down the hallway. She asked if she had permission to walk beside me. "In my culture," she said, "it's considered respectful to walk a few paces behind the teacher."

What these students articulated is that, in their cultures (which tend toward more authoritarianism), there is an expectation of a clear positional power structure. For many, this offers an element of safety because when they understand the hierarchy, they can apply a set of cultural rules about how to treat the people within that hierarchy. They don't have to wonder if/when they're doing the wrong thing.

It also offers them the element of trust (at least a certain kind of trust) because they believe that the person in authority will set the expectations for behaviour, protect them from harm, and take control in a crisis. In such an understanding of power and hierarchy, the person in charge must be competent, strong, unwavering, and unquestioned.

We had long conversations in another class I taught on the cultural relevance of public apologies offered by governments or corporations. For many, especially those from Eastern countries, it was unthinkable that a person in authority would apologize. This means that, while they trust the person in power to take charge and protect them in a crisis, they don't necessarily trust that they will admit their mistakes or take responsibility for repairing those mistakes.

It also means that they wouldn't trust that a person in authority would hold space for them if they found themselves in liminal space. It was an interesting dynamic when students became aware that I was modelling a different kind of leadership in my classroom and could be trusted differently than the leaders they were more accustomed to. Some of them shared surprisingly vulnerable stories with me once they'd shifted their perspective of me. One young man confided that his wife had cheated on him, and then told me I was the only person he'd told. He was quite surprised to be trusting his story to a person in authority.

In Western cultures (at least the ones I'm most familiar with), there is not as much overt signalling of the power hierarchy. That doesn't mean the power structure doesn't exist; it simply means that, from childhood, we need to learn the covert/hidden power structures and pay attention to the subtle cues as they present themselves. A professor, for example, may not expect you to refer to him as "Mr. Professor," and may dress as casually as the students in the classroom. However, that doesn't mean he doesn't have power over what grades you get or that he can't punish you for poor behaviour in the classroom. Ignore that power dynamic at your peril.

We have many subtle indicators of power that we're often not aware of. Consider how, at conferences, speakers often wear a special ribbon on their name tag so that you will know they hold some authority. Or consider the way that the chairs are arranged in boardrooms or classrooms.

Not long ago, I had a conversation with my older brother in which he asked me about my spirituality. Although I have always been an articulate person and don't have trouble talking about the topic, I found myself quickly triggered by his question. I became emotional and defensive. I lost much of my capacity to articulate, mumbling my way through a half-hearted explanation. He, on the other hand, remained cool and composed and didn't understand why the conversation was affecting me in the way it was.

It took me about a week, which included an ongoing email exchange with him, to understand what had happened and to communicate that to him. I was triggered not because he was abusive or had ever been abusive to me. I've never had any doubt that he loves me and has my best interests at heart. I was triggered because I was put into a position where the covert power imbalance made me feel suddenly wobbly and childlike.

At the simplest level, he's my older brother. From childhood, I always assumed he had more experience and more knowledge than I. Not only is he older, but he's always been more confident and less concerned about what others think of him. Some of this is about being born a male in a patriarchal culture; some of it is being the oldest child; and some of it is simply his personality.

But it goes much deeper than that. Being raised in a conservative Christian home, I was socially conditioned to believe that the male voice was more acceptable and trustworthy than the female voice. Though I was born with natural abilities in leadership and communication, those things were never fully accepted or trusted in church. I could teach Sunday school to young children, but I couldn't speak from the pulpit or hold any leadership positions. I had little authority or influence. My brother, on the other hand, never had anyone get in the way of his natural abilities; he could speak from any platform he wanted and could step into any position of authority he was inclined to seek out.

So, when it came to a conversation about my spirituality, I was brought face to face with a well-ingrained (though covert) power structure. Although I no longer choose to live within that type of hierarchy, I was still easily triggered from many years of social conditioning.

In that moment, when I was triggered by the intrinsic familial and religious power imbalance between my brother and me, I could not trust him to hold space for me (especially when it concerns the way my spiritual path has deviated from his) and so I didn't offer an honest answer to his question. Though I couldn't articulate it at the time, I had deeply ingrained beliefs around the dangers of trusting someone with more power than me. Fortunately, over time, that has shifted. When I explained the way I was triggered by the power imbalance, he was willing to hear it, acknowledge the imbalance, and learn from the situation. We have since had several follow-up conversations in which I found myself better able to trust him, largely because he demonstrated a willingness to expand his understanding and shift the balance.

Whether we recognize it or not, there are either overt or covert aspects of power imbalance in nearly every relationship we have. With a boss or teacher, there are overt imbalances of power, because one person's title gives them authority over the other. With a police officer or judge, the imbalance is even more overt. That's why police officers wear uniforms—to make it explicitly clear that they have authority.

With a friend or sibling, the power structure can be much more covert because there is no explicit indication of the hierarchy. The relationship may, in fact, be quite complex, because one person in the relationship may have power in some areas but not others. One person may possess more intellectual power due to a higher level of education while the other person has power due to other factors, like being part of a dominant societal group such as male, white, able-bodied, and cisgender.

It should be noted that power, as I describe it here, is heavily intertwined with privilege (which we'll discuss in greater detail in the next chapter). Those with privilege usually have access to more power, and vice versa. They can influence who has access to privilege, who is marginalized, who must serve as the shock absorbers, and who is kept safe. Those with power have more opportunity to change the rules in a society. And the closer *we* are to power, the more inclined we are to maintain the status quo so that we don't experience the discomfort of losing that power.

It is always the people with less power who have to pay more attention to the power structure and rules associated with it, because they are at greatest risk. They have to spend some of their emotional labour trying to decode the system, trying to figure out the unwritten rules imposed by those with more power, and trying to adjust their behaviour to ensure their own safety.

Meanwhile, those with power can be largely oblivious. My brother, for example, was caught off guard by my reaction because he had no reference point that would help him empathize with my intimidation in the face of his familial and religious power.

According to the article "Power Causes Brain Damage," power changes a person's brain. Those with power are more inclined to have an "empathy deficit" and are less aware of other people's emotions or needs:

> *Power lessens the need for a nuanced read of people, since it gives us command of resources we once had to cajole from others ... Less able to make out people's individuating traits, they rely more heavily on stereotype. And the less they're able to see, other research suggests, the more they rely on a personal "vision" for navigation.*[71]

If this is true, it's not hard to understand why those with power often become the most complicit in upholding the system, oppressing those with less power. Fortunately, as the article says, this "empathy deficit" is not irreversible.

• • •

> *At 26,000 feet above sea level, your body starts to die. Here, at an altitude known as the "death zone"—only 3,000 feet below the summit of Mount Everest—oxygen levels are a third of what they are at sea level. You have about two days before you run out of air.*
>
> *As your body starts to deteriorate, your mind abandons you. Hypoxia, low atmospheric pressure, means less oxygen is entering your brain. Your judgement is impaired. You become confused, your balance starts to falter, and you begin to hallucinate. You are losing your mind—right when you need it most.*
>
> *Just like the oxygen-thin atmosphere on the upper reaches of Mount Everest, the rarified atmosphere of high power and status alters our minds, diminishing our judgement and distorting our perceptions. As we attain power, we develop an illusory sense of control. Our belief in our own ideas increases while our interest in others' feedback and emotions decreases.*[72]

JULIE DIAMOND

If you find yourself with an "empathy deficit," it may be a good indicator that you've been granted a considerable amount of power, either by virtue of your position in a hierarchical organization or in the way that the culture in which you live privileges you. It may be time to grow your empathy muscle by spending more time "in the trenches," hearing the stories of those who have less access to power, learning from them, and using your power to help correct the imbalance.

If you wish to hold space for people but fear that the power imbalance will make that impossible, take heart. It will likely make it more difficult, but it won't make it impossible, as long as you (and the people with whom you're in relationship) are willing to meet each other humbly, courageously, and with an openness to learn and be changed by each other.

You may not be able to dismantle the existing power structure (especially if it is well ingrained in the culture), but you might at least be able to create a more level playing field in the relationships and places in which you hold space. When I think of the way that my brother and I have managed to change patterns that were deeply conditioned into our relationship (which we were oblivious to for many years) and meet each other differently, I am encouraged to believe that, through our commitment to holding brave space, we can change the systems.

In the next chapter, we'll unpack some of these imbalances more fully and talk about how to hold space in spite of them.

22

privilege, oppression, and intersectionality

I N ORDER FOR us to hold brave space for the kind of transformation needed in the world, we need to grow our awareness of the cultural systems that create and uphold the
imbalances we talked about in the last chapter. This awareness
serves two purposes: a) it helps us to be more equitable, just, and
compassionate in how we treat the people we are in relationship with; and b) it helps us to see what work needs to be done
to dismantle the systems so that we can live in a more just world.

According to *Everyday Feminism*, "privilege" is defined as
"a set of unearned benefits given to people who fit into a specific social group."[73]

Social privilege is a primary source of power imbalance.
Everyone has some social privilege. It can be because of the
colour of our skin, the way our bodies move in the world (i.e., are
we able-bodied?), our gender, our religion, our physical appearance, our access to wealth, or the language we grew up speaking.
Even if we grew up disadvantaged in some respects, we still
likely possess some sort of privilege that we did nothing to earn.

Those with the most privilege are often the least aware that they have it. When we are the ones in possession of social privilege, we rarely need to give it attention because the world is designed to work best for us. It's easy to assume our privilege is the norm. However, when we begin to question it, and have our eyes opened to the ways other people are oppressed so that we can enjoy that privilege, our view of the world will be changed.

It won't be easy, though, especially if you are new to this work. This new understanding can quickly cause reactions ranging from guilt and shame to defensiveness and fragility, so it may feel safer and easier to simply pretend it doesn't exist. ("Fragility" is a term made popular by Robin DiAngelo in a paper on "White Fragility,"[74] and later in a book of the same title, and describes the reactivity that comes in the form of defensiveness, argumentativeness, belligerence, etc., when we find the challenge of facing our own biases to be so intolerable that we do what we can to shut down or sideline the conversation.)

Peggy McIntosh, one of the original scholars writing about white and male privilege, describes privilege this way:

> *I have come to see white privilege as an invisible package of unearned assets that I can count on cashing in each day, but about which I was "meant" to remain oblivious. White privilege is like an invisible weightless knapsack of special provisions, assurances, tools, maps, guides, codebooks, passports, visas, clothes, compass, emergency gear, and blank checks.*[75]

Consider the last time you went clothes shopping. Was it easy for you to get what you needed or were there barriers? Were you able to drive to the store in your own car or did you have to take public transit? Did you have to seek out special transportation that would accommodate a wheelchair? Was it difficult for you to leave the house because of your mental health? Did you have to find a babysitter to care for your children before you could leave the house? When you stepped into the store, did a security guard follow you around because the colour of your skin made them suspect that you might shoplift? Did you have trouble communicating with the sales clerk because you don't speak the same language? Did you have trouble finding clothes that suit you because you don't fit the gender binary presented by the store? Did you have enough money in your bank account to pay for the clothes or did you have to use a high-interest credit card?

If there were few barriers to finding and buying what you needed, then it's a good indication that you have access to at least some level of privilege. If there were barriers, then you may be part of a social group that experiences some form of oppression within your culture.

The term "oppression" has a big role in this discussion of power imbalance. In the past, oppression was known within the context of a grander scale, perhaps as the way authoritarian regimes subjugated and controlled people, for example. But with the emerging discussions of privilege in recent years, the understanding of oppression has changed. Dictionary.com now defines "oppression" as "prolonged cruel or unjust treatment or control."[76]

The "unjust treatment" portion of the definition is worth highlighting. Though the term "oppression" might seem to imply something overt and obvious (the oppression of the Jews during the Holocaust, to take one of the most extreme examples), there are much more subtle—but still destructive and dangerous—ways that people experience oppression in our cultures. Consider the way that Hollywood oppresses women, for example, by giving them far fewer roles than men and by over-sexualizing many female characters in movies. Consider the way that shopping malls oppress trans people by only making washrooms available according to the gender binary. And consider the ways that people of colour are oppressed by a police system that subjects them to greater scrutiny, less protection, and more chance of being harmed or killed.

Just as we all have privilege, nearly everyone faces some form of oppression. You may have been born a white male who has privilege because of both skin colour and gender. But if you're gay or trans, you'll still face oppression. Or if you were raised in poverty, your socio-economic status imposes some oppression on you. The same holds true if you have a disability or if you've never had access to higher education.

"Intersectionality" is another important word in this discussion. Intersectionality is the place where privilege and oppression meet. It's the whole picture of who you are within the gridwork of systems relative to the way culture favours some and disfavours others.

Kimberlé W. Crenshaw, who coined the term "intersectionality" as a way of talking about discrimination against Black women, said:

> Consider an analogy to traffic in an intersection, coming and going in all four directions. Discrimination, like traffic through an intersection, may flow in one direction, and it may flow in another. If an accident happens in an intersection, it can be caused by cars traveling from any number of directions and, sometimes, from all of them. Similarly, if a Black woman is harmed because she is in an intersection, her injury could result from sex discrimination or race discrimination . . . But it is not always easy to reconstruct an accident: Sometimes the skid marks and the injuries simply indicate that they occurred simultaneously, frustrating efforts to determine which driver caused the harm.[77]

Your intersectional identity is a mix of race, gender, sexual orientation, socio-economic status, physical and mental ability, religion, language, age, physical attractiveness, occupation, and education. All of these (and more) are factors for consideration in that identity. They all contribute to the amount of culturally sanctioned power to which you have access.

None of these factors are inherently "good" or "bad." Instead, culture assigns value to them and creates systems that favour one over the other. It's not "good" to be white and "bad" to be Black; it's that our culture has centred whiteness while marginalizing Blackness. It's not "good" to be male and "bad" to be female or non-binary, but it's easier to walk in the world as a male because that's who a patriarchal system rates as the most valuable.

Here are just a few other ways privilege can work: Consider an office building with lots of stairs and no ramps or elevators—that's a building constructed within a system that centres and gives privilege to able bodies while marginalizing differently abled bodies. Consider a camera filter designed to view white skin as the norm and, by default, distort Black or brown skin—it's designed by a system that centres and privileges whiteness and marginalizes Blackness. Consider a church built at the perimeter of a city, in a place without public transportation—this is a church designed to favour those with the financial resources to afford cars while marginalizing those without.

We didn't choose our privilege or our oppression. We had no choice over whether we were born male, gay, poor, beautiful, or rich—or whether the culture we were born into privileged or marginalized those things. We *are* responsible for what we do with the cultural privileges into which we were born. We can't be expected to single-handedly overturn a system that favours one over another; that's our collective responsibility.

To fully honour and support the people for whom you hold space, it's imperative that you have some understanding of the intersectional identities of all parties, yourself included, and how these identities might influence your relationship within the space. It's also important that you pay attention to whether you are upholding—or helping dismantle— a system which privileges some and oppresses others.

The writers of *Beyond Inclusion, Beyond Empowerment* refer to those with higher or lower status, power, and privilege in a culture as "Agent" and "Target" groups:

Members of the Agent group are overvalued and receive unearned advantage and benefits. Examples of Agent groups include adults, heterosexuals, whites, biological males, or the U.S.-born. As members of Agent groups, we receive affirmation and support and have ready access to rewards. As Agent group members we have an easier time getting jobs, are more likely to see people "like us" on television and can expect that our concerns will be taken seriously by public institutions.

Members of Target groups are devalued, "otherized," and subject to marginalization:

Examples of Target groups include children/elders, gay/lesbian/bisexual people, People of Color, women, and people born outside the U.S. As members of Target groups, our access is limited and our movement restricted. For example, we experience difficulties finding work appropriate to our education and abilities, we often see people "like us" depicted negatively in the media, and public institutions rarely address our concerns.[78]

Consider how you may fit into either the Agent or Target group depending on various social rank categories: age, disability, religious/spiritual orientation, ethnicity, social class culture, sexual orientation, nationality, and gender. It may look different depending on where you live, but in a North American culture those with the greatest agency are white, cisgender, educated, able-bodied, heterosexual, male adults (aged eighteen to sixty-four) who are culturally Christian.

The Agent group is the one that is most normalized and centred in a culture. When a person is a white male, we rarely see the media refer to him as anything other than "male" because whiteness is assumed. If, however, the person is a Black male, his ethnicity is often referenced because it is outside the "Agent" ranking. His ethnicity comes into the story even more specifically if he is deviating from what the media considers to be socially acceptable behaviour.

If you saw a picture of me walking with my friend who happens to be Muslim, there's a good chance that you would add the descriptor "Muslim" to that of "woman." (She wears a hijab.) *My* religion wouldn't be a factor because it's assumed to be the cultural norm. If you meet a transgender person and you tell the story of your meeting to another friend later, you'll probably mention their gender (if it's apparent). This might not come up if they weren't outside the norm. I remember my mom telling the story of how a member of our community had an affair with "an Indian woman," as though her race had something to do with why the woman had an affair with a married man. It's a subtle thing, but it's rooted in a system that privileges whiteness. Start paying attention to your own tendencies and I'm certain you'll find ways that you do the same.

Especially if you have agency in many of the aforementioned categories, this information can feel like an affront to your sense of who you are. Perhaps you fit into more of the Agent groups than you expected and yet don't think of yourself as someone who has power or privilege. Or maybe you have a lot of personal power and don't want to think of yourself as a Target. Remember that your personal journey and experience of the world is your own; you can never be fully defined by these titles. These categories serve to help us understand and illuminate the factors delineating cultural power structures; they're not meant to be a road map.

Those with the most privilege have the greatest ease moving about in whatever space they choose, and so they can ignore the limitations or threats that those spaces hold for other people. They also have the greatest ease when entering conversations. They experience the least fear of reprisal, so they don't have to give much consideration to how unsafe another person might feel.

Sometimes, for example, when I invite people to share their vulnerable stories in a sharing circle, I forget that for some, vulnerability feels very risky because they've been socially conditioned to believe their stories or emotions don't have value—or are dangerous. For example, the automatic stereotype and marginalization of an "angry Black woman" might make some women of colour reluctant to become emotional in a public space.

Even when your intentions are good, it's simply easier and more comfortable to overlook the things you've been socially conditioned to ignore, especially things that privilege and centre you. If you are able-bodied, for example, you likely won't think twice about inviting a friend to meet you for coffee in a building with stairs. But what if that friend has a mobility issue that makes stairs difficult? If you're white and living in the suburbs, you probably wouldn't hesitate to book a meeting space in your neighbourhood. But what if the meeting participants are of a race or religion that doesn't feel safe in your part of town? If you're male, you probably won't notice when 90 percent of the people in the boardroom are men like you.

But what if your friend is a female manager who feels isolated and ignored? If you're cisgender, you may think nothing of inviting a friend to a sporting event where the washrooms are clearly gendered. But what if that friend is trans or non-binary and doesn't feel safe in those spaces?

When I was co-hosting race relations conversations alongside an Indigenous co-host a few years ago, we gave considerable thought to the space we were inviting people into. Which space would be most welcoming to people of all intersectional identities? Because the primary race issue we were dealing with was between white settlers and Indigenous people, we were especially concerned about where people from both communities would feel comfortable gathering. We settled on the Forks, a cultural centre and public market in the downtown area of Winnipeg. The Forks is a historic area that has a lot of meaning and history for local Indigenous people, with some areas designated as sacred sites. It is also the site where settlers arrived and first established the fur trade with Indigenous tribes. It is easily accessible by public transit, has ample parking for people from the suburbs, and is walkable from downtown neighbourhoods (which tend to have the highest concentration of Indigenous people). It's also wheelchair accessible.

In addition to the space considerations, we took other steps to reduce the barriers for attendance. We arranged to have a meal available for everyone, we welcomed children, and we made it a free event. We set up the room with small round tables to encourage intermingling and minimal hierarchy.

While we wanted all to feel welcome, we paid most attention to how accessible it would feel to the most marginalized. Because people with privilege—in this case, mostly descendants of white settlers—have fewer barriers, they don't need the focused attention in this regard. They can move about in almost any space without feeling their skin colour is a barrier.

We had a good turnout at our first event, with nearly fifty-fifty representation from each community, plus some from other communities, including newcomers to the country. We also had a good mix of people from different socio-economic categories. This wouldn't have happened if we had planned the event in an expensive hotel in the suburbs that would likely feel like foreign territory for some.

Our second event turned out differently. This time, we centred the Indigenous community by hosting the event at an Indigenous social work school, in a primarily Indigenous part of town that is also an economically challenged neighbourhood. We provided soup and bannock (a traditional Indigenous bread). Attendance was smaller this time, with Indigenous participants outnumbering white settler participants. Few people from the suburbs attended—probably because they didn't feel comfortable venturing into what they considered an unsafe neighbourhood.

However, what *did* happen this time is that several members of the Filipino immigrant community were in attendance, more of whom live in and feel comfortable in the downtown area, and an unexpected bond formed between them and the Indigenous community. Several events emerged out of the bond that began at this gathering.

Whenever we hold space, part of our work is to consider who might be privileged and who might be oppressed, and how we might be perpetuating these imbalances. The spaces that we choose, the way we introduce topics of conversation, the stories we share, the expectations we have for other people—all of these can enhance privilege or oppression for different people.

Even in one-on-one relationships, there will be subtle—and sometimes not so subtle—elements of privilege and marginalization. A friend might have less privilege than you in their skin colour but more privilege in their socio-economic upbringing.

They may have more privilege in their gender but less privilege because they're a newcomer to the country we live in.

One of my close friends, for example, is a Black man from Nigeria. Segun and I have long conversations about what it means to be male or female in our culture, and what it means to be Black or white. Sometimes he has to acknowledge unearned privilege in his gender and historic access to power (he was born into a ruling-class family in Nigeria), and sometimes I have to acknowledge unearned privilege in the colour of my skin and the fact that I was born in Canada. Our friendship is rich because we are both prepared to acknowledge and unpack our intersectional identities, while trusting that the other person won't make us feel threatened or marginalized. We have found enough common ground upon which to build a friendship.

One important question to ask, one for which there may not be an easy answer, is this: Is it automatically our responsibility to help the people for whom we're holding space to recognize their own privilege and/or oppression? There is not one answer to that question. It depends upon the relationship, the situation, and whether there's harm being done.

Sometimes, for example, we might work with privileged white cisgender men who are consistently marginalizing other people in the workplace, and it may be important to assist them in understanding their privilege in order to minimize damage. But if we are among the people being marginalized, it may feel too risky or require too much emotional labour on our part to bring them to that understanding. In that case, it might be more successful to transfer that labour to management or bring in a consultant to bear the responsibility of providing education around it.

In another example, perhaps we are in a one-on-one relationship with someone we see as marginalized—a single mother who is Muslim and/or has a disability, for example—but who is determined not to feel like a victim. She may not benefit from our understanding of privilege or oppression, in which case holding space for her might mean supporting her when there are barriers while also allowing her to come to her own understanding of what those barriers are.

In my coaching work, I try to support people in making their own discoveries about themselves, in their own time. Once or twice, in my eagerness to bring my own understanding to the conversation, I've opened someone's eyes to oppression they hadn't yet identified with, and it threw them off balance because they weren't ready to process it. From those experiences I've learned to trust each person's intuitive sense of where their journey needs to take them.

One thing that I know for certain: It is not helpful to offer sympathy when holding space for those whose intersectional identity is more marginalized than mine. Sympathy comes from a place of superiority, not genuine compassion. Sympathy is patronizing, a one-way street that broadens the gaps between people. Instead, try empathy. Empathy requires that you be willing to imagine the world through the other person's eyes. It involves risk in listening deeply and feeling deeply. It dares to sit in the mess with the person. It does not look from above, nor judge, nor patronize.

One of the greatest gifts of my life has been the many relationships I have that cross the culturally imposed boundaries between race, gender, religion, etc. Those relationships are as deep as they are only because I chose to muster up the courage to work through my shame and fragility, to take responsibility for the impact rather than just the intent of my words and actions, to pick myself up after I fumble, and to lean into the discomfort of learning more and more about the places where I continue to have unconscious bias and privilege. I hope that you will find the courage to do the same. I know that you will be immeasurably blessed.

*If I participate, knowingly or otherwise, in my sister's oppression
and she calls me on it, to answer her anger with my own only blan-
kets the substance of our exchange with reaction. It wastes energy.
And yes, it is very difficult to stand still and to listen to another
woman's voice delineate an agony I do not share, or one to which
I myself have contributed.*[79]

AUDRE LORDE

• • •

To give you a sense of my own personal journey of waking up
to my intersectional identity and to how layers of both oppressor
and oppressed are part of my personal narrative, here's a piece I
wrote a few years ago.

Waking Up Is Hard to Do

First, you wake up to your own oppression,
to the ways you've been silenced,
to the many little stories you carry about why
your words are worth less than those who
benefit most from the old story.

You wake up to the truth that
your view of yourself wasn't only constructed by you.
It was shaped for a purpose—to keep you small,
to keep you silent.

Then you wake up to your own anger,
to the fierce determination not to obey,
not to listen to the stories,
not to stay small.

But then, one day later on,
after you've learned to speak,
there's another awakening.
You wake up to the fact that
your frustration taught you to adapt rather than to rise above.
You shape-shifted to be more like them,
to work in their hallways of power,
to survive in a world that didn't want your voice.
You became one of them to be heard by them.

Then your anger wakes up once again,
and you have a new determination.
This time, you speak with your true voice
whether or not it is heard.
You begin to live in the centre of your true life
whether or not it is acceptable to them.
You risk dismissal and disdain
because you are no longer willing to go back to sleep.

But then, one day later on,
you realize that there is something else going on,
and this will require yet another awakening.
This will require that you look with more clear eyes
and speak with an even more clear voice.

You begin to wake up to other people's narrative,
other people's oppression, other people's silence.
You begin to see that those whose skin
is different from yours,
whose gender and love are different from yours,
are waking up too,
and their waking up is asking you to be uncomfortable.

Their waking up
is asking you to look more clearly and unblinkingly
at your own life.

Then you begin to wake up to your own privilege,
to the ways that you have benefited from their oppression.
You begin to wake up to the pain in them,
and you begin to hear the cries of the silenced,
"We want to be heard too!"

This waking up is the hardest,
and you want to ignore it,
to resist it, to deny what you now see.
You want to return to your own narrative,
to your own uprising,
because in that you can feel victorious and liberated.
In that, you don't have to face the truth
that maybe you, even you, are holding the keys
to someone else's chains.

But finally, you can deny it no longer.
Your awakened eyes see that you are only truly free
if they are free too.

And so you wake up,
and you face the hard truths.
And you feel the hurt
when your micro-aggressions
and white fragility are pointed out.
And you do the hard work to peer with unwavering eyes
on yourself,
and to see both the shadow and the light,
and the space in between.

And when you are awake,
you begin to see it all,
and you can't look away.
And finally, you see
that when you are truly awake
and truly honest about your place in the world,

it is no longer threatening to stand by those
who are also waking up.

And your anger burns anew.
And your fierce determination rises once again.
And this time, your love is big enough
to hold their hurt along with your own.
And this time, your voice is strong enough
to speak their truth along with your own.
And this time, your courage is deep enough
to let them speak a truth that is
different from your own.

23

holding space at the intersection

W E NOW HAVE a clearer understanding of how power, privilege, marginalization, and intersectionality play into our relationships and how our social conditioning helps to determine how we respond to others based on their—and our—rank within these systems. The next question we must ask is, "What impact does this understanding have on the way we hold space?"

Does it matter that the person we're in relationship with fits into different Agent and Target categories than we do? Does it change the way we communicate with them? Does it matter that the people in the room where we're hosting a conversation or retreat are from different races and/or religions and/or genders? Will it alter the way we facilitate the conversation?

The simplest answer to this is yes, it does matter. Our identities, our social ranks, and our differences matter. While they might not always play out overtly in our conversations and interactions, they are definitely significant. When we overlook or ignore them, we risk causing harm.

If you choose to do the work of holding space where the complexities of privilege and oppression might come into play, it will require of you that you do your own work to recognize and take responsibility for your own unearned privileges, unconscious biases, and areas in which your defensiveness and fragility get triggered. This is intense work that is not for the faint of heart because it will likely bring up shame over past behaviours and fear that you'll do the wrong thing in the future. You might be inclined to simply stay away from complex conversations where you might fumble or someone might call you out for a statement that reveals an unconscious bias you didn't know you had—but that act of distancing yourself will limit your relationships and shrink the size of your world.

If you are holding space at the intersection, where there are imbalances of power and privilege, or where there are differences in race, gender, etc., here are some things to consider:

1 **Recognize difference.** You might think that statements such as "I don't see colour" or "We're all the same inside" are inclusive and compassionate, but their impact may be the opposite of your intention. They can make people feel erased, as though their differences and unique struggles are not important.

You don't necessarily need to make a point of naming or drawing attention to the differences (especially if the more marginalized person chooses not to), but at least be aware of them and open to discussing them if they become relevant. If someone needs to express their differences and let you know how that presents a unique challenge for them (for example, if a workshop participant wants to let people know of a hidden disability that is a limiting factor for them), listen with openness and compassion and treat them as they ask to be treated.

2 **Acknowledge your limitations.** You can only see the world through your particular lens, bias, and social conditioning, and

though you may do your best to be compassionate, you'll never fully understand another person's experience. Don't pretend that you do. I, for example, can only ever experience the world as a white, cisgender, Canadian, able-bodied woman. And even though I travel a lot and talk to people to try to expand that view, I will always have some limitations in how I hold space for people with very different experiences from mine.

In many long conversations, my friend Saleha and I have found remarkable similarities between her Muslim upbringing in Saudi Arabia and my Mennonite one in Canada—such as our rules around "don't drink, don't dance, dress modestly"— but that doesn't mean I have any right to try to claim some understanding of her experience.

Recently, a prospective client spoke to me about doing work around exploring her identity as a person of colour, and how that came with layers of shame and trauma. While I was happy to work with her, I was careful to also say, "I want us both to be clear that I may not be the right person to hold space for you. As a white woman, whose skin colour represents your people's oppressors, there may be some limitations in what you feel comfortable expressing to me, and some unconscious bias in either of us. I don't want this to get in the way of the work you need to do, so if it feels like a limitation, I'm happy to help you find another person to work with." Speaking that aloud, early in the relationship, gave us both more freedom to talk about those things when they came up.

It's better to be honest about the limitations and differences than to stay silent and allow them to get in the way as the "elephant in the room" later. *But note: Be careful not to centre yourself in this conversation. If you go on and on with, "I'm so sorry I can't be of adequate support to you. I try so hard, but I always seem to fall short . . ." then you're making it about you and not the other person's needs. This is a form of hijacking, forcing the other person to feel that they need to hold space for you instead of the other way around.*

3 **Centre the most marginalized.** In a system of hierarchy (patriarchy, white supremacy, kyriarchy, to name a few) those who fit the most acceptable "norm" (i.e., white, cisgender, heterosexual, able-bodied, Christian male in North America) inevitably are given the most airtime. Their experiences are assumed to be the standard on which all others are measured. Pay attention, for example, to who gets more leading roles in movies or more jobs as TV news anchors; the world is designed for *their* ease and comfort, and everyone else has to find workarounds to function adequately and be heard. (If you're skeptical, look up womenandhollywood.com or look up the article "Does Hollywood Have a Diversity Problem?" on thoughtco.com.)

As someone who holds space, you can disrupt that pattern and give voice to the marginalized, putting their needs ahead of—or at least on an equal footing with—those with power and privilege. Consider, for example, what a community meeting might look like if it were centred on the needs and barriers of a disabled Indigenous transgender individual. How might it change the dynamics of the conversation, the space that was chosen for the meeting, the bathroom facilities? What if that person is given the first opportunity to speak and others from Agent groups are asked to wait until the end? What if, for a change, the issues affecting the Target groups take up the majority of the meeting agenda?

4 **Challenge the abuse of power.** Pay attention to how the people for whom you are holding space, especially if it's within a group, might be knowingly or unknowingly harming people with the way they use their power and privilege. Though holding space is largely a low-intervention practice, there are times when intervention is absolutely necessary, especially if

a marginalized person is being hurt. If, as we said in the point above, you are being intentional about centring the most marginalized, then you must also be prepared to serve as their advocate and ally when they are being harmed in the discourse. In this case, silence equals complicity, so speak up and challenge those who may be clueless about how their actions and words impact others. Though it may feel risky, consider that, as the marginalized person's ally, you are likely putting yourself at less risk than they would be if they spoke.

5 **Use a talking piece when necessary.** Deep and intentional *listening* is a good start in supporting marginalized voices. If you're in a group setting, a talking piece (discussed in more detail in chapter 25) can be a helpful tool to ensure all voices are heard and none are centred more than others. If you begin to notice that some voices are dominating, interject with, "It would be great to hear as many perspectives as possible, so I'm going to pass the talking piece around and give everyone a chance to speak."

Even when you're in a one-on-one conversation, you can use a talking piece, or you can at least hold an imaginary talking piece in your mind, reminding yourself not to interrupt when another person is speaking. I do this for myself when I am coaching people, imagining that my client is holding a talking piece and I don't get to interject until they put it down.

6 **Invite cultural reflection, ceremony, etc.** If you're holding space in, or for, a group that includes a variety of races, cultures, and religions, consider that they each bring wisdom the rest of the group doesn't have access to, and from which the rest of the group can benefit. Perhaps they have an approach to conflict that is unique and healing. Perhaps they practise some ritual that can enhance your learning. Perhaps there are

ways of expressing things in their language that add nuance to the conversation.

Once, when I was teaching a class with a lot of students from India, I happened to know that Holi (one of their cultural festivals) fell on the day of our class because I'd been in India during the Holi festival a few years earlier. I brought in some treats from an Indian restaurant and some of the coloured powder that people throw on each other during Holi and invited the students to teach us about their festival. The students were delighted to share their festival with us, and many came to me afterwards to express how honoured they felt that I'd made the effort on their behalf. That small act created an environment in the classroom where students from other countries also felt welcome to share their cultural practices, music, food, etc. We had some delicious potluck lunches in that class.

When I was in New Zealand, there were a few Maori women at the retreat, and they added richness to the learning by sharing the Maori words that aligned with, and offered depth to, concepts I was teaching.

When you create an environment where this wisdom is welcomed and honoured, people will feel freer to give of themselves. Don't, however, ask them to speak on behalf of their entire race, gender, etc.; that's serving the opposite purpose.

7 **Listen to and read many voices.** Do your homework. Expose yourself to many perspectives so you can be more compassionate when you encounter people who are different from you. Read books by people from other cultures, other religions, other genders, other socio-economic backgrounds. Walk in the world with curiosity and humility, listen when friends share their stories, follow links when people share articles about their countries on social media, go to lectures from visiting professors.

When you are used to listening to, and reading about, other voices, you will be much more prepared to hold space for people whose reality is different from yours. When my Zimbabwean friend needed to talk about the challenges of his marriage, I felt I could offer him better support because I've been intentional about expanding my understanding of how marriages are viewed differently in our two cultures. If I only considered an ethnocentric, North American view of marriage, I would have missed some of the nuance of what he shared.

8 **Don't be afraid to flounder.** You will make mistakes in this work. I have, and will continue to. It's hard to break the patterns of our social conditioning. We've been well trained to exist within the roles that were assigned to us, so it will be challenging to mindfully break away from established categories and automatic behaviour.

We might occasionally and inadvertently hurt people's feelings. And sometimes *our* feelings will get hurt too, especially if others need to express their anger over injustice or not being seen. Some days we'll feel like failures, as if we'll never get it right. That's all part of the work it will take for us to dismantle the systems in which we're so embedded. But we have to keep trusting that the sacrifices are worth it. We can put our hurt feelings into perspective by reminding ourselves that there will always be people with less agency who are being forced to make greater sacrifices than we are making.

9 **Invite bravery.** As we discussed earlier, cultivating a "brave" environment rather than a "safe" one can help people to express themselves, challenge each other, and work together toward positive change. When those who are marginalized are invited to be brave enough to challenge those with power and privilege (and to trust that they will not be met with violence), and those with power and privilege are invited to be brave

enough to recognize and address these things within themselves, then transformation can happen. This is not an easy task; it requires that whoever is holding space be prepared to hold strong emotions and enforce firm boundaries. But it *is* possible with commitment and a willingness to keep trying.

10 **Share the work.** If you are holding space in complex situations, don't do it alone. It's not weakness to ask for help in this situation—it's wisdom. Nobody should carry the burden of complex space-holding alone, partly because it can burn you out, partly because it can become an ego trip causing you to lose sight of another person's best interests, and partly because it can trigger your own trauma, insecurities, and fears.

This is why, in circle work, we try to always have a guardian who works alongside the host. When at least two people are paying attention to the group's energy, needs, or conflict, there's a better chance the container will be strong enough to hold it all. For more about this, read *The Circle Way: A Leader in Every Chair* by Christina Baldwin and Ann Linnea.

Even if you are providing one-on-one support, it's important to ask whether the person you're supporting has other people in their corner. When I do complex coaching work, I usually check in with the person to see who else is in their support circle in the form of family, therapists, body workers, friends, pastors, and others.

11 **Disrupt the narrative and do things more mindfully.** While tradition sometimes has a place, much can be said for the value of breaking with tradition when it gets in the way. Sometimes tradition is simply an excuse for "doing things the way we've always done them" and upholding an oppressive system.

When tradition results in the same people being overlooked repeatedly, and the same people being put in positions of power repeatedly, it's time for disruption. Shake up the status quo. Change the seating plan. Invite those with the lowest rank to speak first. Consider using The Circle Way to run business meetings. Use artmaking or movement practice to engage people in non-linear thinking.

12 **Maintain a heart at peace.** When our hearts are at war, we view other people as objects or obstacles. When our hearts are at peace, we view them as people with dignity and value.

> *Seeing an equal person as an inferior object is an act of violence. It hurts as much as a punch in the face. In fact, in many ways it hurts more. Bruises heal more quickly than emotional scars do.*[80]

When our hearts are at war, we cannot hold space, especially in a complex situation where there are people who are different from us. A heart at peace means that each individual we encounter is as worthy of dignity and respect as we are. If we are facilitating a group, not only do we have to seek to have a heart at peace, but we have to create a space where everyone in the room can respond to each other from hearts at peace. If we objectify people in the room, the group must share the responsibility for having "hearts at war."

You can practise having a heart at peace at any time. Go for a walk in a neighbourhood you're uncomfortable in (perhaps an area with a lot of poverty or where people from different ethnic backgrounds live). When you encounter people who make you nervous, do some self-inquiry about why that person threatens you. And then ask yourself how you would respond differently if your heart were at peace. Stop to have a conversation with a homeless person and notice what changes when you see that person as equal and fully human. (But don't objectify them by expecting them to give you their time or attention.)

13 **Stand at the intersection of power and love.** Adam Kahane says that, in order for social change to happen, both power and love must be brought into the work. He quotes Martin Luther King Jr.: "Power without love is reckless and abusive, and love without power is sentimental and anemic." Kahane brings this into practice when facilitating major conversations in complex situations, including the post-apartheid era in South Africa:

> *When I am facilitating at my best I am using my power and my love to help the group use their power and their love: to grow and unite their self-realizing in the service of the self-realizing of the whole system of which they are a part. On one level, I am active and attentive—moving around at the front of the room, managing the agenda, inviting people to contribute, writing on flip charts, helping to synthesize and advance the content of the work. But at another level I am inactive and inattentive, present only to the emerging self-realization of the whole of the group and to my next step. I have intent without content. A participant in one of my workshops observed, "Beneath his visible activity, Adam has a deeper, quieter, intentional, invisible energy that is not really there and so is not a target. This is the energy that pulls us along."*[81]

14 **Pay attention to the barriers.** For anyone who isn't part of the dominant culture, for whom the world's comfort and ease have not been designed, there are barriers to consider, both seen and invisible. Consider building design: is there wheelchair accessibility, or support for those who are visually impaired? The meeting date: does it fall on someone's religious holiday? Meeting timing: do children have to be picked up at school or does child care need to be provided? The neighbourhood: do marginalized groups feel safe there? Costs involved to attend: is there a fee that's out of reach for those on welfare?

The more we eliminate barriers, and the more welcoming and accessible a space is, the richer and more diverse a group experience will become—and the more potential there is to help create positive change. Instead of thinking about the burden of overcoming these barriers, think about what an asset it will be to have these people involved. When people feel valued and the barriers are removed, they can show up in authentic and generous ways. Everyone benefits.

15 **Consider that the impact may be different from the intent.** Despite our best intentions, there will likely be times when we cause harm. Our implicit bias, for example, might mean that we judge someone based on a stereotype we're not even aware that we're holding. It's worth considering that if we have agency in a relationship, we have to take responsibility, not only for the intent, but also for the impact. Hiding behind our intent ("I didn't *mean* to hurt your feelings") centres *us* and dismisses what might be a valid reaction from the person hurt.

An article entitled "Intent vs. Impact: Why Your Intentions Don't Really Matter" is helpful in understanding why the impact is more important than the intent:

> *For people of identity privilege, this is where listening becomes vitally important, for our privilege can often shield us from understanding the impact of our actions. After all, as a person of privilege, I can never fully understand the ways in which oppressive acts or language impact those around me. What I surely can do is listen with every intent to understand, and I can work to change my behavior. Because what we need to understand is that making the conversation about intent is inherently a privileged action. The reason? It ensures that you and your identity (and intent) stay at the center of any conversation and action while the impact of your action or words*

on those around you is marginalized. So if someone ever tells you to "check your privilege," what they may very well mean is: "Stop centering your experience and identity in the conversation by making this about the intent of your actions instead of their impact." That is: Not everything is about you.[82]

TAKE RESPONSIBILITY for your biases when they are pointed out, apologize and make repairs when the impact is different from the intent, and stay humble enough to continue learning from those who take the time to invest in you enough to help you see where you need more learning and growth.

When you make a choice to hold space at the intersection, you will find yourself on a steep learning curve that will challenge and stretch you. I know this because I am still on this learning curve, still being stretched and challenged, and may, someday, look back at this book and recognize the gaps where I still had much to learn. Keep investing, though, because the potential results are worth it. You will find yourself in much deeper conversations and in much richer relationships, with greater and greater capacity to handle difficult situations and foster brilliance and creativity.

24

when there
is conflict

WHO AMONG US would say they are comfortable with conflict? I haven't yet encountered anyone who is; most of us have a strong aversion toward it. Some of us have learned, after a great deal of practice, to stick around for the hard stuff, and a rare few might actually enjoy certain types of conflict (those with personality disorders that thrive in chaos, for example). But for the most part, people will avoid it, try to redirect it, or unintentionally escalate it in an effort to protect themselves or justify their own violence.

Few have the skills to address it well.

Conflict aversion is a cultural problem that limits the way we develop as individuals and communities. It limits the way we communicate across differences. It limits our intimacy and our friendships. When we are conflict averse, we avoid having hard conversations, getting into uncomfortable disagreements with those we love, and upsetting those we don't understand. Because of our avoidance, we often tell half-truths and live half-authentic lives.

Few of us have any training in dealing with conflict. Most of us did not have parents who modelled conflict well. Many of us watched our educators enforce rules in the classroom that would shut down conflict rather than help us work our way through it. When we watch our politicians or other community leaders in action, we often see them jockeying for power and occasionally yelling at each other, but we rarely see them *working through* the conflict to a healthy resolution. If that happens at all, it's usually behind closed doors.

For a good indication of how conflict-avoidant our culture is, check out the nearest bookstore. On a recent visit, I was struck by how few books teach about conflict. In the relationship section there were a couple of books that had chapters on conflict in marriage, and in the fairly large business section two books taught leaders how to address conflict in what appeared to be a top-down "boss imposes peace" model. But no books addressed the kind of conflict that we deal with on an almost daily basis in our workplaces, neighbourhoods, or Facebook pages. In a bookstore the size of a large department store, there was next to nothing worthy of my investment.

Conflict is uncomfortable because it triggers our fear and unmet needs for safety and belonging. Especially for those who've been through trauma, conflict can trigger memories of abuse, injury, or insecurity. As Sarah Schulman says:

> *a traumatized person has been profoundly violated by some-
> one else's cruelty, overreaction, and/or lack of accountability.
> The experience could be incident-based (rape by a stranger or
> being hit by a drunken driver), or it could be ongoing over a
> long period of time (being constantly demeaned and beaten by
> a stepfather, paternal sexual invasion, alcoholic or mentally
> ill parents), or systematic (intense and constant experiences
> of prejudice, denial of one's humanity, deprivation, violence,*

occupation, genocide). The traumatized person's sense of their ability to protect themselves has been damaged or destroyed. They feel endangered, even if there is no actual danger in the present, because in the past they have experienced profoundly invasive cruelty and they know it is possible. Or in the case of ongoing oppression, they receive cruelty from one place, and project it onto another. [83]

There's another side of conflict aversion that we also need to consider: conflict avoidance is part of the social conditioning we receive in our supremacist culture. We were never taught healthy methods for addressing conflict, because if we had been, we wouldn't be as willing to uphold the current patriarchal, white supremacist culture. If we were more conflict equipped, those with social agency and status would not maintain as much control over us as they do.

Kyriarchy is the social system—or set of connecting social systems—built around domination, oppression, and submission. This system benefits from a conflict-averse culture, allowing those with the most power to enforce the rules that benefit them and use their power to intimidate and control those with lower rank. It keeps people in line because the kyriarchy can't handle the conflict that might emerge from disobedience.

It also helps them stay in control because they can keep members of different social ranks *separate* from each other. For example, if white women, women of colour, and trans women can't learn to communicate effectively due to an inability to handle conflict when it arises (consider the fallout from the Women's March, when more marginalized groups challenged those espousing white feminism), then feminism can never gain enough power to dismantle the patriarchy.

None of us escapes supremacy's skewed view of conflict. If we *have power*, we're more likely to shut conflict down when it threatens our access to power, or we may choose to escalate conflict and use it as a tool. If we *lack power*, we're likely to run from conflict because it threatens our safety, or we may escalate it to try to protect ourselves. According to Schulman:

> we have all experienced the patriarch, the male supremacist, the nationalist, the racist, or just the local provincial big man who will not tolerate any opposition. He can never be wrong. He can never apologize. He explodes in rage whenever there is another experience being presented. He belittles others but can't stand any criticism of himself. He may use criticism or cruelty to tear others apart, but his understanding of emotional life is shallow. He won't allow people to talk to him about what is going on. He doesn't seek resolution, which means to him that he would have to acknowledge having made a mistake, which is an impossibility. He is petty, the kind of person who sends an attacking email and then, when the recipient phones to discuss the conflict, won't take the call. He denies complexity, and the people around him do not challenge him directly. His partner, his friends, the people who feel protected by, elevated by, or who benefit from his power, organize other people to not oppose him. They deflect criticism from him. They are careful around him and are rewarded. He doesn't ask other people, "What are you feeling?"; never says, "I don't understand what is going on. How do you see it?" He acts as though others should follow his orders, and when they refuse he punishes, bullies, shuns, makes false accusations, organizes group exclusion, distorts narratives, and may threaten and use the law or even violence. He expects that once he asserts his position, everyone else will obey, fall in line, and that this is how the moment is resolved: through obedience.[84]

The two primary reasons why conflict is often escalated rather than addressed, says Schulman, are supremacy and trauma. I would add that these two things usually result not only in escalation but also in shutting down and avoidance. If we are viewing the world through the lens of either supremacy or trauma (or both), we tend to interpret conflict as "abuse" or "threat," and so our fight, flight, freeze, or tend-and-befriend mechanisms kick in. In both situations, we are doing our best to protect ourselves, either from future harm or from a loss of social rank in the supremacy. Both supremacy and trauma make us closed and self-centred.

When I talk about conflict aversion, I'm not just talking about some abstract concept; I'm talking about myself. I avoid conflict as avidly as anyone, perhaps even more. My Mennonite upbringing taught me to be a pacifist, but in my experience pacifism often provides an excuse for avoidance. My patriarchal upbringing taught me that women shouldn't rock the boat or talk too loudly or dare to confront the men in charge. My own insecurity and trauma imprint taught me that conflict is dangerous and that I would be rejected and/or harmed if I didn't stop it or run from it.

When I look back at my thirteen years of formal leadership in director positions of government and non-profit organizations, one of my greatest weaknesses was my conflict avoidance. I wanted everyone to get along, so I didn't welcome opinions that introduced too much contrariness. I was afraid to challenge people for bad behaviour, especially if they were confident white males, who were the most likely to trigger me. I overlooked instances where, in retrospect, I now recognize that bullying and mistreatment were happening. I was generally well-liked by my staff and didn't want to risk losing that affection, so I didn't push them as much as I should have, or challenge them when they treated each other badly.

I think I tell a common story, especially among women (and more specifically, I would say, among white women). But now that I have been out of that environment for several years, I can identify my blind spot with much more clarity. Sadly, I have also become aware of how my daughters learned to become conflict avoiders from me. I'm hoping they will witness my self-work on changing this.

My fragility and unwillingness to step into the discomfort of conflict helps uphold the patriarchy and white supremacy. I've seen this even more clearly since then, especially when I've participated in difficult conversations around race. If I am too easily offended by people who challenge my socially conditioned racism, then I will never dare to address it in myself and in the system that I benefit from. In that way, fragility perpetuates supremacy.

To be a more effective leader, facilitator, and coach, and to participate in effectively dismantling the patriarchy and other systems of supremacy, we need to become conflict equipped. This is a crucial skill for those who hold space in *all* its forms, not just for these deep discussions.

The journey to becoming more conflict equipped begins with a journey inward. Until we understand at least some of the roots of our own conflict aversion, we will likely continue responding to it with the same fight, flight, freeze, or tend-and-befriend reactions as we always have.

Start by taking a look at your own past to see more clearly what memories and fears are triggered when your first reaction is to run from—or escalate—conflict.

- What do you carry around in your subconscious about the dangers of conflict?

- What are you afraid will happen to you in conflict?

- What unmet needs are being triggered?

- What needs to be healed so that conflict becomes less of a flashpoint?

- How might it help to use the "noticing, labelling, being curious, and letting it pass" mindfulness practice mentioned in chapter 16 the next time conflict arises?

- How can you retrain yourself to pause long enough and choose a healthier response?

Begin considering how our aversion to conflict allows us to be complicit in upholding systems of supremacy. Do you turn a blind eye to bullying in your workplace because you're afraid to challenge it? Are there voices that aren't being heard because advocating for them would stir up conflict in your community? Is someone in your family getting hurt because you're afraid to be in conflict with the abuser? Does your fragility in difficult conversations mean that you withdraw and avoid future confrontations?

Once we understand our triggers and instances of complicity (and/or victimhood) in flawed systems, we can begin to seek out tools and resources to help us develop healthier relationships with conflict. Two of the people whose work I found helpful in this regard are John Paul Lederach and Marshall B. Rosenberg.

John Paul Lederach, who wrote multiple books on conflict and peace building, believes the very language we've adopted to address conflict is problematic:

> *"Conflict resolution" implies that conflict is bad—hence something that should be ended. It also assumes that conflict is a short-term phenomenon that can be "resolved" permanently*

through mediation or other intervention processes. "Conflict management" correctly assumes that conflicts are long-term processes that often cannot be quickly resolved, but the notion of "management" suggests that people can be directed or controlled as though they were physical objects. In addition, the notion of management suggests that the goal is the reduction or control of volatility more than dealing with the real source of the problem.[85]

Instead of conflict management, Lederach teaches conflict *transformation*, which allows us to see the *potential* in the conflict. Rather than simply seeking a resolution, he feels we should look for the ways that the conflict can transform the individuals involved, including the relationship between them and the culture of which they are part. When we develop a healthier relationship with conflict—and don't simply view it as a problem to be fixed—we can peer into it more deeply and imagine the better world it might reveal.

For example, I remember a relationship I had with a housemate in university. For reasons neither of us entirely understood or acknowledged, there was a simmering conflict in nearly every interaction we had. We each became annoyed with little things the other person would do around the house, like leaving dishes in the sink, using the other person's towels, and so on. And though we never had big blowups, we sniped at each other almost daily in passive-aggressive ways.

Finally, one of us (I can't remember who) decided that we needed to sit down and try to figure out why this was present in our relationship. We started by laying our frustrations on the table, and then we took it deeper. Slowly and tenderly, each of us opened up about how we were intimidated by the other person. She was an accomplished musician with obvious talents that everyone admired, and so I always felt inferior to her since my talents were of the less tangible/overt variety; I was sure people didn't find me as interesting or special as her. On the other hand, I had an easy way with people, natural leadership skills, and several close friendships that intimidated her because she felt awkward around people and was sure they didn't find her as likeable as me.

We talked long into the night, entering a level of vulnerability and trust that neither of us had experienced much of in other relationships. After that, we were inseparable friends, and other people expressed admiration for the depth of our friendship. When she got married a couple of years later, I was her maid of honour. Our relationship was dramatically transformed because we dared to step into the conflict and dig deeper for the potential it opened up. If we'd simply "resolved" it—found excuses or compromises for the little annoyances so that we could live together in relative harmony—we would never have discovered the potential for a life-changing friendship.

My housemate and I had fairly equal power and social rank, so the transformation of our conflict did not have far-reaching effects on the culture we were part of. But imagine a similar situation where this approach could change the fibre of a community. Imagine if the same work we did was being done by people within a community with racial or gender divides. I'm not suggesting the conversation would be the same as ours, because power imbalance changes the nature of the conflict, but a *transformed* conflict can heal divides and change relationships and power structures.

When I worked in non-profit management, I once confronted someone whose actions had irritated me for quite some time. It was a board member who often made sexist remarks that made me feel dismissed, especially since he had more power and social rank than I. Remarkably, when I finally confronted him, his attitude changed, and he began treating me with much more respect. At the very next board meeting, he became the champion of an idea I put forward, something I never would have imagined possible. (Note: I wouldn't advocate this kind of confrontation for all situations where a person is abusing their power. Use discernment about the risks involved, and bring in reinforcements, advocates, or allies when necessary.)

Another influential teacher in the field of conflict and peace building, Marshall B. Rosenberg, uses a practice similar to our mindfulness exercise in his work in Nonviolent Communication (NVC). There are four components to his Nonviolent Communication process: *observation, feelings, needs,* and *requests.*

> *First, we observe what is actually happening in a situation: what are we observing others saying or doing that is either enriching or not enriching our life? The trick is to be able to articulate this observation without introducing any judgement or evaluation—to simply say what people are doing that we either like or don't like. Next, we state how we feel when we observe this action: are we hurt, scared, joyful, amused, irritated? And thirdly, we say what needs of ours are connected to the feelings we have identified. An awareness of these three components is present when we use NVC to clearly and honestly express how we are... [The] fourth component addresses what we are wanting from the other person that would enrich our lives or make life more wonderful for us.*[86]

We can contribute to de-escalation and transformation by shifting from *reactionary* mode to *observation* mode, then being honest and vulnerable about our feelings and unmet needs while allowing the other person/people in the conflict to do the same. Everyone in the conflict potentially has the opportunity to have their needs met without there being a "winner" or "loser." (However, it should be noted that NVC does not fully address the power imbalances we discussed earlier, and some have critiqued it as being primarily useful for privileged people. When there is a distinct power imbalance, it will likely be much more difficult for some parties to express their emotions and unmet needs than others. If you want to learn more about these critiques, google "decolonizing Nonviolent Communication.")

One of the best things that practices like NVC teach is the importance of pausing. A pause gives people a chance to shift out of reactivity into a more balanced response. A pause, especially when accompanied with deep breathing techniques, movement, and mindfulness, can help people's brains to shift from amygdala hijacking into prefrontal cortex thinking. For example, if you are facilitating a group where conflict erupts, you could slow the process down by inviting people to pause for a moment and consider what they're feeling and what unmet needs are being triggered in the situation.

I once facilitated a retreat that deteriorated into conflict and shadow. In that case, because it was late in the day when things escalated, I chose not to address it right away but instead invited people to leave the circle quietly and spend the evening in self-care and contemplation. I asked them to hold the discomfort rather than run from it and to seek wisdom in their own mindfulness practices. In the morning we were fresh and ready to transform what happened into meaningful learning and a deepening of relationships. That physical and emotional pause in the gathering had a remarkable impact on the conflict from the night before.

As I deepen my understanding of how to become more conflict equipped, I find myself turning increasingly toward Indigenous practices such as healing circles. At least here in Canada (and probably in other places as well) we can receive many gifts by paying attention to the ways Indigenous nations approach peace building, reconciliation, and community healing.

In the article "Indigenous Centered Conflict Resolution Processes in Canada," I am struck by the way language reflects a culture's approach to conflict:

> As Stó:lō Nation legal traditions do not have a word for "justice," Stó:lō Elders created the word, Qwi:qwelstóm kwelam t' ey (qwi:qwelstóm)—roughly translated as, "they are teaching you, moving you toward the good"—to describe program initiatives developed with the assistance of Wenona Victor in the late 1990s. It is a concept of "justice" centered upon the family and reflects a way of life that focuses on relationships and the interconnectedness of all life. It has four key elements: "the role of elders; the role of family, family ties, and community connections; teachings; and spirituality."
>
> ... When asked to participate in a Circle, participants are also asked to "come prepared to share all four sacred parts of being... the physical, the mental, the emotional, and the spiritual." Preparation for a Circle engages the person's mental, physical, emotional and spiritual lives. Not only are participants asked to come physically ready to participate by being "well-rested, fed, and drug- and alcohol-free for at least four days prior to the Circle date" but they are also asked to be mentally ready by coming to the Circle with "a strong mind, in order to make best use of the words that will be shared." Preparing for participating in a Circle may depend on whether the Circle is a "healing or a peacemaking Circle" since in healing Circles the focus is "almost exclusively on restoring balance to an individual(s)" where a peacemaking Circle focuses mostly on gaining an "understanding by all Circle participants regarding a specific incident."[87]

At the heart of the Stó:lō Circle is community and family. The purpose of their healing and peace building is always to reconnect a person or people to the relationships that sustain them and hold them accountable.

The same cannot be said for many of the other justice or conflict resolution processes we witness in the world, which are focused more on punishment of the "offender" and protection of the "victim." These systems, as we discussed earlier, tend to support a system of supremacy and dominance. They result in further separation rather than a deepening connection.

The Indigenous ways of addressing conflict that I've been exposed to tend to be highly spiritual and ceremonial, reconnecting those in conflict to their higher selves and their spiritual guides. Elders are brought in to offer teachings and ceremony, and often there is a deep connection to Mother Earth. In a Navajo healing ceremony, for example, a sand painting is created on the earth by a shaman or "chanter" and the person who is out of balance (ill or in conflict) is placed in the middle of the painting. After the painting is finished, the chanter rubs their skin with sand from the images, bringing them back into the balance depicted by the painting.

In the book *Connecting to Our Ancestral Past*, Francesca Mason Boring writes about how she uses a combination of family constellations and Indigenous ceremony and ritual to support people in healing the conflict within themselves and their families or communities: "Relationship with creation, the Creator, and the ancestors has often been surgically removed from many Western healing movements." She goes on to say that each of us, whether we know our roots or not, should tap into our "Indigenous knowing field" in order to access the wisdom of our ancestors and Creation.

> *That all people have within their ancient roots some indigenous field allows an opening to wisdom arising within our individual family fields. Citizens of the United States, Canada,*

and Australia (countries of immigrants and descendants of immigrants) still have within their knowing "fields" the motherlands that hold their ancestors' blood and bones. A person may, on the surface, have no history, no roots, and no remembrance of traditions. However, within the family field, our ancestry, our genetic memory, and within our blood, there is a remembrance of old songs and ceremonies and a different way of knowing. The ancestries that refugees and transplanted people deny or dismiss still contain within their fields truths, teachings, and secrets that can restore strength and release our sense of isolation.[88]

In my experience with the Indigenous peoples of Canada, I am struck by their willingness to gather and be in right relationship with people who represent their colonizers and oppressors. Their approach is often one of conflict transformation, seeking to reconcile and grow something beautiful together rather than to blame and shame. After our city, Winnipeg, was named the most racist in Canada, I attended an Indigenous sharing and drumming circle, and when I walked into the room, the elder leading the circle handed me a drum. It did not concern him that I was a settler; he simply saw me as someone willing to be in relationship with him.

At a talk I attended, Murray Sinclair, head of the Truth and Reconciliation Commission on residential schools (a topic that is part of our history in which Indigenous children were taken from their families, placed in residential schools, and forced to assimilate and give up their culture and language), said, "Settlers don't need to be afraid of us. It's not like we want to send you all back where you came from. On the contrary—we need you!" He also said, "Reconciliation turns on one very simple concept... *I want to be your friend.* And I want you to be mine. That way, when something goes wrong, we'll figure out how to fix it together."

This, I believe, is at the heart of conflict transformation: a recognition that we need each other, that we're stronger together, and that when something goes wrong, we'll figure out how to fix it together.

In your own exploration of holding space for conflict, I encourage you to explore the tools that will help you peer into it, face it, learn from it, and heal and transform it. Perhaps there are healing rituals to help you move past conflict, tools that you can adopt or develop together with your community. Avoid appropriating practices from outside your own cultural experience; instead, look for people from within that culture to guide and teach you. Perhaps there are ways to gather people into circle for deeper, more vulnerable conversations. Perhaps there is new language that will help you move from "fix-it" mode into "transformation" mode.

25

the circle as container

THERE IS ONE practice that has become, for me, the embodiment of holding collective space.

That practice is the circle.

Several years ago, the Canadian government apologized to our First Nations people for the injustices of residential schools. I had the privilege of participating in a sharing circle for the Truth and Reconciliation Commission, a circle that offered all of us an opportunity to seek healing as a country.

In the circle, we were asked to share how we were personally impacted by residential schools, what we believe reconciliation means, and how our countries and communities could heal. Only a few of the people in the circle had been to residential schools themselves, but all of us were influenced by the deep wounds our country bears.

One woman shared how bewildered she was as a four-year-old when her older sister disappeared from their home, and then how she too was eventually taken. Another woman talked about the abuse she suffered at the hands of her alcoholic husband who was a residential school survivor. A young man, who worked as a videographer at sharing circles similar to the one we were in, talked about how the priests and nuns at some of the residential schools put needles into the tongues of children who were caught speaking their Indigenous languages while at school.

Almost every First Nations person who talked expressed the shame that the residential school system instilled in their culture. Whether they were in residential schools themselves or raised by parents or grandparents who were survivors, each one of them carried the burden of being an oppressed people made to feel less than their oppressors. It was a poignant reminder that healing from oppression takes many generations.

An interesting thing happened around the diverse and multicultural circle. Those who shed the most tears were often people of settler descent. It was clear that the shame and pain in the circle was not only among the Indigenous people. Those who are descendants of oppressors also needed healing from the pain their ancestors caused. (In retrospect, I also recognize the tendency some of us have to centre on our own pain when we feel uncomfortable with the depth of others' pain.)

As I sat in that circle, I opened myself up to the pain I carried and the pain that I and my lineage have caused. I felt the pain of both colonizers and the colonized. I held space in my heart for the pain stories that all of us carry and continue to perpetuate, even in small and seemingly harmless ways.

When the talking piece came to me, I shared a story about how some of my own racism had emerged after I'd been raped by an Indigenous man. After years of healing, though, I was able to see that that man was likely acting out his own pain as a result of the generations of trauma of his people. I said that I was choosing not to hold hatred toward that man, but instead seek healing. At the end of the circle, two young Indigenous men came to hug me and I knew that healing had happened for each of us.

The last question we were asked in that circle was about how we thought our country could be healed, a question far too big for me. I don't yet know how to hold space for the healing of a whole country. I don't think anyone does. However, I do know that what heals *me* begins to heal a country. And what continues my healing is the opportunity to sit in circle, to hold space for grief, pain, and transformation.

Sharing stories offers us the opportunity to see each other through new lenses, to peel away the layers of power imbalance, hierarchy, and pain. Sitting in circle with people who are different from us helps shift our paradigms and change the world, one relationship at a time. That's why the circle is my methodology of choice when holding collective space.

Circles give us the chance to sit in equal positions, look into each other's eyes, listen deeply to each other's stories, and build or rebuild trust. Circles help us hold the complexity of power imbalances, conflict, and deep collective grief and fear. Circles teach us to be present for each other's pain and share the burden of it without projecting it onto each other.

Years ago, not long after Matthew was born and died, I searched for a leadership model different from what I saw in the government job where I worked as a manager. I came across the book *Calling the Circle: The First and Future Culture* by Christina Baldwin. As soon as I found it, I knew my life would be forever changed. In the years since, I have spent a lot of time learning about The Circle Way from Baldwin and her partner, Ann Linnea. (They've since written another book called *The Circle Way: A Leader in Every Chair.*) I've incorporated the teaching into my own work.

In the circle, there is "a leader in every chair." Each person is invited to take responsibility for what they bring into the circle, what they contribute to the energy and wisdom of the circle, and what they take out. Imagine, if you will, that there are many cells that have come together to serve a common purpose, drawn together by the sensors on their psychic membranes. These cells form a circle to hold space collectively, yet each cell still maintains and takes responsibility for its own psychic membrane. The circle then becomes a new type of membrane—like the "membrane" of skin that covers your body, made up of millions of cells—that holds space for work which needs to happen in that space. Like the psychic membrane, the circle collectively decides what to allow in, what to keep out, and how to seek out what is needed in order to maintain homeostasis inside.

When we sit in circle, we speak to the centre, placing our emotions, stories, and questions into that sacred space rather than projecting them at others. We use a talking piece to ensure that all voices are heard. It focuses our listening, and keeps us from cross-talking, interrupting, or trying to fix each other. We have shared agreements that help guide how we interact with each other and what values we hold collectively.

The circle slows conversations and invites us to deeper listening and more intentional speaking.

When I was teaching in university, considerable conflict once bubbled up in a group project in which the whole class was involved. I had no idea how to resolve it, only a sense that a circle would help us hold space for the hurt feelings and anger that were present. I invited the students to push the tables against the walls and bring their chairs into a circle. Then I passed a talking piece (a flip chart marker, the only thing I could find in the classroom), inviting people to share what they were experiencing in the group project.

The first time around, people shared tentatively, but I knew there was more that needed to surface, so I passed the talking piece around again. This time, the person who came to me with the most grievances, a young man who was both gay and a person of colour, paused for a moment when the talking piece came to him, and then decided to dive in and admit how marginalized he felt and how he often didn't feel listened to in the group project.

As soon as he shared, I could sense the energy of the circle changing. People started to lean in more. When it was their turn, they followed his lead and opened up with more vulnerability. Some cried, some admitted that they too were feeling marginalized, ignored, or pushed aside, and some took responsibility for contributing to the conflict and apologized.

When the talking piece came back to me again, I had a sense that it needed to go around one more time, so I passed it on. This time, students—many of whom had wanted to drop out of the group—began recommitting themselves to the project, recognizing what they could learn from it, and expressing determination to work together in a more generative way. By the end of the third round of sharing, the conflict was transformed and there was excitement about what lay ahead.

I said very little in our time together and didn't give any instructions on how to resolve what showed up. I simply offered invitations each time I passed the talking piece. The students collectively held space for their own pain, fear, and frustration, and figured out how to move forward together. The wisdom came from the *circle*, not from a teacher at the front of the room.

Circles don't always work that quickly or have the same outcome. Sometimes the shadow takes many iterations to fully reveal itself. Sometimes there are people in the circle who won't let go of their pain or face their blind spots in order to move forward. Sometimes the power imbalance is too great to allow the most marginalized to feel safe. And sometimes there is a realization that the circle is complete in its purpose and it's time for people to part ways. But time and again I see how circles deepen conversation, transform conflict, grow relationships, generate collective wisdom, and allow us to hold space for very complex challenges.

There are many sources of information about how to practise circle, and I encourage you to explore multiple teachings or find one you love and dive in. I spent a lot of time learning, practising, and teaching The Circle Way, and I'm a long-time member of Gather the Women, an organization that supports women's circles all over the world. I've also had the privilege of being in several circles led by Indigenous elders using an ancient practice of circle that has been part of their culture since time immemorial.

Circle is part of cultures all over the world, and you may find a tradition indigenous to the place where you live, or from your own lineage. You can find teachers to guide you in how to host a circle. (The Circle Way has workshops listed on their website, and Gather the Women has useful resources about starting and hosting women's circles.) You can also begin simply by inviting people to arrange chairs in a circle and passing a talking piece from hand to hand. It starts with a simple concept, but it opens the door to complexity and opportunity for growth and transformation.

We need more circles. We need circles in our classrooms, circles in our governments, and circles in our homes. Collectively, if we hold space in the circle, the circle can hold our transformation.

26

seeking sovereignty

AFTER A COUPLE of years spent working with, and writing about, holding space, it suddenly dawned on me that there was an important aspect of this concept that I'd missed earlier. Everything I wrote about, taught, and contemplated came down to one profound realization. The heart of holding space is this: *freedom*.

| We hold space so that all may be free.

Free of judgment, free of fear, free of injustice, and free of discrimination, prejudice, and shame. Free to emerge from a liminal space journey with pure, powerful truth.

This is no small thing, holding space. Because no matter its size—for one person or for a group—we hold space to give each other the freedom to do hard and liberating soul work. To heal trauma. To feel deep emotions and express unspoken needs. To transform conflict and rewrite stories of abuse. We hold space to accommodate both light and shadow, agony and delight. To find our path in the world.

| When we hold space, we create a container for liberation.

Freedom is not an easy thing to hold space for. It's not an airy-fairy, pie-in-the-sky ideal that we attract if we think good thoughts and send out love and light. It takes hard work and drags us through dark and chaotic places. As any freedom fighter will tell you, it comes at a high cost. Freedom from oppression, fear, injustice, indignity, poverty, supremacy, violence, discrimination, exploitation—all these require that we make strong commitments, take risks, put our bodies on the line, and stay in the struggle even when it gets ugly.

Nelson Mandela, a man whose twenty-seven years in prison taught him more about freedom than most of us will ever know, once said, "To be free is not merely to cast off one's chains, but to live in a way that respects and enhances the freedom of others."

As we learned earlier, we hold space for our own freedom within our own psychic membranes. That, in turn, allows us to hold space for the journeys of others. Our strong psychic membranes first protect us and give us space for growth. Once we have found, fought for, and claimed our own freedom to be authentically, courageously, fiercely ourselves, we can then extend it to other people so that we all may be free.

• • •

No one is free until we all are free.[89]

MARTIN LUTHER KING JR.

• • •

| A container that holds space for liberation also holds
| space for sovereignty.

According to Wikipedia, sovereignty is "the full right and power of a governing body over itself, without any interference from outside sources or bodies."[90]

To bring a practical analogy to the concept of sovereignty, let's look at the work I used to be part of in ending global hunger. At the non-profit in which I worked, we often talked about the three categories used for food-related support: food aid, food security, and food sovereignty. If you give a man a fish (food aid), he'll eat for a day. If you teach a man to fish (food security), he'll have food for a lifetime. But what if you put a fence around the pond and only allow him to fish on certain days and he has to go hungry in between? Ensuring he has *agency* over his food choices and accessibility to the sources of that food is food sovereignty. In the non-profit world, we supported food sovereignty by funding projects where people advocated for their right to adequate food and agricultural resources.

With full sovereignty, a woman can fish at the pond if and when she wants. She can make decisions about that pond and choose whether or not to share the pond with her neighbours. She is not at the mercy of oppressive or colonizing systems.

Largely, the term "sovereignty" is associated with nations and their governments. But how might it apply to our own lives? How does it change our relationship with ourselves and with others if we consider ourselves to be sovereign alongside those we're in relationship with? How does it impact the integrity of how we hold space for each other?

To claim sovereignty means that I get to decide what happens to my body, heart, and mind. It means I have agency and autonomy and am not controlled or manipulated by anyone. I get to make my own decisions and live with the consequences. I get to choose who I am in relationship with and how much space to give them in my life. I can choose to end relationships that cause me harm and walk away from situations and communities that don't honour my sovereignty. A sovereign being has a healthy psychic membrane.

If I treat you as someone entitled to your own sovereignty, it means that I assume you have the same right to self-govern your life as I. You get to tell me how you want to be treated and I can choose to accept those boundaries or walk away.

Sovereignty is what we've been talking about throughout this discussion on holding space—that we offer love to each other without attachment, manipulation, control, or boundary crossing. It's the starting point to developing healthy, strong social contracts between us.

For me (and possibly for you) it feels quite foreign to think of myself as sovereign. I have all kinds of old scripts running in my head, telling me that it's selfish to claim the "full right and power" of my own "governing body" without "any interference from outside sources or bodies." Shouldn't I be nicer and more agreeable than that? Shouldn't I accommodate other people's needs before my own and extend grace to those who interfere? Shouldn't I overlook the boundary-crossers if they offer me safety, protection, resources, or employment? Aren't they entitled to certain rights if I need what they have to offer?

Recently, I had an opportunity to claim my sovereignty in a relationship with someone who didn't always respect it in the past. This person was going to be in my house, and I was nervous about it because of past experience. They would fix things without being asked and make judgments about my choices on how I arrange and maintain my house. As the time approached for the visit, I realized that I had a choice: say nothing and risk further violations or claim my sovereignty and communicate what kind of behaviour I found unacceptable in my space.

I chose the latter. With a simple text, I let the person know what the ground rules would be for the visit. If they wished to comply, they were welcome, but if they didn't, they could choose not to come. They chose to comply.

In essence, what I did was establish a "treaty" with this person, claiming my sovereignty in the relationship and in my space and laying out the expectations for what was acceptable.

A treaty is an agreement under international law entered into by actors in international law, namely sovereign states and international organizations.[91]

If we can bring the definition of sovereignty into our own lives, perhaps we can also consider how sovereignty can be negotiated via treaty between sovereign individuals in a relationship. The problem, as I see it, is that few of us have an embodied understanding of sovereignty because we have been socially conditioned by colonial systems.

Colonization is a process by which a central system of power dominates the surrounding land and its components.[92]

Colonizers are not respecters of treaties. They may create them, but they use their power to manipulate what the treaties contain and/or ignore them to take the resources they want. In a colonial system, everyone is impacted. Both the colonizers and the colonized become shaped by the imbalance of power and the lack of respect for boundaries and sovereignty. Some learn to take what's not theirs; others learn that their rights are easily violated and resources easily taken. In a colonial system, nobody walks away unscathed. Nobody ends up with a well-balanced understanding of what it means to hold sovereignty as a core value in a relationship.

Most of us find ourselves somewhere at the intersection, having power in some relationships and no power in others.

As a result of this ingrained concept of colonization, people the world over develop a warped sense of how to be in relationships with each other, both on small and large scales, not only community-to-community and country-to-country but also in one-on-one relationships. We cross boundaries and downplay our own rights to have those boundaries. We fail to communicate our expectations of how we want to be treated. We are victimized, we hijack space, we manipulate. We run away from conflict because we haven't been adequately prepared for the work it takes to negotiate and maintain fair treaties. We harm each other and suffer from the wounds inflicted on us. Consequently, we face the kind of actions being challenged by social movements such as #MeToo, Idle No More, and Black Lives Matter. And those who challenge the status quo face the resulting backlash. When colonized and/or oppressed people rise up to claim their sovereignty, it makes those in power nervous.

How do we change this? How do we decolonize ourselves and our culture to reclaim and honour sovereignty in our relationships and communities?

It is a problem on every scale, large, small, and in between. There is no one-size-fits-all solution. We have to do the hard work of claiming our own sovereignty piece by piece, and that needs to be accompanied with a lot of self- and community-care. We have to do the hard work of dismantling our imbalanced systems of power. We have to practise negotiating and communicating better treaties in our personal relationships. And we have to address the ways in which the colonizers in our countries have ignored and/or failed to negotiate and ratify treaties with other sovereign nations and people groups.

It is inevitable that dismantling these power structures— on every level—means encountering tremendous resistance and fear from those who benefit from that power. Because of that, holding space for this transformation requires knowing how to enter into conflict in more generative ways so that all parties emerge with their sovereignty intact. Practised skills are needed to have harder conversations and not run away whenever we feel attacked for violating another person's sovereignty. We need to learn how to communicate expectations and boundaries and not be offended when other people communicate theirs. And we most certainly have to evolve in the way we raise our children so that new generations can grow up with a better sense of their own sovereignty.

I've begun the slow and sometimes painful work of decolonizing my relationships and I know I still have a long way to go. Sometimes I feel the way I did when I first started dancing—as though I'm stumbling across the room, stomping on people's toes while trying to find a rhythm that fits us both.

Just as dancing isn't a natural act for someone raised with Mennonite roots, claiming sovereignty doesn't feel natural for someone raised with colonial roots. But when we learn to dance together well, we learn to respect each other's space, honour each other's bodies, and stay out of the way of each other's brilliance. We find intimacy without violating each other's space, spending many hours in practice, negotiating the space between us, and holding that space for each other. We might still step on each other's toes now and then, but we commit to staying on the dance floor and trying again. When one person violates the social contract we've made, we each take responsibility and figure out how to move on.

The better we become at dancing together, the closer we are to being truly free.

27

holding space for human evolution

A S I MENTIONED in the introduction, when I first started writing about holding space, I was determined to give credit where credit was due. (I didn't want to colonize anyone else's ideas.) I searched for the originator of the concept, but the lineage wasn't entirely clear.

I learned about it from the work of Harrison Owen, who first started talking about it in the facilitation field, but Donald Winnicott was speaking similar language in the education and child development field. And then I heard that it showed up in *other* fields, including yoga and spiritual direction. There seems to be no straightforward thread connecting all these areas (at least not one that's apparent to my limited research capacity), but there is clear indication the concept travelled and met responsive audiences.

My friend TuBears, in whose home I write these final chapters, is a Choctaw elder and shamanic practitioner. We have had many conversations about the concept of holding space, and she recently told me about the time it first emerged for her.

When she hosted vision quests in the early nineties, she took people into the woods, and for each individual quester, she drew a circle on the ground. She instructed them to stay in the circle for four days without food or water, with only a sleeping bag to shelter them.

She recognized early on that she couldn't do this work alone, so she brought in helpers who checked in on the questers periodically. Each helper was responsible for two questers.

The first thing TuBears did before the quests began was to light a fire at the base camp where she and her helpers stayed. The fire was kept burning throughout the quest, and it served as the hub of the circle. It held a connection to all the questers, moving energy and strength out to their separate locations.

To assist the helpers to understand what they were doing in support of the questers, TuBears started using the term "holding space." It's not a term she remembers learning from anyone specific; it just emerged for her and felt like the right way to describe it. She told the helpers to be very responsive to the needs and emotions that showed up in their own bodies, because those were very likely the same needs and emotions the questers sent out, even though they didn't actually see or speak with the questers.

"If you feel hunger or fear," she would tell them, "hold that in your body, because you are doing it in support of the questers you're holding space for. You are feeling their feelings for them and responding to their needs accordingly. When one of the questers comes into your mind, it's likely because they are crying out for support. Hold them in your heart and send out the energy they need."

TuBears also told me about the times when she was a dancer at the sun dance, where they would dance for several days in the hot sun without food and water. At each sun dance, there were people around the edges who provided care for the dancers. Though they didn't use the term "holding space," it was much the same concept.

TuBears told me, "The cooks working in the kitchen sometimes get cravings, and they eat those foods, knowing that the craving came from one of the dancers." When TuBears worked in the kitchen one year, she craved celery and later learned that one of the dancers craved celery during the dance. When TuBears danced another year, she craved watermelon, and later heard about someone in the kitchen who ate it on her behalf.

I've also heard about concepts related to holding space from Maori people who've attended my retreats in New Zealand, and was told it resonates with my friend Nestar's Ugandan culture. Talking to TuBears convinced me that the wisdom of holding space is ancient wisdom that has always been present and available to us, but which—except for those most connected to an ancient way of knowing—lay dormant, waiting for humanity to recognize the need for it again. Because it's a universal truth available to all, we see its resurgence not just in one place but in multiple places at the same time.

When TuBears was a young child, she remembers her grandfather telling her, "White people have had their throats cut." It took her many years to understand what her grandfather meant, but she finally got it. "White people have had their heads severed from their *hearts*," she said. "You've lost the connection and you don't know how to stitch it back together again. What I think this work can do is stitch it back together so there can be wholeness again. You're holding space for spirits to heal."

A shiver moved through my body when she said that to me. I knew exactly what she was talking about. Just that morning, I'd written in my journal about how, when I find myself getting close to some deep and potentially disruptive wisdom in this work, I often feel my throat start to constrict. I never understood what that was about. Her words helped me recognize that what was showing up in my throat was the ancient trauma of disconnection. This disconnection runs so deep in our culture that not only have we severed our heads from our hearts, we have severed ourselves from Mother Earth. We have let our disconnected heads lead us into our own destruction—a trauma that still resides in our bodily memory.

We are so disconnected that we don't know how to stop this harmful course we're on. We don't know how to return to a relationship with our hearts and with Mother Earth. As a result, we've been on a destructive path leading to climate change, species extinction, and huge islands of plastic in the ocean.

In evolutionary biology, the term "convergent evolution" describes the process whereby unrelated organisms independently evolve similar traits as a result of having to adapt to similar environmental challenges. For example, insects, birds, and bats all evolved into winged creatures in response to similar environmental shifts. In the same way, different groups of people in different parts of the world find similar wisdom and characteristics evolving in response to the environmental challenges they face.

I believe this is what's happening with the emergence of holding space; the same concept is being recognized in different communities simultaneously without any direct, traceable link. My blog post went viral in 2015 because millions of people around the world immediately recognized and connected to it. The post tapped into a hunger and readiness waiting to be awakened. It was a hunger for a different way of walking in the world and a different way of being in relationship with each other, the earth, spirit, and ourselves. Environmental conditions created the perfect space in which this wisdom could grow.

The challenges we now face—including climate change, out-of-control consumerism and economic growth, increased conflict, the threat of extinction, and the rise of patriarchy and white supremacy in response to movements that challenge it—

see us being thrust into a liminal space journey that leaves us frightened and disoriented. If we don't evolve, we risk extinction.

We must figure out how to walk through the chaos of this liminal space together in order to emerge into the next spiral of human existence.

What I offer in this book is not new wisdom. Instead, I have, to the best of my ability, tapped into a source of ancient wisdom that has evolved to meet the challenges we now face.

Holding space is what we need for this time. We can return to it and grow it, letting it change us. We can let it reveal new practices and revive old ones. We can turn to the wisdom-keepers who can bring us back into relationship with Mother Earth. We can gather in circle and grow new collective wisdom in the spaces between us.

Another thing TuBears said to me in one of our many conversations is that we must return to ceremony. "All ceremonies we put together are about holding space," she said. "When I get up in the morning, for example, I greet Mother Earth and Grandfather Sun. I ask them to hold space for me, and they always do. They show up every day and hold space for us."

She also told me of a time when the grandmothers in her childhood community gathered one night after someone in their village lost a loved one. They sat all night in a sweat lodge in the dark, wailing on behalf of the grieving family. "They wailed and they pushed that pain down into Mother Earth," she said. "Mother Earth knows how to take that pain, mix it with mud and water, and transform it into compost so something beautiful can grow out of it."

That's the kind of ceremony we need more of right now—wailing for the pain and grief of humankind, releasing it into Mother Earth, and asking Her to transform it into something beautiful. Perhaps, if we learn to hold space for such a ceremony, we can emerge from this liminal space journey transformed.

AS I WRITE this final chapter, I sit in the sacred space where TuBears writes and where she guides people on shamanic journeys into the spirit world. It was an act of great generosity on her part to offer it to me. Her sacred objects surround me: drums, medicine wheels, a walking stick with the head of a hawk on the top, rattles made of animal skin, a medicine pouch made from a turtle shell and a coyote head, cedar branches and sage, the wings of a hawk, and paintings of bears and Native dancers. I curl up in a big chair covered with a buffalo hide that TuBears received from an elder at sun dance. Just outside the door of this beautiful space is a Native princess carved out of the trunk of an old tree, standing as a guardian for what happens here. Around the corner is a tree that TuBears whistles to each morning when she walks into her space. When she whistles, ravens come to perch in the tree.

This is the perfect place to complete this book. In this space I am grounded and supported, held by the natural world and a lineage of dancers and warriors and elders and gardeners who held space on this land for centuries before I arrived. While I am here, I am reminded to stay humble and serve not as a self-made expert but as a channel for the wisdom asking to flow through me. I am not indigenous to this land, so I sit with deep gratitude that I was welcomed into this space and given access to wisdom severed from my own lineage.

I humbly offer this to you and hope the teachings in this book stretch you, change you, challenge and inspire you. I hope that you will show up differently as a result, going even deeper than I have so far. Holding space is an evolving work meant for an evolving world, and I trust that those who come after will hold space for it to grow even further to meet the coming needs.

Thank you for showing up and for being willing to hold space with me.

acknowledgements

I T'S IMPOSSIBLE TO grow a body of work around a topic like holding space without a large community of support. There are many, many people who have held space for me and for this work and it is in relationship with them that I have done some of my deepest learning on the topic.

To my editor, Brenda Dammann... You held this work so tenderly and helped it to blossom into an even more beautiful version of itself. Thank you for believing in it from the beginning and for being the kind of person I could trust so explicitly.

To everyone at Page Two... I knew that I'd found the right publishing company to entrust this work to the moment I sat down with Trena at the Gumboot Café in Roberts Creek, BC. Thank you for pouring yourselves into this project with such big, open hearts. Thank you for offering such a wonderful mix of skills and kindness and commitment to the work. Thank you for giving it a broader reach than I could have imagined on my own. Thank you to Trena, Jesse, Amanda, John, Alison, Annemarie, Gabrielle, Taysia, Deanna, Brian, and Michelle.

To my friends Lorraine Lima and TuBears... Not only have you been my cheerleaders from the moment I met you, but you lovingly provided a special space in your backyard where I could write the final pages. Thank you, Lorraine, for all of the nourishment and kindness, the cups of tea and the fruit smoothies in the middle of my afternoon slumps. Thank you, TuBears, for the buffalo rug to curl up in, for the many wise conversations, and for the moments of ceremony that blessed me and the work.

To my "work-wife" who evolved from assistant to business manager to business partner, Krista Folkers Dela Rosa... None of this would have been possible without your steadfast support. You showed up at just the right time, when I could no longer bear the weight of this work alone, and you graciously and smoothly took more and more of it onto your own shoulders. Thank you for loving this work as much as I do, for holding it with me even when it was hard, and for being willing to evolve as the work keeps calling us into bigger and bigger spaces.

To the teaching/mentorship team that has helped to support this work as it has evolved: Sharon Wichman, Susan Dupuis, Joy Onyschak, Emily Gillies, MaryJo Burkhard, Celeste Inez Mathilda, and Brenda Barritt... Thank you for your commitment to this work and for all of the ways in which you have enhanced it. Thank you for your willingness to grow and to stretch along with the work and to hold space so that others can learn alongside you.

To the early readers of this book, Saleha Alshehri, Dr. Jo Ann Unger, Shameeka Smalling, Sharon Simon, and Celeste Inez Mathilda... Thank you for helping to make the book as accessible as possible to diverse audiences, for making sure I didn't make too many blunders from a scientific or psychological perspective, and for ensuring I used gender-inclusive language throughout. You helped to make the book more beautiful and meaningful.

To all of those who have stretched this work into international spaces... There are now too many to name, but I want to mention the early adopters—those who believed in it enough near the beginning to trust their intuition and invite me to their countries and communities: Georgia Bailey of Welcome to the BIG House in Australia, Brenda Zwinkels of Davotes in the Netherlands, Kelly Townsend in New Zealand, Lynn Thomas of EAGALA in the United States, and the team at the Bert Hellinger Institute in the Netherlands. Thank you for your ongoing support and friendship and for your belief that this work is needed in your parts of the world. Thank you for the ways in which you each uniquely hold space for your own work so that collectively we can make the world a little kinder.

To the learning communities that helped shape this work and the concepts in this book (especially in the early days when I was just waking up to what it means to hold space): ALIA, The Art of Hosting, The Circle Way, and Gather the Women . . . Thank you for all that you have taught me and that we have learned together. Thank you for being the communities in which I felt so at home when I needed such a home, where my ideas suddenly made more sense because others were having similar ones. Thank you especially to my teachers, Christina Baldwin and Ann Linnea, for the many ways that you have modelled the art of holding space.

To all of the friends who've sat with me in long conversations that helped shape this work throughout the years . . . Again, there are too many to name and I'm afraid to miss some, but I need to at least mention Beth Sanders, Saleha Alshehri, Desiree Adaway, Segun Olude, Jo Ann Unger, Pamela Slim, and Amanda Winn, who helped me find clarity and truth in my quest to put words to these concepts. Your friendship means the world to me.

To the people all over the world who have been participants in my online and in-person workshops and retreats . . . You helped this work grow, you helped me develop concepts and fine-tune ideas, and you generously shared your stories and wisdom. Thank you for showing up and for holding space in such beautiful, authentic ways.

To the various circles that hold space with and for me—my women's circle, my sporadic circle of friends, my online mastermind, and the "spectacular six"... Thank you for your love and support, for many open-hearted and thought-provoking conversations, and for holding space for my growth and the emergence of this work.

To my siblings and their spouses, Brad and Sue, Dwight and Lorna, and Cynthia and J-L... Thank you for your ongoing love and support. Thank you for walking with me through the hard times that taught me so much about the meaning of holding space—especially the deaths of our parents and my son, Matthew. Thank you for being such a solid and dependable place for me to turn whenever I need shelter, laughter, kindness, or a moment of nostalgia over our memories of growing up on the farm.

To my beautiful, unique, courageous daughters, Nicole, Julie, and Madeline... You give my life more meaning and you teach me more about holding space than anyone else in the world has. You help me see the world through a lens that's broader than my own. You continue to stretch me, challenge me, and nudge me to be the best version of myself that I can be. When necessary, you forgive me for the ways I still fumble. You are each uniquely gifted and you each bring something special to my life. I am immensely grateful that I get to be your mom and that I get to share this life with you. Thanks for putting up with my long hours of writing and the many times when I needed to be away from home to write or teach.

To those who've already passed on but who will always be an important part of this work: my mom, Margaret; my dad, Arthur; and my son, Matthew... You will always have a special place in my heart. Your deaths were some of the hardest moments of my life AND they taught me such incredible lessons in how to live and love and hold space. This book wouldn't exist without you.

notes

1. Harrison Owen, *Open Space Technology: A User's Guide*, 3rd ed. (San Francisco: Berrett-Koehler Publishers, 2008).
2. D.W. Winnicott, *The Child, the Family, and the Outside World*, 2nd revised ed. (Boston: Da'Capo Lifelong Books, 1992).
3. "Donald Winnicott (1896–1971)," GoodTherapy (website), goodtherapy .org/famous-psychologists/donald-winnicott.html.
4. Dr. Seuss, *Oh, the Places You'll Go!* (New York: Random House, 1990).
5. "Liminality," Wikipedia, en.wikipedia.org/wiki/Liminality.
6. Richard Rohr, "Grieving as Sacred Space," *Sojourners*, January–February 2002, sojo.net/magazine/january-february-2002/grieving-sacred-space.
7. Richard Rohr, *Everything Belongs: The Gift of Contemplative Prayer* (Chestnut Ridge, NY: Crossroad Publishing, 2003).
8. Parker J. Palmer, *Let Your Life Speak: Listening for the Voice of Vocation* (Hoboken, NJ: John Wiley & Sons, 2015).
9. Parker J. Palmer, "The Gift of Presence, the Perils of Advice," On Being (website), April 27, 2016, onbeing.org/blog/the-gift-of-presence-the-perils-of-advice.
10. Mark Nepo, *The Book of Awakening: Having the Life You Want by Being Present to the Life You Have*, 20th anniversary ed. (Newburyport, MA: Red Wheel, 2020).
11. Mary Pipher, *Letters to a Young Therapist: Stories of Hope and Healing* (New York: Basic Books, 2003).
12. M. Scott Peck, *The Different Drum: Community Making and Peace*, 3rd ed. (Toronto: Simon & Schuster, 2010).

13. Pipher, *Letters to a Young Therapist*.
14. Brené Brown, *The Gifts of Imperfection: Let Go of Who You Think You're Supposed to Be and Embrace Who You Are* (Center City, MN: Hazelden Publishing, 2010).
15. "Allyship," The Anti-Oppression Network (website), theantioppression network.com/allyship.
16. Thank you to my friend, psychologist Dr. Jo Ann Unger, for this addition and for pointing me to the work of Marsha Linehan, the creator of DBT.
17. Brené Brown, *I Thought It Was Just Me: Women Reclaiming Power and Courage in a Culture of Shame* (West Hollywood, CA: Gotham Books, 2007).
18. Mark Nepo, *The Exquisite Risk: Daring to Live an Authentic Life* (New York: Harmony, 2007).
19. Susan Silk and Barry Goldman, "How Not to Say the Wrong Thing," *Los Angeles Times*, April 7, 2013, latimes.com/opinion/op-ed/la-xpm-2013-apr-07-la-oe-0407-silk-ring-theory-20130407-story.html.
20. "Emotional Labor," Wikipedia, en.wikipedia.org/wiki/Emotional_labor.
21. Rainer Maria Rilke, *Letters to a Young Poet*, trans. Søren Filipski (Hythloday Press, 2014).
22. Tina Fossella, "Human Nature, Buddha Nature: An Interview with John Welwood," *Tricycle Magazine*, Spring 2011, tricycle.org/magazine/human-nature-buddha-nature.
23. "Episode 19: Conversation with Gordon Neufeld," *Conversation with Alanis Morissette* (podcast), Google Podcasts, September 11, 2018, bit.ly/2UzDNvO.
24. "Personal Boundaries," Wikipedia, en.wikipedia.org/wiki/Personal_boundaries.
25. *Marion Woodman: Dancing in the Flames*, directed by Adam G. Reid (Toronto: Martinelli Films, 2018), Vimeo.
26. Richard Rohr, *Falling Upward: A Spirituality for the Two Halves of Life* (New York: Jossey-Bass, 2011).
27. Ibid.
28. Carl Jung, *Collected Works of C.G. Jung: Development of Personality*, vol. 17, trans. Gerhard Adler and R.F.C. Hull (Princeton, NJ: Princeton University Press, 2014).
29. Stephen Levine, *A Year to Live: How to Live This Year as If It Were Your Last* (New York: Three Rivers Press, 1998).
30. Palmer, *Let Your Life Speak*.
31. John O'Donohue, *Anam Cara: A Book of Celtic Wisdom* (New York: HarperCollins, 2009).

32. Starhawk, *Dreaming the Dark: Magic, Sex and Politics*, 15th anniversary ed. (Boston: Beacon Press, 2012).

33. Robin Wall Kimmerer, *Braiding Sweetgrass* (Minneapolis: Milkweed Editions, 2013).

34. Shonda Rhimes, *Year of Yes: How to Dance It Out, Stand in the Sun and Be Your Own Person* (New York: Simon & Schuster, 2015).

35. Lauren A. McCarthy, "Evolutionary and Biochemical Explanations for a Unique Female Stress Response: Tend-and-Befriend," Great Ideas in Personality (website), February 2005, personalityresearch.org/papers/mccarthy.html.

36. Dr. David Berceli, TRE (website), traumaprevention.com.

37. Foundation for Human Enrichment, Somatic Experiencing Trauma Institute (website), traumahealing.org.

38. Leticia Nieto with Margot F. Boyer, Liz Goodwin, Garth R. Johnson, and Laurel Collier Smith, *Beyond Inclusion, Beyond Empowerment* (Olympia, WA: Cuetzpalin, 2010).

39. Christina Baldwin, *The Seven Whispers: A Spiritual Practice for Times Like These* (Novato, CA: New World Library, 2010).

40. Gabor Maté, *When the Body Says No: Exploring the Stress-Disease Connection* (Hoboken, NJ: Wiley, 2011).

41. Christopher Germer, *The Mindful Path to Self-Compassion: Freeing Yourself from Destructive Thoughts and Emotions* (New York: Guilford Press, 2009).

42. Ibid.

43. Ellen J. Langer, *Mindfulness*, 25th anniversary ed. (Boston: Da Capo Lifelong Books, 2014).

44. Ibid.

45. Ibid.

46. Chögyam Trungpa, *Mindfulness in Action: Making Friends with Yourself through Meditation and Everyday Awareness*, reprint ed. (Boulder, CO: Shambhala, 2016).

47. Karen Casey, *Let Go Now: Embrace Detachment as a Path to Freedom* (Newburyport, MA: Conari Press, 2019).

48. Thomas Ryan, ed., *Reclaiming the Body in Christian Spirituality* (Mahwah, NJ: Paulist Press, 2004).

49. Charles Eisenstein, *The More Beautiful World Our Hearts Know Is Possible* (Berkeley, CA: North Atlantic Books, 2013).

50. Elizabeth Renzetti, "Life of Solitude: A Loneliness Crisis Is Looming," *Globe and Mail*, November 23, 2013, theglobeandmail.com/life/life-of-solitude-a-loneliness-crisis-is-looming/article15573187.

51. Caroline Beaton, "Why Millennials Are Lonely," *Forbes*, February 9, 2017, forbes.com/sites/carolinebeaton/2017/02/09/why-millennials-are-lonely/#5eb6646f7c35.

52. Saul McLeod, "Attachment Theory," *Simply Psychology*, February 5, 2017, simplypsychology.org/attachment.html.

53. Robert Weiss, "The Opposite of Addiction Is Connection," *Psychology Today*, September 30, 2015, psychologytoday.com/us/blog/love-and-sex-in-the-digital-age/201509/the-opposite-addiction-is-connection.

54. Peter Block and John McKnight, *The Abundant Community: Awakening the Power of Families and Neighborhoods* (Oakland, CA: Berrett-Koehler Publishers, 2012).

55. bell hooks, *All about Love: New Visions* (New York: William Morrow, 2018).

56. "john a. powell: Opening to the Question of Belonging," *On Being with Krista Tippett* (podcast), June 25, 2015, onbeing.org/programs/john-a-powell-opening-to-the-question-of-belonging-may2018.

57. Deepak Chopra, Debbie Ford, and Marianne Williamson, *The Shadow Effect: Illuminating the Hidden Power of Your True Self* (New York: Harper-Collins, 2011).

58. Michael Jones, *Artful Leadership: Awakening the Commons of the Imagination* (Victoria, BC: Trafford Publishing, 2006).

59. Chopra, Ford, and Williamson, *The Shadow Effect*.

60. Ibid.

61. Ibid.

62. Brian Arao and Kristi Clemens, "From Safe Spaces to Brave Spaces: A New Way to Frame Dialogue around Diversity and Social Justice" in *The Art of Effective Facilitation: Reflections from Social Justice Educators*, ed. Lisa M. Landreman (Sterling, VA: Stylus Publishing, 2013).

63. Robert Boostrom, "'Safe Spaces': Reflections on an Education Metaphor," *Journal of Curriculum Studies* 30, no. 4 (1998), doi.org/10.1080/0022027 98183549.

64. everylevelleads.com

65. desireeadaway.com

66. diversityisanasset.com

67. Betty J. Barrett, "Is 'Safety' Dangerous? A Critical Examination of the Classroom as Safe Space," *Canadian Journal for the Scholarship of Teaching and Learning* 1, no. 1 (2010), ir.lib.uwo.ca/cjsotl_rcacea/vol1/iss1/9.

68. Ibid.

69. Jamie Marich, "Please Don't Tell Me 'I'm in a Safe Space,'" *Decolonizing Yoga* (website), November 19, 2016, decolonizingyoga.com/please-dont-tell-im-safe-place.

70. Arao and Clemens, "From Safe Spaces to Brave Spaces."

71. Jerry Useem, "Power Causes Brain Damage," *Atlantic*, July/August 2017, theatlantic.com/magazine/archive/2017/07/power-causes-brain-damage/528711.

72. Julie Diamond, *Power: A User's Guide* (Santa Fe, NM: Belly Song Press, 2016).

73. Sian Ferguson, "Privilege 101: A Quick and Dirty Guide," *Everyday Feminism*, September 29, 2014, everydayfeminism.com/2014/09/what-is-privilege.

74. Robin DiAngelo, "White Fragility," *International Journal of Critical Pedagogy* 3, no. 3 (2011), libjournal.uncg.edu/ijcp/article/viewFile/249/116.

75. Peggy McIntosh, "White Privilege: Unpacking the Invisible Knapsack," *Peace and Freedom*, July/August 1989, psychology.umbc.edu/files/2016/10/White-Privilege_McIntosh-1989.pdf.

76. "Oppression," Dictionary.com, dictionary.com/browse/oppression.

77. Kimberlé W. Crenshaw, "Demarginalizing the Intersection of Race and Sex: A Black Feminist Critique of Antidiscrimination Doctrine, Feminist Theory and Antiracist Politics," *University of Chicago Legal Forum* 1, no. 8 (1989), chicagounbound.uchicago.edu/cgi/viewcontent.cgi?article=1052&context=uclf.

78. Nieto et al., *Beyond Inclusion*.

79. Audre Lorde, *Sister Outsider: Essays and Speeches* (London: Penguin Modern Classics, 2019).

80. Arbinger Institute, *The Anatomy of Peace: Resolving the Heart of Conflict*, 2nd ed. (Oakland, CA: Berrett-Koehler Publishers, 2015).

81. Adam Kahane, *Power and Love: A Theory and Practice of Social Change* (Oakland, CA: Berrett-Koehler Publishers, 2010).

82. Jamie Utt, "Intent vs. Impact: Why Your Intentions Don't Really Matter," *Everyday Feminism*, July 30, 2013, everydayfeminism.com/2013/07/intentions-dont-really-matter.

83. Sarah Schulman, *Conflict Is Not Abuse: Overstating Harm, Community Responsibility, and the Duty of Repair* (Vancouver: Arsenal Pulp Press, 2016).

84. Ibid.

85. John Paul Lederach, *Preparing for Peace: Conflict Transformation across Cultures* (Syracuse, NY: Syracuse University Press, 1996).

86. Marshall B. Rosenberg, *Nonviolent Communication: A Language of Life*, 3rd ed. (Encinitas, CA: PuddleDancer Press, 2015).

87. Nisha Sikka, George Wong, and Catherine Bell, "Indigenous Centered Conflict Resolution Processes in Canada," 2016, nawash.ca/wordpress/wp-content/uploads/2016/10/Web-version-Final-Indigenous-Centred-Conflict-Resolution-app.pdf.

88. Francesca Mason Boring, *Connecting to Our Ancestral Past: Healing through Family Constellations, Ceremony, and Ritual* (Berkeley, CA: North Atlantic Books, 2012).

89. This is possibly based on the Emma Lazarus quote, "Until we are all free, we are none of us free."

90. "Sovereignty," Wikipedia, en.wikipedia.org/wiki/Sovereignty.

91. "Treaty," Wikipedia, en.wikipedia.org/wiki/Treaty.

92. "Colonization," Wikipedia, en.wikipedia.org/wiki/Colonization.

about the author

HEATHER PLETT IS an international speaker, facilitator, and co-founder of the Centre for Holding Space. Participants of her Holding Space Practitioner Program have come from six continents to join her online and at in-person workshops around the world. Her writing on the subject of holding space has appeared in publications such as *Harvard Business Review* and *Grist* magazine and has been quoted in multiple books as well as curricula for nurses, hospice care workers, yoga teachers, facilitators, and military chaplains. She lives in Winnipeg, Manitoba, Canada, with her three daughters.

• • •

Learn more at **heatherplett.com**.